GEORGE F. KENNAN'S STRATEGIC THOUGHT

George F. Kennan
Photograph appears courtesy of George F. Kennan

GEORGE F. KENNAN'S STRATEGIC THOUGHT

The Making of an American Political Realist

Richard L. Russell

Foreword by Kenneth W. Thompson

Westport, Connecticut
London

Library of Congress Cataloging-in-Publication Data

Russell, Richard L., 1961–
    George F. Kennan's strategic thought : the making of an American
political realist / Richard L. Russell ; foreword by Kenneth W.
Thompson.
      p. cm.
    Includes bibliographical references and index.
    ISBN 0–275–96402–7 (alk. paper)
    1. Kennan, George Frost, 1904– . 2. United States—Foreign
relations—1945–1989—Case studies. 3. United States—Foreign
relations—Philosophy—Case studies. 4. World politics—1945- —
Case studies. 5. Strategy—History—20th century—Case studies.
6. Realism—Case studies. I. Title.
E748.K374R87   1999
909.82′1′07202—dc21   98–33625

British Library Cataloguing in Publication Data is available.

Library of Congress Catalog Card Number: 98–33625
ISBN: 0–275–96402–7

First published in 1999

Praeger Publishers, 88 Post Road West, Westport, CT 06881
An imprint of Greenwood Publishing Group, Inc.
www.praeger.com

Printed in the United States of America

The paper used in this book complies with the
Permanent Paper Standard issued by the National
Information Standards Organization (Z39.48–1984).

10 9 8 7 6 5 4 3 2 1

Voor mijn mooie vrouw Lilian

Theory exists so that one need not start afresh each time sorting out the material and plowing through it, but will find it ready to hand and in good order. It is meant to educate the mind of a future commander, or, more accurately, to guide him in his self-education, not to accompany him to the battlefield; just as a wise teacher guides and stimulates a young man's intellectual development, but is careful not to lead him by the hand for the rest of his life. If the theorist's studies automatically result in principles and rules, and if truth spontaneously crystallizes into these forms, theory will not resist this natural tendency of the mind.

—Carl von Clausewitz, *On War*

CONTENTS

FOREWORD

We have waited too many years for a book on the strategic thought of George F. Kennan. Too many earlier studies of Kennan seek to engage the historian-diplomatist on some idiosyncratic point with which the critic differs. These treatises challenge Kennan on points of agreement and disagreement, however insignificant.

At last a young scholar and public official has looked in great detail at the essentials of Kennan's strategic doctrine. Those of us who have known and respected Dr. Russell's career are not surprised he would lead this way. His interest is tracing with exquisite care what Kennan really meant and how consistent he is in proceeding from one issue to another. He finds that from the Long Telegram, the Mr. X article, and his University of Chicago lectures entitled *American Diplomacy*, Kennan has followed a reasonably steady course in assessing American strategy and foreign policy.

Whenever a writer has a strong opinion or proposes a specific policy, he is fair game for the critics. Even though Richard Russell has been closer to policy making than most who praise or blame "the man from Milwaukee," he eschews the vocation of punditry. What Russell seeks to elucidate are the principles on which Kennan grounds his thought. What are the core propositions that go to the heart of his approach? How consistent is he in holding those core principles? When and how does he depart and why? How consistent are his policies, and how committed is he to the fundamentals of his philosophy of foreign policy? Is there a red thread that connects the main elements of his strategic thinking? These are some of the essentials that his forerunners were overdue in examining as they wrote about Kennan.

Russell, more than many of his predecessors, chooses to take Kennan at his word rather than looking for hidden meanings, as is the work of some political philosophers. It turns out that Kennan's views are, for the most part, transparent. He says what he means and means what he says, especially in his more careful scholarship. At the same time, he recognizes the importance of diplomatic restraint. Yet as Russell indicates, Kennan pays a high price for his candor when he lapses into heedless or ill-considered language, particularly in his comments about Soviet totalitarianism while traveling to Moscow to take up his post as U.S. ambassador. In these and other ways, Russell compares theory and practice in Kennan's conduct of diplomacy. Kennan is a romantic as well as a realist, and he breaches diplomatic restraint when he is crusading.

Russell makes few extravagant claims for Kennan, and the book is often marked by understatement. That quality enables Russell to steer a course somewhere between too much praise and excessive criticism. He patiently traces the high and low points in Kennan's career and wherever possible allows the facts to speak for themselves. Although he finds Kennan's perspective illuminating and sometimes inspiring, Russell stops short both of canonizing his subject and of condemning him to outer darkness.

Not many pages into the work go by before one senses that the author has a pedagogical purpose. A principal strength of the work is Russell's determination to view Kennan in a context, which is not to judge with finality his doctrine but to consider it in relation to the circumstances about which he is writing. In this respect, the book is a refreshing departure from studies in black and white, whose authors seem compelled to reveal successive flaws in Kennan's thought without ever disclosing what the historian-diplomat is undertaking to explicate. From the outset, Russell has no higher goal than to "get it right" in describing Kennan's strategic views and policies. Here again he aims at nothing so much as an honest account of Kennan's strategic views.

This study, then, fills a vacuum left by the previous studies of Kennan. It is less interested in revelations or discoveries than in clarity and coherence. Russell is a realist writing about another realist, George F. Kennan. He leaves to others the deconstruction of Kennan, the historian-practitioner. Yet there can be no doubt that Russell has a grip on his subject that few polemicists are likely to attain. This is an old-fashioned book in which the ultimate aim is clarification. Kennan's life and work are not a vehicle Russell seeks to use to ride into prominence with startling new findings. He has no argument, as the theorists put it, to construct a new Kennan before our eyes. The book is good, solid narrative and analysis. Its virtue is its relative simplicity of purpose. It should be judged on that basis.

Kenneth W. Thompson
J. Wilson Newman Professor of
Government and Foreign Affairs
University of Virginia

PREFACE

This study uses George F. Kennan's thought for a case study in political realism for an approach to international politics and American foreign policy. It attempts to more accurately capture the essence of realist thought than that presented by scholars who would mine the tradition for inconsistencies at the margins to the neglect of the greater weight of consistencies that lie at the core of the school. The study delineates the key concepts and principles of realism. In so doing, the study presents a theoretical model of political realism that could be used to critically examine alternative philosophies and to inform the post–Cold War debate in the international relations theory and American foreign policy fields.

The study attempts to discover the enduring validity of the concepts in the realist school for interpreting international politics and guiding American foreign policy. Its objective, in part, is to escape the phenomenon by which each generation of scholars and statesmen forgets or neglects the wisdom of preceding generations. Contemporaries often cast old wisdom aside and dismiss it as obsolete and unsuited for the conduct of today's affairs, only to relearn lessons lost and take them as their own discoveries. Unfortunately, the relearning of painfully acquired wisdom often entails enormous costs. This study aims at perpetuating wisdom acquired and practiced in the Cold War by one wise diplomat-scholar who shared many ideas with like-minded realists for present and future generations in hopes of avoiding the pitfalls of forgotten wisdom.

More specifically, the study explores George Kennan's realist worldview as a theory of American foreign policy. It seeks to illuminate the principles and concepts that underpin Kennan's thoughts on international politics and American foreign policy to see if they might be relevant for contemporary foreign policy. Historian John Lewis Gaddis has noted that the test of lasting relevance is "the extent to which principles developed in one context can be fruitfully applied in others. If the continued pertinence of the ideas Kennan worked out during the early years of the cold war is any guide, his strategic concepts, like those of Clausewitz, may find application in circumstances far removed from those which give rise to them."[1] The illumination of a theory in Kennan's thought might enable contemporary and future foreign policy scholars and practitioners to more readily comprehend the essential features of international politics and the opportunities and dangers posed to American foreign policy in the post–Cold War period.

Although Kennan has been the subject of extensive scholarship, this book attempts to fill a niche not entirely covered by any previous study. Two important studies have anticipated the focus of this book. David Mayers, in his biography of Kennan, devoted only one chapter—albeit a fine one—to Kennan's thought.[2] Barton Gellman treated Kennan's ideas more fully and examined his concept of "how the world works and how things ought to be done within it."[3] Gellman's work comes the closest of all the literature on Kennan to the focus of this study. This study, however, seeks to both expand and deepen the exploration of Kennan's thought contained in Gellman's work as well as to draw linkages between Kennan's thought and that of other political realists. Mayers and Gellman do not examine *per se* the tenets of realism as an approach to American foreign policy.

This study uses Kennan as a window through which to view the American realist school of thought on international politics as relevant to American foreign policy. Two significant works on the school by Michael Smith and Joel Rosenthal examined numerous realist thinkers including Kennan.[4] The scope of this study in comparison to the studies by Smith and Rosenthal is both narrower, in that it focuses on Kennan's thinking, and broader, in that it examines a wider array of his thoughts. This study broadens the focus to include Kennan's realist thought on political theory, geopolitics, diplomacy, the use of force, and the Cold War superpower rivalry.

This book is distinct from other studies in several important respects. First, this study is not a biography. Mayers's book is an intellectual and political biography as well as a critical review of Kennan's service in government and subsequent political counsel.[5] Michael Polley's work purports to offer an interpretation of Kennan's realist thought, but more closely resembles a chronological biography than an illumination of realist concepts or principles in Kennan's worldview.[6] Professor Gaddis has written—but not yet published—Kennan's authorized biography.

Second, this study is written by a political scientist, not by a historian or journalist. The study does not aim at the historical reconstruction of American foreign policy during Kennan's service in government. Rather, it aims at a systematic treatment of Kennan's lifetime of thought. Wilson Miscamble has written an excellent study of Kennan's involvement in the policy-making process. He used Kennan's involvement as a prism through which to view the formulation of policy during the postwar period from 1947 to 1950, a crucial period in American foreign policy.[7] Gaddis's excellent history, *Strategies of*

Containment, primarily focused on Kennan's foreign policy-making role rather than on his thought, although Gaddis does make many insightful observations on the latter, and they will be drawn upon in this study. Walter Isaacson and Evan Thomas focused their study on the history and interrelationships of the establishment elites, including Kennan, who were the most influential in the formulation of American foreign policy in the aftermath of World War II.[8]

Third, this book is not an examination *per se* of Kennan's views on the policy of containment or the Soviet Union. Anders Stephanson sought to "subject Kennan's historical texts to serious theoretical examination" and largely focused on his views on the nature of Soviet foreign policy.[9] Walter Hixson's work is a critical interpretation of containment and of Kennan's place in American diplomatic history.[10] Kennan's writings on the Soviet Union will be primarily drawn upon in this study to illuminate his general principles of international politics and American foreign policy.

In a review of the large body of secondary research on Kennan, the author has come to the conclusion that, although Kennan has been much studied and written about, few have understood what he was trying to say. Much of the secondary literature is focused on Kennan's role in the debate over the origins, interpretation, and implementation of the policy of containment. Kennan's realism as a philosophic approach to American foreign policy is mentioned only in passing and has received no sustained analysis in much of this literature. This study, written in the aftermath of the Cold War, is perhaps able to make a more dispassionate analysis of Kennan's thought than those studies written largely in the midst of the Cold War. Although authors then aimed at clear-headed analysis, human beings will always be unable to completely divorce themselves from the emotionally and politically charged atmosphere of their times. As students, scholars, and policy makers increasingly look to the Cold War not as the battle at hand today but as a passing phase of history, a fresh, objective look at Kennan's work to search for the governing principles that underpinned his thought may now be more readily possible.

WORLDVIEWS AS FOUNDATIONS FOR THEORY

One methodology for the construction of theory in the field of international relations is the study of past statesmen and thinkers. Many historical figures possessed implicit theories or philosophies of international relations that governed their thought and foreign policy prescriptions. As Kenneth Thompson has suggested, scholars might "distill from past international politics as viewed by some of our wisest interpreters a body of common principles or a core of residual truths reflecting the essence of their approach."[11] Along similar lines, Greg Russell pointed out that "The Actor on the political stage carries within his mind a political philosophy, however inchoate and fragmentary and unacknowledged. That philosophy makes him understand the political scene and act with regard to it."[12] Great statesmen and master thinkers share acute worldviews through which they have surveyed the landscape of international politics. These worldviews consist of generalizations and principles that act as a filter to simplify reality. Hans Morgenthau observed that "the great statesman differs from the run-of-the-mill diplomatist and politician exactly in that he is able to see the issues confronting him as special cases of general and objective—that is, theoretical—propositions."[13]

Statesmen operate in the foreign policy realm on the basis of their simplified perceptions of reality. As Louis Halle explained, "What the foreign policy of any nation addresses itself to is the image of the external world in the minds of the people who determine the policy of that nation. That image may approximate the reality more or less closely, but at best it can never be quite the same thing."[14] He noted that "The fact is that none of us has much absolute knowledge of 'the vast external realm' to which every nation pretends to shape its foreign policy. But the human mind finds it almost impossible to live with the unknown or the uncertain. Its tendency, therefore, is to fill the vacuum of ignorance by legend, by a view of the unknown world around which belief can crystallize."[15] Halle was by no means alone in identifying the "legendary image," or worldview, of a statesman as an important element in the foreign policy of a nation-state. As Walter Lippmann viewed this phenomenon, "Human behavior takes place in relation to a pseudo-environment—a representation, which is not quite the same for any two individuals, of what they suppose to be—not what is—the reality of things."[16] Alexander George referred to a worldview as an "operational code," which he defined, in part, as a political leader's beliefs about the nature of politics and political conflict.[17]

The accuracy of the perception of statesmen is a function of the sophistication of their worldviews. The most astute students of international politics share worldviews that come close to objective reality, while the poorest analysts suffer from badly distorted images of the external environment. Professor Thompson has cited Winston Churchill as an example of a statesman with a finely honed worldview: "What a theory such as Churchill's provides is a map for finding one's way across unknown terrain. It brings together disparate aspects of reality. It establishes the interconnectedness of action or policies that would otherwise be perceived in isolation."[18] In contrast, Saddam Hussein—who launched an ambitious bid to occupy Kuwait in 1990 only to face broad international political and military opposition to his move—might be cited as an example of a leader with a poor worldview that formed a warped vision of reality outside Iraq.

Worldview acuity is sharpened by contemplation as well as by practical political experience. Morgenthau attested to this point when he wrote that enduring political thought "is developed out of the concern of a politically alive and committed mind with the concrete political problems of the day. Thus all great political theory, from Plato and Aristotle and from the biblical prophets to our day, has been practical political theory, political theory which intervenes actively in a concrete political situation with the purpose of change through action."[19] Thompson shared Morgenthau's observation and wrote: "In political theory in general, at least in Western civilization, and in the theory of international politics in particular, the lasting contributions have come from men who resisted the fateful divorce of theory from practice."[20]

Sharply focused worldviews have successfully projected the broad outlines of the future course of international politics. Alexis de Tocqueville, in his masterwork *Democracy in America*, in 1835, appeared to anticipate the Cold War: "There are at the present time two great nations in the world, which started from different points, but seem to tend towards the same end . . . Their starting-point is different and their courses are not the same; yet each of them seems marked out by the will of Heaven to sway the destinies of half the globe."[21] Similarly, Nicholas Spykman's prose in 1942, before the close of World War II, foreshadowed the coming of the Cold War: "A Russian state from the Urals to the North Sea can be no great improvement over a German state from the North Sea to the Urals."[22]

Kennan's projections of the course of international politics attest to the acuity of his worldview. It enabled him to see beyond the clouded visions of those within government and the public who were awash in the events of international politics but lacked a theory to see broader trends and implications. Throughout his career, Kennan was often able to leap beyond the bounds of accepted wisdom to be prophetic in his analysis of international politics. Kennan's foresight begs the question, What factors account for the clarity of his worldview which informed his recommendations for American foreign policy?

This study sifts through Kennan's writings to try to discover and then make explicit his worldview that constitutes a realist theory of American foreign policy. The approach used to analyze Kennan is similar to a survey of the literature approach used in more general works. This study, however, confines the survey to literature on Kennan. It quotes from a wide body of work produced by Kennan from the late 1940s to 1997. Much of the previous scholarship devoted to Kennan has focused on a much narrower selection of his work, particularly his famous "X article." The present study allows Kennan to speak for himself. For this reason, the study does more than describe Kennan's ideas; it gives the reader full quotes to more accurately capture the content of Kennan's thought.

Indeed, one of Kennan's long-standing complaints against his critics was that they frequently misrepresented his views. As an illustration of this problem, Kennan wrote of one critic that "In a number of instances he has done me the favor to quote one or more whole sentences from things I have said or written. But in a far greater number of instances he has taken isolated words or phrases out of the sentences in which I used them and has inserted them, in quotes, into his own."[23] This practice caused Kennan to be "startled by the quoted phrases and the inferences conveyed by the way they were used, for they seemed extremely, almost grotesquely, out of accord with what I have always thought to be my own views."[24] This study's approach—in an effort to redress shortcomings identified by Kennan—reduces the risk of quoting out of context and misrepresenting Kennan's ideas.

The question may be asked, What does this study offer that a reader cannot obtain by reading Kennan's work? Although Kennan was a prolific writer and speaker, he never compiled in any comprehensive way the theoretical principles and concepts that run throughout the corpus of his work into a single text. Kennan, of course, made important strides toward a theory of American foreign policy in his books *American Diplomacy* and *Realities of American Foreign Policy*, and more recently in his *Around the Cragged Hill*, as well as in a recent article, "On American Principles," published in *Foreign Affairs*. Nevertheless, these works taken separately do not constitute the robust theory that underpins Kennan's collective work. This study essentially attempts to do for Kennan what Morgenthau had done for himself in *Politics among Nations*, that is, to marshal the most pertinent theoretical components of his thought into one work. Although Morgenthau focused on a theory of international politics, this study ties Kennan's thought more closely to American foreign policy. Indeed, it might be argued that an outside observer might be better able to take a cold, analytic and objective look at an author's life corpus to find overarching theoretical linkages than the author himself. In other words, a neutral observer might be better positioned to see the "forest," as the author may be wandering amongst the "trees."

STUDY OUTLINE

Chapter 1 discusses the relationship between international relations theory, political realism, American foreign policy, and Kennan's thought. It argues that international relations theory should inform the conduct of American foreign policy. Political realism as established by Hans Morgenthau in the United States is a classical theory of international politics that links theory and practice. Kennan's thought moves in lockstep with that of Morgenthau, although Kennan never explicitly developed a theory to the extent that Morgenthau had. Nevertheless, this chapter suggests that Kennan was conscious of the need to develop principles to govern the conduct of American foreign policy. These principles, which are suspended in Kennan's worldview and are illuminated in the course of subsequent chapters, collectively constitute a classical theory of American foreign policy.

To dissect Kennan's worldview, chapter 2 examines Kennan's thought on politics along the levels of analysis approach used by Kenneth Waltz in his *Man, the State and War*.[25] It discusses Kennan's humanistic commitment to the idea that any discussion of politics must begin with an examination of the nature of man, the first of Waltz's three images. For Kennan, the drive for power inherent in all men sets the context for political intercourse. Kennan's understanding of the nature of man and his drive for power is the foundation of his thought on politics. Man needs the state or government, Waltz's second image, to harness, control, and channel his drive for power. Various forms of government are able to meet these requirements, but each, in Kennan's view, has a tendency to produce unique characteristics. This chapter also discusses the realist understanding of practical morality, which seeks to reconcile competing interests of power and morality. In the international realm, no entity or government is able to harness, control, or channel the competition for power among nation-states, Waltz's third image of analysis. Consequently, Kennan looked to the operation of the balance of power to hold competing nation-states in check to preserve their political autonomies.

Armed with an understanding of Kennan's general precepts toward man, power, morality, and politics, chapter 3 turns to an examination of American foreign policy. It discusses Kennan's appreciation for the origins of American power—the means in foreign policy—and the national interest or end for which American power should be used. In the realm of international politics, the United States is forced to equate means and ends within the geopolitical constraints and opportunities posed by the global balance of power.

American statesmen are unable to frame foreign policy exclusively on a realist's geopolitical calculus. They are forced to operate in realms other than those of power, national interest, and balance of power calculations. As the United States competes for power in the international balance of power, it is under the influence of the domestic struggle for power. Foreign policy is inextricably linked to domestic politics. Chapter 4 discusses the unique characteristics of American democracy, identified long ago by Tocqueville and echoed in Kennan's work, which pose challenges for the formulation and implementation of foreign policy. Only the executive could effectively articulate guiding principles for foreign policy as well as meet the exacting demands for policy implementation. Kennan argued that the diffusion of power to the legislature and submission to whims of public opinion were a prescription for floundering in foreign policy.

Divided powers in American democracy present unique problems to policy makers and diplomats alike trying to craft and implement foreign policy within the context of the domestic competition for power. Chapter 5 explores the theory of diplomacy and the contemporary American philosophy of diplomacy, which has sharp differences with its traditional conception. Kennan devoted considerable study to the contemporary American philosophy of diplomacy and contrasted it to the diplomacy exercised by the Founding Fathers, who, for Kennan, had a fine grasp of the art that has eluded many contemporary statesmen. American philosophy has been seized with international law and organizations as the key means to advance diplomatic efforts to mitigate the circumstances conducive to the outbreak of war. For Kennan, however, international law and organizations, to the extent that they have any efficacy in world politics, are shadows of power realities—the real substance of diplomacy. American statesmen and diplomats are prone to deal with law and organizations to the neglect of power realities, and thereby decrease the prospects for achieving the national interest via means short of war.

Chapter 6 discusses Kennan's views on the ubiquity of force and war in international politics. It examines Kennan's thought on war as an instrument for advancing the American national interest. Although Kennan saw utility in conventional military power, he regarded nuclear weapons as instruments largely unsuitable for the promotion of U.S. interests. This chapter explores Kennan's views on American foreign and military policy in the world wars, Korea, Vietnam, and in Europe during the Cold War. Kennan's principles of war and foreign policy are consistent with Clausewitz's view of war as continuation of politics by other means.

The relationships between major powers have an enormous impact on the stability of the international system. Chapter 7 takes a close look at the dynamics at play in relations between major powers competing for power in the international arena. A review of Kennan's writings on the Cold War reveals a pronounced concern over heightened tensions, or the "security dilemma" in the American–Soviet relationship. The pursuit of power by rival nation-states causes a spiral of insecurity referred to in international relations theory literature as the security dilemma. Kennan was acutely concerned that the security dilemma in the superpower competition threatened to propel both powers down the path to direct military conflict despite the absence of any political objectives that would have justified such a conflict. This chapter explores the security dilemma in the American–Soviet relationship during the Cold War as viewed through Kennan's eyes. It discusses the factors that Kennan believed were the most significant in the formulation of Soviet foreign policy as well as the strengths and weaknesses of the Soviet state. An appreciation of Soviet power and its limits allowed Kennan to initially take a confident view of the West's ability to meet the Soviet challenge. This chapter then looks at Kennan's recommendations for American foreign policy—from the Truman to the Reagan administrations—that flowed from his view of the Soviet Union and his desire to ameliorate the security dilemma between the Soviet Union and the United States.

Chapter 8 undertakes to synthesize the principles and concepts discussed in the preceding chapters to construct Kennan's realist theory of American foreign policy. It juxtaposes Kennan's thought with the realist principles laid out by Morgenthau. The study concludes that Kennan's realist principles constitute a practical theory of American foreign policy that is relevant for statesmen faced with policy dilemmas in the post–Cold War period.

NOTES

1. John Lewis Gaddis, "Containment: A Reassessment," *Foreign Affairs* 55, no. 4 (July 1977): 887.

2. David Mayers, *George Kennan and the Dilemmas of U.S. Foreign Policy* (New York, NY: Oxford University Press, 1988), 317.

3. Barton Gellman, *Contending with Kennan: Toward a Philosophy of American Power* (New York, NY: Praeger Publishers, 1984), 20.

4. See Michael Joseph Smith, *Realist Thought from Weber to Kissinger* (Baton Rouge, LA: Louisiana State University Press, 1986) and Joel H. Rosenthal, *Righteous Realists: Political Realism, Responsible Power, and American Culture in the Nuclear Age* (Baton Rouge, LA: Louisiana State University Press, 1991).

5. Mayers, *George Kennan and the Dilemmas of U.S. Foreign Policy*, vii–viii.

6. Michael Polley, *A Biography of George F. Kennan: The Education of a Realist* (Lewiston, NY: Edwin Mellon Press, 1990).

7. Wilson D. Miscamble, *George F. Kennan and the Making of American Foreign Policy, 1947–1950* (Princeton, NJ: Princeton University Press, 1992), xi.

8. Walter Isaacson and Evan Thomas, *The Wise Men: Six Friends and the World They Made* (New York, NY: Simon & Schuster, 1988).

9. Anders Stephanson, *Kennan and the Art of Foreign Policy* (Cambridge, MA: Harvard University Press, 1989), viii.

10. See Walter L. Hixson, *George F. Kennan: Cold War Iconoclast* (New York, NY: Columbia University Press, 1989).

11. Kenneth W. Thompson, *Political Realism and the Crisis of World Politics: An American Approach to Foreign Policy* (Lanham, MD: University Press of America, 1982), 8.

12. Greg Russell, *John Quincy Adams and the Public Virtues of Diplomacy* (Columbia, MO: University of Missouri Press, 1995), 66–67.

13. Hans J. Morgenthau, "The Nature and Limits of a Theory of International Relations," in William T. R. Fox (ed.), *Theoretical Aspects of International Relations* (Notre Dame, IN: University of Notre Dame Press, 1959), 25.

14. Louis J. Halle, *American Foreign Policy: Theory and Reality* (London, UK: Bradford & Dickens, 1960), 316.

15. Halle, *American Foreign Policy*, 317.

16. Walter Lippmann, *Essays in the Public Philosophy* (Boston, MA: Little, Brown and Company, 1955), 92.

17. Alexander L. George, "The 'Operational Code': A Neglected Approach to the Study of Political Leaders and Decision-Making," *International Studies Quarterly*, Volume 13, Number 2, June 1969, 197.

18. Kenneth W. Thompson, "Unity and Contradiction in the Theory and Practice of International Relations," *The Review of Politics*, Volume 44, Number 3, July 1982, 330.

19. Hans J. Morgenthau, *Politics in the Twentieth Century*, Abridged Edition (Chicago, IL: University of Chicago Press, 1971), 293.

20. Thompson, *Political Realism*, 7.

21. Alexis de Tocqueville, *Democracy in America*, Volume I, Henry Reeve Text, Revised by Francis Bowen, and Further Corrected and Edited by Phillips Bradley (New York, NY: Vintage Books, 1990), 434.

22. Nicholas John Spykman, *America's Strategy in World Politics: The United States and the Balance of Power* (New York, NY: Harcourt, Brace and Company, 1942), 460.

23. "George F. Kennan Replies," *Slavic Review*, Volume 35, Number 1, March 1976, 33. The response was written to C. Ben Wright's "Mr. 'X' and Containment," published in the same volume.

24. "Kennan Replies," 33.

25. See Kenneth N. Waltz, *Man, the State and War* (New York, NY: Columbia University Press, 1959).

ACKNOWLEDGMENTS

I would like to express my appreciation for financial support for my doctoral studies and this project. A Dupont Fellowship from the University of Virginia's Woodrow Wilson Department of Government and Foreign Affairs enabled me to complete my course work in the Ph.D. program. A generous fellowship from the White Burkett Miller Center of Public Affairs at the University of Virginia allowed me to take time from work to finish the research for this study. Without the Miller Center's support, I doubt that I would have been able to complete my dissertation, which served as the foundation for this book. Equally important, the Miller Center provided me with a congenial place to hang my hat and escape from the tactical whirlwind pace of life in the national security community to ponder larger, strategic questions facing American foreign policy.

I was fortunate to have a dissertation committee composed of individuals who are both distinguished scholars and gentlemen. Most doctoral candidates are not so lucky. I greatly appreciated the help of Professor Allen Lynch, who impressed upon me the importance of geopolitics in his class on Soviet and Russian foreign policy. Mr. Lynch was instrumental in shaping and sharpening the focus of this study. His marching orders to make a unique contribution to scholarship were in the forefront of my mind as I researched and drafted the study. I am indebted to Professor Inis Claude for his willingness to take time from his busy schedule to graciously serve on my committee. His landmark studies—*Power and International Relations* and *Swords into Plowshares*—have had a lasting influence on my understanding of the balance of power and collective security. Professor Claude's close reading of a draft caught more errors and inconsistencies than I would care to admit. I can only marvel at the penetration and clarity of Professor Claude's thought. Likewise, I am indebted to Professor Norman Graebner for his generosity in taking time from his research and writing of an important study of the Cold War to serve as the dean's representative on my committee. His critical eye and mastery of the

American Constitution were especially helpful in identifying numerous shortcomings in an initial version of chapter 4. I particularly owe Professor Graebner thanks for exposing me to the deep tradition of realism in American foreign policy, both in his dynamic lectures on Cold War history and in his suggested readings from earlier periods in American diplomatic history.

I owe the lion's share of thanks for help with this study to my mentor and friend Kenneth Thompson, the director of the Miller Center. He was the intellectual wellspring for this study and a constant source of support, advice, and good humor as I stumbled along a rocky road to finish my studies. I consider myself fortunate to have had the opportunity to study and work under a man who is a model of Christian humility and civility. I am forever indebted to Mr. Thompson for pointing out the rich path of political realism; this study is but a small, first step along this journey. The only way I could possibly begin to repay my personal and intellectual debt to Professor Thompson is to do what I can to perpetuate political realism as a vibrant school of thought in international relations and American foreign policy.

I also owe thanks to others beyond the grounds in Charlottesville. Ambassador George F. Kennan graciously granted me permission to quote from his personal papers deposited at the Seeley G. Mudd Manuscript Library of Princeton University Library. I appreciated Ambassador Kennan's kind words about one chapter as well as his identification of numerous errors littered throughout an earlier draft. I also must thank the Mudd Manuscript Library for permission to quote from the George F. Kennan Papers and the Hamilton Fish Armstrong Papers. University archivist Ben Primer's efficiency and professionalism in this regard were always appreciated. Special thanks go to Professor John Lewis Gaddis, who kindly accepted a request for an interview from a stranger. His comments provided unique and important insights into the origins of Kennan's thought. I particularly want to thank Professor Gaddis for his careful reading of a draft and his words of encouragement, which came at a time when I needed a morale boost.

My family also played an important role in this study. I am grateful to my parents, Dick and Sue Russell, for their support of what must seem to them to be an endless pursuit of education and books. Without their help, I never would have been able to return to school after a long hiatus to pursue my ambitions of earning a doctorate and writing a book. Across the Atlantic in The Netherlands, my in-laws Bert and Kathy Immers have been unceasingly supportive. They have helped us make our house a home. Kathy's stays with us were a godsend because she unselfishly took over responsibility for many—if not most—of my household chores and allowed me time to finish the manuscript. I am sorry that my grandmother Eleanor Boyce—who had hoped to see me earn a doctorate one day—did not live long enough to see me start.

My grandparents Leavitt and Mildred Moulton are due enormous thanks for their insistence on buying me books throughout my undergraduate and graduate career. I recall a return home for a holiday during my first semester of college.

I remember trying to relate to my grandfather some esoteric insight gleaned from an introductory course in philosophy. After a long discourse that failed to evoke a response from my grandfather, I paused to solicit his comments. He replied, "That is all well and good. But, if you found yourself in the middle of the woods, how would your philosophy help you then? You'd have to eat your books!" My grandfather's New England pragmatism has been my ever present guide in this study. It aims, in part, at drawing *practical* insight from political theory and history to inform and strengthen the quality of American foreign policy in the face of concrete problems. I hope that my grandfather will approve.

Lastly, and most significantly, I owe a thank you to my wife Lilian. In the past several years Lilian frequently found herself trapped inside a house with a man who would habitually jump out from behind his computer to pace around the house complaining that he could never finish this study. During these episodes, our golden retriever Dutchess—my wife's more consistent companion—could look on only in confusion. Lilian's encouragement—coupled with our son Daniel's impending arrival—gave me the boost that I needed to finish the last part of the project. Our son Ryan's arrival further pushed his father to put the finishing touches on the book. I am especially grateful to Lilian for shouldering the burden of preparing the book for publication. Without her computer expertise, this book would not have become a reality. For Lilian's tolerance, support, and love this work is dedicated to her. I regret only that the study is hardly of sufficient merit to thank her for our life together.

1

POLITICAL REALISM AND AMERICAN FOREIGN POLICY

The United States emerged as a major power in international politics in the twentieth century. American military intervention in World War I reestablished a fragile peace on the European continent. The United States again intervened in Europe in World War II to repair the failed peace of the Treaty of Versailles. In the war's ruins, Germany and Japan, the aspirants for world power during the Second World War, were defeated, while England and France, although on the winning side of the conflict, were exhausted and had lost their claims to great power status. The United States and the Soviet Union stood alone as the dominant powers, and their Cold War rivalry was the most pronounced feature of the landscape of Europe and international politics for the subsequent forty-five years.

The field of international relations developed in the United States during the post-World War II period. Scholars within this field of study sought to develop theoretical frameworks to inform American foreign policy. This chapter discusses the contending "scientific" and "classical" approaches to theorizing. In the latter approach, the competing schools of liberalism and conservatism are examined. Attention then turns to the development of political realism as a classical and conservative approach to the theory of international relations. These discussions provide a context for an examination of George Kennan's place in this tradition and his call for principles to guide American foreign policy.

INTERNATIONAL RELATIONS THEORY:
SCIENTIFIC AND CLASSICAL APPROACHES

The United States' emergence from World War II as a great power fueled the growth of international relations as an American academic discipline. Many of the founding fathers of the discipline sought to overcome the shortcomings of the prevalent American schools of thought during the interwar period, when international law and organizations were viewed as the central features of international politics. These schools proved woefully inadequate for grappling with the issues of war and peace, as the Second World War painfully demonstrated.[1] The quest of the new discipline was a theory of international relations that would simplify complex reality to inform, shape, and guide American foreign policy.

Many practitioners and scholars have been disappointed by the progress made in the past fifty years toward a theory of international relations. Professor Inis Claude observed, for example, that "There is admittedly a certain element of presumptuousness in this reference to 'the theory of international relations,' for it is unfortunately true that there exists no well-defined body of systematic thought which clearly deserves that rather dignified title."[2] Martin Wight had judged that "international theory, or what there is of it, is scattered, unsystematic, and mostly inaccessible to the layman."[3] In a more recent review of the literature, Yale Ferguson and Richard Mansbach summed up that "students of international relations should recognize the modest progress that has been made on the long road to theory, as well as admit frankly that a much longer road still lies ahead."[4]

One might attribute this disappointment, in part, to overly high expectations for a theory of international relations. Scholars who advocated a "scientific" approach to theorizing held out the prospect that a successful theory of international relations could predict the behavior of nation-states. They had anticipated that international relations approached as a science would make mathematically measurable progress toward a theory, similar to that witnessed in the natural sciences. Raymond Aron described a social scientific theory of international relations as "a hypothetical, deductive system consisting of a group of hypotheses whose terms are strictly defined and whose relationships between terms (or variables) are most often given a mathematical form."[5] Hans Morgenthau characterized this approach as "the attempt to use the tools of modern economic analysis in a modified form in order to understand international relations."[6] The approach, however, largely overlooked the debate among economists over the uses and limitations of formal mathematical models for predicting market behavior. Endeavors in the scientific approach, moreover, have yielded no grand theory that satisfies its goals. These shortcomings led John Lewis Gaddis to conclude that "The efforts theorists have made to create a 'science' of politics that would forecast the future course of world events have produced strikingly unimpressive results."[7]

More damaging to the school's objectives is the fact that statesmen and policy makers rarely, if ever, rely on the burgeoning body of "scientific" theoretical literature to guide them in the day-to-day conduct of foreign policy. As Alexander George has noted, "not a few policy specialists exposed to the scholarly literature have concluded that most university professors seem to write largely for one another and have little inclination or ability to communicate their knowledge in terms comprehensible to policymakers."[8] Morgenthau had much earlier concluded that "Politics is an art and not a science, and what is required for its mastery is not the rationality of the engineer but the wisdom and the moral strength of the statesman. The social world, deaf to the appeal to reason pure and simple, yields only to that intricate combination of moral and material pressures which the art of the statesman creates and maintains."[9] More recently, Ambassador David Newsom commented that jargon and scientific quantification limit the readership and influence of much academic research.[10]

Although a scientific approach to the study of international relations stresses the quantifiable as the basis for theory formulation, the "classical" approach relies on philosophy and history for its foundation. The classical approach to international relations theory, as Hedley Bull described it, "is characterized above all by explicit reliance upon the exercise of judgment and by the assumptions that if we confine ourselves to strict standards of verification and proof there is very little of significance that can be said about international relations, that general propositions about this subject must therefore derive from a scientifically imperfect process of perception or intuition, and that these general propositions cannot be accorded anything more than the tentative and inconclusive status appropriate to their doubtful origin."[11] Advocates of the classical approach, therefore, take a less sanguine view than their scientific approach counterparts of the prospects for predictive capability in international relations theory.

The classical approach is further distinguished from the scientific approach by its normative nature. The adherents to the scientific approach seek to divorce value judgments from their study of politics. In contrast, advocates of the classical approach argue that values are integral and defining elements that need to be at the core of the study of politics. Kenneth Thompson stressed this point: "Every time the student raises a basic question of ends and means in the realm of war and peace, he very likely (whether implicitly or explicitly) is posing a value question. He is making normative assumptions, formulating positions regarding good or bad, better or worse, evil or more evil; and there are important benefits to be gained from bringing this fact to consciousness, both for him and for those who rally around."[12] This concern about values succinctly captures the essence of the classical approach to international politics.

Advocates of the classical approach view theory as synonymous with philosophy. From the classical perspective, Aron conceived of "Theory as contemplative knowledge, drawn from ideas or from the basic order of the world, [which] can be the equivalent of philosophy."[13] Louis Halle, a scholar and former American diplomat, observed that "Anyone who, trying to understand the practical questions of national policy, explores below the surface, discovers that they are rooted in questions of philosophy."[14]

In the quest for a theory or philosophy, adherents to the classical approach search for recurrences in history while they remain cognizant that history never fully repeats itself. The Prussian strategist Carl von Clausewitz is an example of a classical approach theorist. The use of history to separate the unique from the recurrent in human affairs lies at the heart of Clausewitz's theory of war. In Clausewitz's judgment, "Whenever an activity deals primarily with the same things again and again—with the same ends and the same means, even though there may be minor variations and an infinite diversity of combinations—these things are susceptible of rational study. It is precisely that inquiry which is the most essential part of any *theory*, and which may quite appropriately claim that title."[15]

Theory is nurtured by history in the classical approach. As Thompson explained the relationship, "History is past politics and as such provides the raw stuff of theory."[16] Henry Kissinger grasped this relationship and observed that "One of the most difficult challenges a nation confronts is to interpret correctly the lessons of its past. For the lessons of history, as of all experience, are contingent: they teach the consequences of certain actions, but they leave to each generation the task of determining which situations are comparable."[17] The use of history to generate international relations theory is useful for extrapolating from past politics the parameters for future international politics, but its use is insufficient for predicting the contingent inherent in human affairs. The distillation of the recurrent in history provides the intellectual foundation for a theory to govern the conduct of future action.

A general body of knowledge grounded in the classical approach should meet a number of criteria to be considered a philosophy or theory of international relations. Some scholars and practitioners agree that the function of theory is threefold; it gives order and meaning to a mass of phenomena that without it would be disconnected and unintelligible, it requires that the criteria of selection of problems for intensive analysis be made explicit, and it can be an instrument for understanding not only uniformities and regularities but contingencies and irrationalities.[18]

A theory of international relations, moreover, should be readily usable and accessible to policy makers and statesmen. Francis Bacon wrote that the "Philosophers make imaginary laws for imaginary commonwealths, and their discourse as the stars gives little light because they are so high."[19] Accordingly, Thompson warned that the unity of theory and practice may be destroyed when theories are "too remote and exalted," which is most often the case with theories conceived in the scientific approach. Policy makers are always on the verge of being overwhelmed by the rush of day-to-day demands and cannot develop the specialized analytic tools needed to interpret scientific models of international relations. Kissinger, in appreciation for the competing demands of the scholar and the policy maker, pointed out that "What is relevant for policy depends not only on academic truth but also on what can be implemented under stress."[20] Esoteric models or theories that are impenetrable to policy makers will not be read, understood, or used to formulate and implement policy.

A theory or philosophy consisting of a general body of ideas that simplify reality may lack the specificity demanded by many scholars, but this shortcoming is overshadowed by its potential practicality for policy makers. As Thompson observed, "Practical men with first-hand diplomatic experience point to the need for rational generalizations and intellectual structures to extract meaning from the jet stream of contemporary events."[21] Alexis de Tocqueville wrote of this trade-off long before the advent of the discipline of international relations: "The chief merit of general ideas is that they enable the human mind to pass a rapid judgment on a great many objects at once; but, on the other hand, the notions they convey are never other than incomplete, and they always cause the mind to lose as much in accuracy as it gains in comprehensiveness."[22] A philosophy of international relations enables scholars and statesmen alike to sift out the relevant from the mass of information to grasp reality more readily.

A classical theory or philosophy of international politics consists of an interrelated set of principles. One may turn to Clausewitz for a definition of principle in the classical tradition. He wrote that "*Principle* is also a law for action, but not in its *formal, definitive meaning*; it represents only the spirit and the sense of the law: in cases where the diversity of the real world cannot be contained within the rigid form of law, the application of principle allows for a greater latitude of judgment. Cases to which principle cannot be applied must be settled by judgment; principle thus becomes essentially a support, or lodestar, to the man responsible for the action."[23] The importance of principles to guide political action was eloquently captured by the conservative philosopher Edmund Burke. He wrote that "without the guide and light of sound, well-understood principles, all reasonings in politics, as in everything else, would be only a confused jumble of particular facts and details, without the means of drawing out any sort of theoretical or practical conclusion."[24]

A practical and applicable theory of international relations comprised of principles tempered by political judgment would sharpen the focus and improve the quality of American foreign policy. William T. R. Fox argued that "Theory is useful because it organizes social science so as, marginally at least, to heighten the rationality of choice, official and unofficial. It does not do this directly; it does it by clarifying doctrinal positions, by pointing to the most efficient means to move toward desired ends, and by minimizing the area of contingency and sheer ignorance which the policy-maker can never hope completely to eliminate."[25] Thompson similarly pointed out that "Theory may serve to enhance the rationality of choice of decision-makers by helping them in the articulation of a more fully consistent view of the factors of the external environment. Yet the statesman is bound to a world of contingencies and pressures. He must express his philosophy from time to time as rough guides and rules-of-thumb that can only be limited and restricted in character."[26]   In Halle's bottom-line assessment, "If we are to have an effective foreign policy, we need to base it on a conceptual scheme that reveals and explains the world in terms that bear the test of practical application."[27]

CONTENDING CLASSICAL APPROACHES:
LIBERALISM AND REALISM

Within the classical approach to the study of international relations there are two major contending schools of thought. Political realism, as Robert Gilpin reflected, "must be seen as a philosophical disposition and set of assumptions about the world rather than as in any strict sense a 'scientific' theory."[28] Political realism is often defined by contrasting it with its rival philosophy of international politics—political idealism.   Edward Carr during the period between the world wars distinguished political realism from political idealism. He noted that, whereas the idealist or utopian "makes political theory a norm to which political practice ought to conform," the realist "regards political theory as a sort of codification of political practice."[29]   John Herz pointed out that the term political realism commonly "has been used in connection with theories claiming to be concerned with the observance and analysis of political 'facts,' the often sober and hard-boiled 'what is' of history and politics, while the term 'political idealism,' in this usage, has referred to those theories which have dealt with the ideals of a 'better' world, a 'better' state, 'better' politics, etc.—in short, the often utopian 'what ought to be' of history and politics."[30]

Political realism and political idealism are often cast as conservatism and liberalism, respectively. As Thompson broadly characterized these political philosophies, "Liberalism is steeped in the principles of the Enlightenment and in faith in man's essential goodness and his capacity to subdue nature. The articles of faith of the Enlightenment creed include the beliefs that civilization is becoming more rational and moral, that injustice is caused by ignorance and will yield to education and greater intelligence, that war is stupid and can be overcome through reason, that appeals to brotherhood are bound to be effective in the end and that conflict is simply a matter of misunderstanding. Liberalism as a philosophy of life accepted the Enlightenment view of human progress and perfectibility."[31]   In contrast, "The corrective to these liberal illusions in Western civilization has been conservatism.   Conservatism speaks for the skeptical and cautious side of human nature that sees all about it too many examples of man's sinfulness, frailty and caprice. It is full of the grave doubts about the goodness and rationality of man, the sagacity of the majority and the wisdom of reform. It seeks to put the calipers on the possibilities of human attainment. It tends toward pessimism and displays a natural preference for stability over change, continuity over experiment, the past over the future."[32]

Despite the conservative-liberal dichotomy, a theory based on a foundation of realism coupled with a limited dose of liberalism is a formula for political action. As Thompson observed, "England's political advance must be attributed at least partly to the creative interplay between its traditions of Lockean liberalism and Burkean conservatism. The one has a keen sense of justice; the other is more aware of all the inescapable aspects of community life that are organic in character."[33] The view that conservatism or realism needs an infusion of liberalism is consistent with the thought of many realist thinkers. From Carr's point of view, for example, "The utopian who dreams that it is possible to eliminate self-assertion from politics and to base a political system on morality alone is just as wide of the mark as the realist who believes that altruism is an illusion and that all political action is based on self-seeking."[34] Likewise, Herz argued that "While all political action and endeavor should be based firmly on a sound foundation of 'realist' facts and insights, the guiding star of all such action should be one that moves man to try to push developments in a different direction. They should be built, not on the sands of wishful thinking but on the rock of reality. On the other hand, they should not be left where the inertia of things would carry them. Within the limits of the attainable, a combination of Political Realism and Political Idealism thus seems to be the political ideal."[35]

If John Locke's *Second Treatise on Government*—which inspired the American Founding Fathers and their Declaration of Independence—spawned modern liberalism, traditional conservatism was born in Burke's thought. Clinton Rossiter judged that "There were brave conservatives before Edmund Burke, but not until this great man and his colleagues faced up boldly to the extravagant radicalism of that event [the French Revolution] did conservatism come to life as a clearly distinguishable school of political thought. Burke's *Reflections on the Revolution in France* (1790) is rightly considered the first and greatest statement of consciously conservative principles."[36]

The conservative, continental Europeans had a fundamentally different outlook on the nature of international politics from their maritime English and American liberal counterparts. Arnold Wolfers related that "As Continental political philosophers saw it, the main problem presented by conditions of multiple sovereignty was that of a deep conflict between morality and raison d'etat. This was in line with the experience common to all Continental countries which in the face of constant external threats to their national existence believed themselves exposed to the compelling impact of forces beyond their control."[37] In contrast, "English and American thought and experience traveled a different road. Even the concepts of necessity of state or reason of state remained foreign to the political philosophers of the English-speaking world. While the Continentals were arguing about the dilemma of the statesmen faced by the irreconcilable demands of necessity and morality, English and American thinkers in turn were engaged in a debate about the best way of applying accepted principles of morality to the field of foreign policy."[38]

The geographic protection afforded the United States and Great Britain by their maritime buffers eroded due to technological advances in the twentieth century and made conservative continental thought pertinent to American and British views on international politics. As Wolfers and Martin had foreseen, "If it was correct to relate the peculiar outlook of the English-speaking theorists—their philosophy of moral choice—to the insular security that their countries enjoyed, the disappearance of this security in our time, now an acknowledged fact, may call for a significant modification of the traditional philosophy. The leeway for choice which the two countries enjoyed in the past has been gravely curtailed. For all practical purposes they have become 'Continental' in terms of the dangers and compulsions pressing upon them from the outside."[39]   The course of the Second World War—with Germany's contemplation of an amphibious assault on England and Japan's attack on Pearl Harbor—demonstrated that technological advances in warfare had reduced the maritime powers' margin of safety. The thought of the continental philosophers—nurtured in the European crucible of conflict—therefore became more relevant to British and American foreign policy.

Political realism as a conservative, classical theory of international politics and foreign policy emerged against the backdrop of the liberal philosophy or Wilsonianism prevalent in the United States. American conservatism was significantly bolstered in the 1930s and 1940s by an influx of philosophically conservative European scholars, many of whom had fled Nazi Germany. The immigration of these scholars represented an infusion of European thought in general and conservatism in particular into the American liberal body politic. These scholars subsequently had an enormous impact on the growth and development of the discipline of international relations in the United States.

Realism and continental European thought emerged as an alternative to liberalism and Wilsonianism in the United States after the Second World War. German immigrant Hans J. Morgenthau, more than any other scholar, laid the conservative foundation for the growth of the American school of political realism in the study of international politics. Morgenthau was the "godfather" of the American realists who were to be nurtured in this philosophy born in traditional conservatism. As Joel Rosenthal recalled, "Although realism did become a collaboration of sorts, a case can be made for distinguishing Morgenthau as the group leader. His work established the range and parameters for all those who would follow. Because he was so deliberate in his explanations and so prolific as a scholar and commentator, Morgenthau's name became synonymous with political realism."[40] As Michael Smith observed, "Morgenthau's project was to turn realism from a critique of utopianism and a characteristic approach to man and politics into a comprehensive theory that would explain the underlying essence of relations among states, illuminate the moral problem in statecraft, and provide a sound basis for evaluating specific, contemporary problems of national policy."[41]

Morgenthau's efforts to move the realist school to the mainstream of American political thought were abetted by others who shared his conservative philosophy. Michael Howard commented that, in the aftermath of the Second

World War, "such 'Realist' political thinkers as Nicholas Spykman, Arnold Wolfers, and Hans Morgenthau had established flourishing schools in American universities which were taking as their bases the very concepts of the national interest, military capabilities and the balance of power on which American political scientists had turned their backs twenty-five years earlier."[42] In the mid-1950s to the mid-1960s, Henry Kissinger and Robert Osgood claimed "to be political theorists dealing in universally valid concepts of international relations," which marked "them as the successors to the 'Realist' thinkers of the 1940s."[43]

Realists view politics—stripped to its bare essentials—as the struggle for power, which Morgenthau defined as one's control over the minds and actions of others.[44] He stressed that "Politics is a struggle for power over men, and whatever its ultimate aim may be, power is its immediate goal and the modes of acquiring, maintaining, and demonstrating it determine the technique of political action."[45] The struggle for power is a universal phenomenon evident in interpersonal relations as well as in relations between nation-states. Thompson wrote in reflection of this realist position that "In all social groups—whether the state or in smaller, more intimate communities—a contest for influence and power goes on."[46] Morgenthau's work set the parameters for political realism as a normative school of thought in which political realists since have dwelt. They strenuously argue that statesmen must recognize the ubiquity of the struggle of power in order to fashion policies that balance competing drives for power in international politics.

A variant school of realism has emerged since the school's formative years under Morgenthau's tutelage. Many contemporary scholars have sought to convert political realism from its classical form into a social scientific form. In so doing, the "structuralists," or "neorealists," have stripped the tradition of its normative contents and reduced the theory to only one facet of traditional realism—the balance of power. Kenneth Waltz laid the intellectual groundwork for the neorealist school in the late 1970s.[47] The significance of Waltz's theory, according to Robert Keohane, "lies less in his initiation of a new line of theoretical inquiry or speculations than in his attempt to systematize political realism into a rigorous, deductive systemic theory of international politics."[48] The neorealist school in many respects has eclipsed traditional realism as a major focus of research in the discipline of international relations. Young scholars today commonly use the terms realism and neorealism interchangeably, which obscures the profound differences between these schools. This study represents, in part, an attempt to reinvigorate contemporary research toward the normative realist tradition.

KENNAN'S CALL FOR AMERICAN FOREIGN POLICY PRINCIPLES

George Kennan was one of the leading figures who worked to nurture the school of political realism in the United States in the aftermath of World War

II.   Ironically, Kennan frequently emphasized to his biographer John Lewis Gaddis that he never intended to become a founding father of realism.[49] Nevertheless, Kennan's intellectual outlook bore all the traits of a conservative approach to international politics and distinguished him from his contemporaries with a Wilsonian or liberal view of politics. Kennan, moreover, was committed to the classical approach to international politics; he rejected a scientific approach to politics and chose for a humanistic one. Halle noted that Kennan was "in the tradition of Gibbon and Keynes, a scholar-humanist."[50] Likewise, David Mayers observed that "Kennan's notions about international policy are strikingly devoid of the scientism and abstruseness that have spoiled so much of international relations theory in recent decades."[51]

Kennan's worldview, which was forged in diplomatic practice and scholarship, informed his recommendations for American foreign policy. As Thompson remarked, "Kennan's career has combined diplomacy and scholarship at a level unmatched by any other public servant" and his "grasp of foreign policy has seldom if ever been matched in American thought and practice."[52] Kennan's experiences as an American diplomat for twenty-six years and as a diplomatic historian mutually reinforced his worldview. His theoretical understanding of international politics was nurtured in the intellectual struggle with practical, concrete problems in American foreign policy. Kennan believed that "part of my strength as a diplomatic historian came from the fact that I had been responsibly involved with contemporary problems of diplomacy, whereas whatever value I had as a commentator on contemporary affairs was derived, in part at least, from the belief on the part of the public that I knew something about history."[53]

Kennan's thoughts on international politics also were nurtured by the work of other members of the American realist school, as well as by philosophers, historians, theorists, and statesmen. Kennan, for example, acknowledged that he followed Morgenthau's work closely. In a personal letter to Morgenthau in 1966, Kennan wrote that "I continue to read with great admiration nine-tenths of what appears from your pen."[54] As Professor Norman Graebner has suggested, Kennan probably read Carr's *Twenty Years' Crisis*, from which he would have instantly grasped the meaning of realism from this concise book.[55] Kennan shared many of the assumptions held by other American realist thinkers, including Bernard Brodie, Reinhold Niebuhr, Walter Lippmann, Louis Halle, and Nicholas Spykman. In a letter to Halle, Kennan wrote that "I don't suppose there is anyone writing in this field, unless it be Herbert Butterfield or Reinhold Niebuhr, whose views of World War II and its aftermath would be closer to my own."[56] Kennan's views also appear to have been influenced by scholars and statesmen such as John Quincy Adams, Burke, Clausewitz, Alexander Hamilton, Edward Gibbon, Halford MacKinder, James Madison, and Tocqueville.

Many commentators have been impressed by the sophistication of Kennan's worldview. David Mayers noted of Kennan that "out of his personal experiences as a diplomat and his findings as an historian, he has produced since the 1950s a rich set of underlying assumptions and principles that in their aggregate amount to theory worthy of comment."[57] Halle viewed Kennan as "a man of Shakespearian insight and vision who saw the international scene as a stage on which those who represented the historic achievements of human civility were challenged by powerful forces of evil."[58] Halle commented that "No one can converse with Kennan long and not perceive that, like de Tocqueville, he is a man in the grip of a personal vision which illuminated everything that comes under his observation. The normative world of this vision presents itself to his mind with such clarity and persuasiveness as to make him react in alarm, time and again, to a world of actuality in which men who are blind to it march toward disaster."[59] Gaddis wrote that Kennan had a "knack for seeing relationships between objectives and capabilities, aspirations and interests, long-term and short-term priorities—rarely found in harried bureaucracies."[60] This trait brought to Kennan's writings "a degree of foresight and a consistency of strategic vision for which it would be difficult to find a contemporary parallel."[61]

Kennan labored throughout his life in a conservative tradition to find a theoretical foundation for American foreign policy. As Kennan wrote in a letter to the editor of *Foreign Affairs*, Hamilton Fish Armstrong, in 1950, "*I have tried to contribute what I could to putting a theoretical floor under United States foreign policy, which seems to me to have been without one since approximately the time of John Quincy Adams. Where my own acumen and influence were inadequate to the task (and between them their inadequacy has covered a big area) I have tried to provoke others into thinking about the theory of American foreign policy and contributing to its development.*"[62] Kennan's book *Realities of American Foreign Policy* was a step along this path and outlined a "personal philosophy of foreign policy."[63] It was, in Kennan's words, the "realization of the lack of an adequately stated and widely accepted theoretical foundation to underpin the conduct of our external relations which aroused my curiosity about the concepts by which our statesmen had been guided in recent decades."[64]

Despite this endeavor, Kennan expressed skepticism about the prospects for a theory of international politics and American foreign policy. Kennan noted that theory to him, "as to Goethe, has always been gray, in contrast to the green quality of what he called 'the golden tree of life.'"[65] Kennan's aversion to "theory" reflected the tendency identified by Clinton Rossiter for conservatives to have a distaste for working out elaborate theories in the scientific sense of the word: "The Conservative's ideas about government display an unusual degree of symmetry, and he is rarely stumped by practical questions about its nature, structure, and purpose. These ideas are not, in any one sense, especially profound. Reluctant theorist that he is, he prefers to live with contradictions (such as between liberty and authority) and to ignore nasty questions (such as that of sovereignty) with which men who like their doctrines neat are feverishly concerned."[66] Indeed, Kennan never viewed himself as a theorist, according to Gaddis, and he appeared always to be surprised by the scholarly attention devoted to his writings as theory.[67]   Kennan's reaction undoubtedly is attributable to his conservative proclivities. Although he rejected the pursuit of a "scientific" theory of international politics and American foreign policy, Kennan probably sought in his mind's eye the construction of a theory or philosophy as understood by the classical approach advocates such as Clausewitz, Burke, and Morgenthau.

General principles help policy makers cope with complexity in international politics. Kennan noted that "The heart of their problem lies—and will always lie—in the shaping and conduct of policy for areas about which they cannot be expert and learned."[68]   Kennan late in life cautioned that "many of these troublesome situations that bother you do not really threaten your interests. And even for those that do, there could be no single grand design—no vast common denominator—that would tell you how each of them should be approached. Each has to be judged on its merit. Discard, then, this traditional American fondness for trying to solve problems by putting them into broad categories. What you need are not policies—much less a single policy. What you need are sound principles: principles that accord with the nature, the needs, the interests and the limitations of our country."[69]   Kennan argued that the use of these assumptions constituted a "conceptual framework more closely related to the realities of the world we live in and that in the long run—in the law of averages—conduct realistically motivated is likely to be more effective than conduct unrealistically motivated."[70]

Kennan's greatest influence during his government service in the course of post–World War II foreign policy is in large measure attributable to his successful construction of governing principles. He was instrumental in the formulation of the Marshall Plan as head of the State Department's Policy Planning Staff. The Policy Planning Staff's primary function then was to "cull out" a "workable recommendation for the principles" for an American approach to post–World War II Europe. The staff worked out three principles for the Marshall Plan: the Europeans should themselves ask for U.S. assistance; all European states, including the Soviet Union should be eligible for aid; and the decisive emphasis of the program should be on the rehabilitation of the German economy.[71]   These principles laid the theoretical foundation for the American foreign policy that successfully contributed to the rebuilding of war-torn Europe.

Likewise, Kennan's articulation of principles in the famous 1947 article published in *Foreign Affairs* on the strategy of containment had an enormous impact on American foreign policy.[72]   Although ambiguities in Kennan's prose coupled with the ideologically charged atmosphere in the United States during the Cold War led to a prolonged and heated debate over the interpretation of the policy of containment, Kennan had in mind a simple set of principles. The policy of containment for Kennan meant; "restoring economic health and political self-confidence to the people of Western Europe and Japan in order that they may be resistant to local Communist pressures—and prove to the men in the Kremlin in this way that they are not going to succeed in extending their rule to further areas by political intrigue and intimidation, that they cannot serve their own interests without dealing with us; and then, when a political balance has been created, to go on to the negotiation with Moscow of a general political settlement."[73]

CONCLUSION

The growth of international relations as an academic discipline in the United States was a result, in part, of the United States' rise to power in twentieth-century international politics. One of the primary goals of the discipline was to inform the formulation and implementation of American foreign policy. The scientific approach that has emerged to dominate the field in the United States is increasingly unable to meet this objective, as policy makers charged with running foreign policy cannot comprehend the school's specialized jargon and methodologies. In contrast, political realism as established by Hans Morgenthau in the United States is a classical theory of international politics that links theory and practice. It offers policy makers a package of principles and concepts to simplify complicated reality to illuminate the most salient features of international politics and the challenges posed to the United States.

Kennan's thought moved in lockstep with that of Morgenthau, although he never explicitly developed a theory to the extent to which Morgenthau had. Kennan was conscious of the need for principles to govern the conduct of American foreign policy, but he failed to sufficiently articulate these principles beyond those in the Marshall Plan and the policy of containment. Subsequent chapters sift through Kennan's work to illuminate and make more explicit the principles suspended in Kennan's worldview, which, taken collectively, constitute a classical theory of American foreign policy. The use of these principles could strengthen the ability of policy makers to comprehend reality and could improve their understanding of the American policy tools needed to navigate the troubled waters of international politics.

NOTES

1. For background on the development of the field, see Kenneth W. Thompson, "Four Decades of International Relations Theorizing," in his *Traditions and Values in Politics and Diplomacy* (Baton Rouge, LA: Louisiana State University Press, 1992), 36–51. Thompson has more fully discussed the evolution of the field in his *Schools of Thought in International Relations: Interpreters, Issues, and Morality* (Baton Rouge, LA: Louisiana State University Press, 1996).

2. Inis L. Claude, Jr., *Power and International Relations* (New York, NY: Random House, 1962), 8.

3. Martin Wight, "Why There Is No International Theory," in Herbert Butterfield and Martin Wight (eds.), *Diplomatic Investigations: Essays in the Theory of International Politics* (Cambridge, MA: Harvard University Press, 1966), 20.

4. Yale H. Ferguson and Richard W. Mansbach, "Between Celebration and Despair: Constructive Suggestions for Future International Theory," *International Studies Quarterly* 35, no. 4 (December 1991): 366.

5. Raymond Aron, "What Is a Theory of International Relations?" *Journal of International Affairs* 21, no. 2 (1967): 186.

6. Hans J. Morgenthau, "Common Sense and Theories of International Relations," *Journal of International Affairs* 21, no. 2 (1967): 210.

7. See John Lewis Gaddis, "International Relations Theory and the End of the Cold War," *International Security* 17, no. 3 (Winter 1992/93): 5-58 for a valuable survey of international relations theory literature.

8. Alexander L. George, *Bridging the Gap: Theory and Practice in Foreign Policy* (Washington, DC: United States Institute of Peace Press, 1993), 8.

9. Hans J. Morgenthau, *Scientific Man vs. Power Politics* (Chicago, IL: University of Chicago Press, 1946), 10.

10. David D. Newsom, "Foreign Policy and Academia," *Foreign Policy* 101 (Winter 1995-96): 62.

11. Hedley Bull, "International Theory: The Case for a Classical Approach," *World Politics* 18, no. 3 (April 1966): 361.

12. Kenneth W. Thompson, "Normative Theory in International Relations," *Journal of International Affairs* 21, no. 2 (1967): 278-279.

13. Aron, "What Is a Theory of International Relations?" 186.

14. Louis J. Halle, *Men and Nations* (Princeton, NJ: Princeton University Press, 1962), vii.

15. Carl von Clausewitz, *On War*, Edited and Translated by Michael Howard and Peter Paret (Princeton, NJ: Princeton University Press, 1989), 141.

16. Kenneth W. Thompson, "Toward a Theory of International Politics," *American Political Science Review* 49 (September 1955): 734. This paper summarized the findings of a group of scholars, analysts, and diplomatists. The group included Robert Bowie, Dorothy Fosdick, William T. R. Fox, Walter Lippmann, Hans Morgenthau, Reinhold Niebuhr, Paul Nitze, Don Price, James Reston, Dean Rusk, Kenneth Thompson, and Arnold Wolfers. Although George Kennan did not attend the conference, he submitted a paper. For a more recent discussion of the relevance of history to the study of international relations, see John Lewis Gaddis, "Expanding the Data Base: Historians, Political Scientists, and the Enrichment of Security Studies," *International Security* 12, no. 1 (Summer 1987).

17. Henry A. Kissinger, *Nuclear Weapons and Foreign Policy* (New York, NY: Harper & Brothers, 1957), 21.

18. Thompson, "Toward a Theory of International Politics," 735-736.

19. Quoted in Kenneth W. Thompson, "Unity and Contradiction in the Theory and Practice of International Relations," *Review of Politics* 44, no. 3 (July 1982): 330.

20. Henry A. Kissinger, *American Foreign Policy* (New York, NY: W.W. Norton & Company, 1969), 22.

21. Thompson, "Toward a Theory of International Politics," 733.

22. Alexis de Tocqueville, *Democracy in America*, Volume II, Henry Reeve Text, Revised by Francis Bowen, Further Corrected and Edited by Phillips Bradley (New York, NY: Vintage Books, 1990), 13.

23. Clausewitz, *On War*, 151.

24. Edmund Burke, "Speech on the Petition of the Unitarians (1792)," in Louis I. Bredvold and Ralph G. Ross (eds.), *The Philosophy of Edmund Burke: A Selection from His Speeches and Writings* (Ann Arbor, MI: University of Michigan Press, 1967), 41.

25. William T. R. Fox, "The Uses of International Relations Theory," in William T. R. Fox (ed.), *Theoretical Aspects of International Relations* (Notre Dame, IN: University of Notre Dame Press, 1959), 49.

26. Thompson, "Toward a Theory of International Politics," 735.

27. Louis J. Halle, *Civilization and Foreign Policy: An Inquiry for Americans* (New York, NY: Harper & Brothers Publishers, 1955), 52.

28. Robert G. Gilpin, "The Richness of the Tradition of Political Realism," in Robert O. Keohane (ed.), *Neorealism and Its Critics* (New York, NY: Columbia University Press, 1986), 304.

29. Edward Hallett Carr, *The Twenty Years' Crisis 1919–1939: An Introduction to the Study of International Relations*, Second Edition (New York, NY: St. Martin's Press, 1966), 12.

30. John H. Herz, *Political Realism and Political Idealism: A Study in Theories and Realities* (Chicago, IL: University of Chicago Press, 1951), 17.

31. Kenneth W. Thompson, "Liberalism and Conservatism in American Statecraft," *Orbis* 2, no. 4 (Winter 1959): 465.

32. Thompson, "Liberalism and Conservatism in American Statecraft," 466.

33. Thompson, "Liberalism and Conservatism in American Statecraft," 476.

34. Carr, *Twenty Years' Crisis*, 97.

35. Herz, *Political Realism and Political Idealism*, 131–132.

36. Clinton Rossiter, *Conservatism in America*, Second Edition (Cambridge, MA: Harvard University Press, 1982), 15–16.

37. Arnold Wolfers and Laurence W. Martin, *The Anglo-American Tradition in Foreign Affairs* (New Haven, CT: Yale University Press, 1956), xx.

38. Wolfers and Martin, *Anglo-American Tradition*, xx.

39. Wolfers and Martin, *Anglo-American Tradition*, xxvi.

40. Joel H. Rosenthal, *Righteous Realists: Political Realism, Responsible Power, and American Culture in the Nuclear Age* (Baton Rouge, LA: Louisiana State University Press, 1991), 12.

41. Michael Joseph Smith, *Realist Thought from Weber to Kissinger* (Baton Rouge, LA: Louisiana State University Press, 1986), 134.

42. Michael Howard, *The Causes of Wars*, Second Edition (Cambridge, MA: Harvard University Press, 1983), 41.

43. Howard, *Causes of Wars*, 43.

44. Hans J. Morgenthau and Kenneth W. Thompson, *Politics among Nations: The Struggle for Power and Peace*, Sixth Edition (New York, NY: McGraw-Hill Publishing Company, 1985), 32.

45. Morgenthau, *Scientific Man vs. Power Politics*, 195.

46. Kenneth W. Thompson, *Political Realism and the Crisis of World Politics: An American Approach to Foreign Policy* (Lanham, MD: University Press of America, 1982), 69.

47. See Kenneth N. Waltz, *Theory of International Politics* (Reading, MA: Addison-Wesley Publishing Company, 1979).

48. Robert O. Keohane, "Realism, Neorealism and the Study of World Politics," in Robert O. Keohane (ed.), *Neorealism and Its Critics* (New York, NY: Columbia University Press, 1986), 15.

49. Interview with John Lewis Gaddis, Woodrow Wilson International Center for Scholars, Washington, DC, 26 October 1995. Hereafter referred to as Gaddis Interview.

50. Louis J. Halle, "George Kennan and the Common Mind," *The Virginia Quarterly*, Volume 45, Number 1, Winter 1969, 47.

51. David Mayers, *George Kennan and the Dilemmas of U.S. Foreign Policy* (New York, NY: Oxford University Press, 1988), 317.

52. Kenneth W. Thompson, *Masters of International Thought* (Baton Rouge, LA: Louisiana State University Press, 1990), 145, 157.

53. George F. Kennan, *Memoirs 1950–1963* (New York, NY: Pantheon Books, 1972), 14.

54. "Correspondence to Hans J. Morgenthau," 6 December 1966, George F. Kennan Papers, Box 31, Seeley G. Mudd Manuscript Library, Department of Rare Books and Special Collections, Princeton University Library.

55. Norman Graebner, Discussion and Correspondence with the Author, 24 April 1996, and 8 October 1996, respectively.

56. "Correspondence to Louis J. Halle," 15 December 1964, George F. Kennan Papers, Box 31, Seeley G. Mudd Manuscript Library, Department of Rare Books and Special Collections, Princeton University Library.

57. Mayers, *George Kennan and the Dilemmas of U.S. Foreign Policy,* 11.

58. Louis J. Halle, *The Cold War as History* (New York, NY: HarperPerennial, 1991), 116.

59. Halle, "George Kennan and the Common Mind," 52.

60. John Lewis Gaddis, *Strategies of Containment: A Critical Appraisal of Postwar American National Security Policy* (New York, NY: Oxford University Press, 1982), 25.

61. John Lewis Gaddis, "Containment: A Reassessment," *Foreign Affairs* 55, no. 4 (July 1977): 886.

62. "Correspondence to Hamilton Fish Armstrong" [italics added], 20 October 1950, Hamilton Fish Armstrong Papers, Box 38, Kennan Correspondence File 1946–1951, Seeley G. Mudd Manuscript Library, Department of Rare Books and Special Collections, Princeton University Library.

63. George F. Kennan, *Realities of American Foreign Policy* (Princeton, NJ: Princeton University Press, 1954), 3.

64. George F. Kennan, *American Diplomacy*, Expanded Edition (Chicago, IL: University of Chicago Press, 1984), ix.

65. George F. Kennan, *Around the Cragged Hill: A Personal and Political Philosophy* (New York, NY: W.W. Norton & Company, 1993), 11.

66. Rossiter, *Conservatism in America*, 31.

67. Gaddis Interview.

68. Kennan, *American Diplomacy*, 38.

69. Kennan, "The Failure in Our Success," *New York Times*, 14 March 1994, A17.

70. Kennan, *American Diplomacy*, 72.

71. George F. Kennan, *Memoirs, 1925–1950* (New York, NY: Pantheon Books, 1967), 343.

72. See X [George F. Kennan], "The Sources of Soviet Conduct," *Foreign Affairs* 25, no. 4 (July 1947).

73. George F. Kennan, *At a Century's Ending: Reflections, 1982–1995* (New York, NY: W.W. Norton & Company, 1996), 38.

2

A REALIST'S POLITICAL THEORY: ON MAN, POWER, MORALITY, AND POLITICS

Kennan's perspective on American foreign policy was, in large measure, informed by a philosophy of man and politics. This philosophy was the infrastructure upon which many of Kennan's foreign policy principles rested. Only by grappling with Kennan's philosophy of man and politics—both within and between nation-states—is one able to come to a full appreciation of his views on the United States' role in world affairs.

To dissect Kennan's political theory, this chapter examines his thought on the levels of analysis set up by Kenneth Waltz in his *Man, the State and War*.[1] It discusses Kennan's humanistic conviction that any discussion of politics must begin with an examination of the nature of man, the first of Waltz's three images. For Kennan, the drive for power—inherent in all men to varying degrees—defines political intercourse. Kennan's understanding of the nature of man and his drive for power is the foundation for his thought on politics. Man needs the state or government, Waltz's second image, to harness, control, and channel his drive for power. For Kennan, morality had to be reconciled with the demands of power politics. Various forms of government are able to meet these requirements, but each, in Kennan's view, has a tendency to produce unique characteristics. No overarching government can harness, control, or channel the competition for power among nation-states in the international system, Waltz's third image of analysis. Consequently, Kennan looked to the operation of a balance of power to preserve the autonomy of nation-states by holding one another in check to prevent their domination by any one or group of nation-states.

Kennan's views throughout each of the three images is marked by conservative philosophy. This philosophy has fallen out of favor with mainstream American political thought, which is more sympathetic to idealism or Wilsonianism than realism. An examination of Kennan's conservative philosophy provides an alternative paradigm through which one can critically examine key tenets of the contemporary Wilsonianism that informs American foreign policy.

THE CORE IMAGE: MAN

The nature of man lies at the core of Kennan's realist thought and is the starting point for understanding his views on American foreign policy.[2] Kennan argued that "The relations between nations are part of the whole great problem of politics--of the behavior of man as a political animal."[3] Kennan elaborated that "International affairs are primarily a matter of the behavior of governments. But the behavior of governments is in turn a matter of the behavior of individual man in the political context, and the workings of all those basic impulses—national feeling, charity, ambition, fear, jealousy, egotism, and group attachment—which are the stuff of his behavior in the community of other men."[4] The British historian Herbert Butterfield similarly argued that "It is a statesman's business to know human beings as they really are and to deal with them as such."[5] To understand the behavior of nation-states, therefore, one must understand the nature of man.

It is this focus on the nature of man that distinguished the thoughts of the traditional realists such as Hans Morgenthau, Reinhold Niebuhr, and Kennan from the neorealists such as Waltz and marked the former's approach to international politics as humanistic. In Kennan's judgment, "Whoever does not understand these things will never understand what is taking place in the interrelationships of nations. And he will not learn them from courses that purport to deal with international affairs alone. He will learn them, rather, from those things which have been recognized for thousands of years as the essentials of humanistic study: from history and from the more subtle and revealing expressions of man's nature that go by the names of art and literature."[6] This emphasis on history and literature is a key distinguishing feature of what Hedley Bull referred to as the "classical" approach to the study of international politics.[7]

Kennan worked in the realm of the classical approach to politics and rejected contemporary approaches that seek to adopt scientific methods for the study of politics. Many scholars since the 1960s have rejected the classical approach and have instead sought to exploit the techniques that give the physical sciences demonstrable success in broadening knowledge. Kennan rebuked such approaches to the study of politics: "Let no one be permitted to think that he is learned in something called a 'science' of international relations unless he is learned in the essentials of the political process from the grass roots up and has been taught to look soberly and unsparingly but also with charity and sympathy, at his fellow human beings. International affairs is not a science. And there is no understanding of international affairs that does not embrace understanding of the human individual."[8] Kennan argued that "the proper study of mankind has always been man; and until it can be shown to me that the scientific advances of this age have relieved man of some of the moral challenges and dilemmas which press themselves upon him, I must continue to pursue what others are at liberty to regard as my outdated ruminations and reactions."[9]

The rejection of the assumption that the tools and techniques used by the natural sciences are directly applicable to the study of politics reflected Kennan's strong commitment to a conservative philosophy. Kennan followed in the footsteps of the great spokesman for the conservative tradition, Edmund Burke. Although Kennan had read Burke, he never viewed himself as a master of Burke's work, according to John Lewis Gaddis.[10] Nevertheless, the similarity of Kennan and Burke's views is striking. Burke, in rejecting the scientific approach to politics, wrote that "The legislators who framed the ancient republics knew that their business was too arduous to be accomplished with no better apparatus than the metaphysics of an undergraduate, and the mathematics and arithmetic of an exciseman. They had to do with men, and they were obliged to study human nature. They had to do with citizens, and they were obliged to study the effects of those habits which were communicated by the circumstances of civil life."[11] Burke influenced other political realists as well. Kenneth Thompson recalled that Niebuhr "in his later years pointed to Edmund Burke as a political thinker who best understood that 'the powers which are in cooperation and conflict in the human community are compounded of ethnic loyalties, common traditions, ancient sanctities, common fears, common hopes and endless other combinations of human motives.' Those who recognize such factors tend toward a historical rather than a purely systemic discussion of politics. Man, the center of the study of politics, is best understood as a historical being rooted in time and place."[12]

Conservative philosophy questions the Enlightenment notion that man is capable of progressively improving his condition through reason. While conservatives acknowledge that man is capable of technological advancement, they see man's capacity for development confined by the limits of his nature. Along these lines, Kennan once remarked that he knew of "no evidence of any important change in man himself since the days of the classical cultures. There is no reason to believe that his intellectual or artistic capacities have undergone any significant change from what they used to be. And as far as his moral nature is concerned the cruelties which have been perpetrated within our own memories have been on a vaster scale, in absolute terms, than anything known for centuries back."[13] Man, from the conservative philosophic perspective, is not perfectible. Accordingly, Kennan asserted that "I have, it is true, no belief in human perfectibility, and hold that many of man's cruelest limitations and frustrations are built into his own imperfect makeup."[14] In Kennan's judgment, "These fissures in the human psyche are profound and elemental. As long as civilized life subsists, it will continue to be marked by them and to be limited by the restraints they impose."[15]

The human condition is marked by a perennial struggle between man's competing traits. Kennan once remarked that "I have no high opinion of human beings: they are always going to fight and do nasty things to each other. They are always going to be part animal, governed by their emotions and subconscious drives rather than by reason. They will always, as Freud remarked, feel a grave *Unbehagen*, a discomfort, at having to live in a civilized framework, and kick against it. But if that is so, the only thing you can do with them is to see that the weapons they have are not too terrible."[16] Kennan's characterization of human nature is reminiscent of that of Machiavelli, who wrote that "one can generally say this about men: that they are ungrateful, fickle, simulators and deceivers, avoiders of danger, greedy for gain."[17] Interestingly, mention of Machiavelli, a political theorist often associated with realist views on human nature, is notably absent from Kennan's writings. Kennan appears not to have devoted special attention to Machiavelli's work.

Mankind is torn by two competing drives, one referred to as "self-love"—or "self-regard" as Reinhold Niebuhr preferred—and the second is the sexual urge.[18] Niebuhr turned to Augustine as the first great "realist" in Western history, given his identification of "self-love" as "the source of evil."[19] Niebuhr pointed out that the Christian doctrine of original sin "asserts the obvious fact that all men are persistently inclined to regard themselves more highly and are more assiduously concerned with their own interests than any 'objective' view of their importance would warrant."[20] Building on Niebuhr's thoughts, Kennan believed that "A central feature of the human predicament is the conflict between these so frequently conflicting impulses—a conflict for which man's own soul constitutes the field of battle."[21] Man's

psychic makeup is the scene for the interplay of contradictions between the primitive nature of his innate impulses and the more refined demands of civilized life, contradictions that destroy the unity and integrity of his undertakings, confuse his efforts, place limits on his possibilities for achievement, and often cause one part of his personality to be the enemy of another. Whipped around, frequently knocked off balance, by these conflicting pressures, he staggers through life as best he can, sometimes reaching extraordinary heights of individual achievement but never fully able to overcome, individually or collectively, the fissures between his own physical and spiritual natures.[22]

In sum, Kennan argued that "Man, to the degree that he tries to shape his behavior to the requirements of civilization, is unquestionably a cracked vessel."[23]

The human condition is further marked by an ever present element of tragedy. Kennan's appreciation of literature and history in his classical approach to politics underscored his view that tragedy always is a companion of man. He sensed that "a measure of tragedy is built into the very existence of the human individual; and it is not to be overcome by even the most drastic human interventions into the economic or social relationships among individuals."[24] Despite this seemingly pessimistic view of the human condition, Kennan was not without a glimmer of optimism over man's fate. The tragic human condition "should not be taken as a reason for despair. The struggle against these handicaps can have, and does have, its glorious moments."[25] Kennan identified a "need underlying the entire historical development of civilizations—to redeem human life, at least partially, of its essentially animalistic origins by lending to it such attributes as order, dignity, beauty, and charity—this last meaning the love of or at least the respect for one's fellow man, and the capacity for compassion."[26] He believed "in the inherent worthiness of the struggle rather than in the visible prospects for success."[27] The challenge for man is to struggle to mitigate evil while strengthening good rather than to achieve human perfection or the end of history in the liberal philosophic sense envisioned by Hegel, Kant, and most recently Francis Fukuyama.[28]

POWER AND POLITICS

The corollary to the realist appreciation for the dual nature of man is the view that the struggle for power is a universal aspect of human nature that permeates everyday life. Hans Morgenthau and Kenneth Thompson spoke of power as "man's control over the minds and actions of other men."[29] Kennan shared this view and wrote in 1993 that "as a projection of the insistent need for indulgence of the individual's self-regard, is the lust for authority, for power, for demonstrated preeminence over others. This urge, assuming an open-ended multiplicity of forms, some relatively innocent and harmless, others more questionable, pervades a great part of personal and organized life."[30] He noted that the struggle for power will be found "in marriages, in families, in youth groups, in social clubs—wherever, in fact, people associate in small ways for personal or other purposes."[31] For Kennan, "This form of self-regard is, in short, a major and unavoidable accompaniment of all organized human activity."[32] Kennan's views here are similar to those of Thomas Hobbes, who "put for a generall inclination of all mankind, a perpetuall and restlesse desire of Power after power, that ceaseth onely in Death."[33] But, as in the case of Machiavelli, there is no evidence to suggest that Kennan paid particular attention to Hobbes's work.

Kennan cautioned about the intoxicating effects of power. He observed that "power is not, in truth, a nice thing. It is very heady stuff. It engenders an excitement which, like some radioactive field, infuses the entire atmosphere in and around any place where it is centered. It is probably not too much to say that all those who become involved with the power of government, whether in the competition for its acquisition or in the enjoyment of it when once acquired, are affected by this excitement, usually quite severely and never very attractively."[34]

The effects of power are more pronounced among collectives than in individuals. Kennan observed that "There seems to have been, from time untold, a universal need for people to feel themselves a part of something larger than themselves, and larger than just the family. Sometimes, in the more distant past, it has been the tribe, or, in other instances, the native valley, or a religious association, or membership in a given caste."[35] As for the struggle for power, "much more prominently and ruthlessly does it come to the fore in larger and more formal associations and hierarchies of every sort: professional, military, bureaucratic, and commercial, among others."[36]

In attempting to retrace the origins of Kennan's thoughts on man and power, the path most directly leads to Niebuhr. The similarity of Kennan's views with those of Niebuhr is too striking to be a coincidence. As Niebuhr perceived man's drive for power,

Man, being more than a natural creature, is not interested merely in physical survival but in prestige and social approval. Having the intelligence to anticipate the perils in which he stands in nature and history, he invariably seeks to gain security against these perils by enhancing his power, individually and collectively. Possessing a darkly unconscious sense of his insignificance in the total scheme of things, he seeks to compensate for his insignificance by pretensions of pride. The conflicts between men are thus never simple conflicts between competing survival impulses. They are conflicts in which each man or group seeks to guard its power and prestige against the peril of competing expressions of power and pride. Since the very possession of power and prestige always involves some encroachment upon the prestige and power of others, this conflict is by its very nature a more stubborn and difficult one than the mere competition between various survival impulses in nature.[37]

Although Kennan was reticent in acknowledging his debt to Niebuhr, Kennan once paid tribute to Niebuhr's intellectual impact on the American realists by referring to him as "the father of us all."[38]

For the realists and Kennan, politics is essentially man's struggle for power writ large. Kennan once contemplated teaching a course on politics in 1964, and in draft lecture notes he wrote: "Politics is the study of the exertion of power by man over man, and particularly of the behavior of man in the political context: as an object of, a competitor for, or a wielder of power."[39] Kennan's thoughts on power and politics echoed those of Max Weber, who defined politics as "striving for a share of power or for influence on the distribution of power, whether it be between states or between groups of people contained within a single state."[40] In Weber's view, "Anyone engaged in politics is striving for power, either power as a means to attain other goals (which may be ideal or selfish), or power 'for its own sake,' which is to say, in order to enjoy the feeling of prestige given by power."[41] Michael Smith perceptively pointed out, however, that "Even if others, particularly Reinhold Niebuhr and George

Kennan, reached their own versions of realism in a way that owed little to Weber directly, the fact remains that Weber's delineation of the issues established the terms of realist discourse that endure to the present day."[42]

The nation-state is a common vessel for the containing and channeling of power in contemporary politics. Kennan described the concept of a nation in these terms: "In the modern world it is the nation—the country—the social, cultural, and political unit in which one was born and brought up or in which, by the force of circumstances, one has been extensively acclimatized."[43] As for the state or government, Kennan wrote that "government always implies and involves power. No government is without it. No government *can* be without it. It is government's most essential attribute. It lies in the very definition of government that it represents the greatest center of power in any national community."[44] Because there is no power above that of the state, the nation-state has become the central focus in the study of politics: "The sovereign state of our age represents, precisely in view of the totality of its power, the most far-reaching and concentrated theatre in which the relationships of power are manifested; as such, it is the one which people most readily associate with the study of politics."[45] Power, therefore, is the adhesive that holds the state to the nation or nations and enables the formation and perpetuation of modern nation-states. Conversely, its absence leads to the disintegration and collapse of nation-states in modern politics.

No matter what its shape or form, government is a universal element of human affairs. In Kennan's view, "Whatever the form it takes, however liberal or oppressive it may be, however large or small the community to which its power extends, government is an absolute necessity. Its adoption or acceptance is not, therefore, a matter of deliberate choice. The only conceivable alternative would be a state of anarchy which would constitute self-destruction for the community in question—which is, in effect, no choice at all."[46] The other functions of government, such as "the maintenance of law and order, the external representation and defense of a national community, or the concern for its health and welfare, the administration of justice, and the regulation of competing and conflicting economic interests," are "rather sad necessities, flowing from the inability of men to govern themselves individually in a manner compatible with the interests of the entire community."[47] In other words, government "is a sad necessity, perhaps—the product of man's weakness, not of his strength (if he were what he should be, you wouldn't have to have it)—but it is a necessity nevertheless. Its absence—by which I mean that state of chaos and of unrestrained violence and willfulness that would ensue if it did not exist at all—would certainly represent a deterioration of the environment for the realization of Christian ideals."[48]

Government serves to constrain the self-love of individuals. As Herbert Butterfield observed, "The essential nature of man may not be altered, but human behavior in general is sometimes improved, by the establishment of an order of things which has the effect of reducing temptation."[49]

Government—based upon traditions and customs, which are the bedrock of its composite institutions—meets this need. The American Founding Fathers held human nature in the forefront of their minds when they crafted the Constitution, and Kennan's periodic references to the Founding Fathers in his work demonstrate his attention to their thoughts. Alexander Hamilton argued that "To judge from the history of mankind we shall be compelled to conclude, that the fiery and destructive passions of war reign in the human breast with much more powerful sway than the mild and beneficent sentiments of peace; and that to model our political systems upon speculations of lasting tranquility is to calculate on the weaker springs of the human character."[50] As James Madison eloquently observed, "If men were angels, no government would be necessary. If angels were to govern men, neither external nor internal controuls on government would be necessary."[51] Human nature at once makes the existence of government possible and necessary.

As nation-states exercise power over citizens, the struggle for power also takes place within the halls of government. In the contest for power and the control of government, individuals align themselves in groups to gain power for its own sake as well as to attain political ends. In Kennan's words, "The competition for power is conducted not just by individuals acting in loneliness but more often, and for very good reason, by groups of persons pooling their efforts at least momentarily with a view to achieving positions of dominant influence. Groups thus motivated will be found in the vicinity of the power center of every political regime, authoritarian or democratic."[52] Preoccupation with the struggle for power within government leads politicians to neglect the interests of their citizens. Kennan observed a disconnect between the government elite and the population of a nation-state. He believed that "the interests of the populace at large will normally be no more than a secondary consideration for those in power. Closer to the heart of any governing regime will normally be its own political fortunes, actual or potential, in the face of whatever significant internal-political opposition it confronts or fears to confront. However seemingly securely installed at any given moment, a governing regime is always only one of the players in the internal political power game, and never forgets it."[53]

Any group's position at the summit of power in government will be momentary. Kennan observed that "One will almost always find at or near every center of power, democratic or authoritarian (and here is where the uniformity comes in) a single group of this nature, momentarily successful, installed (however precariously) in the positions of influence to which it has aspired, and controlling most, if not all, of the instrumentalities of power."[54] He stressed the words "momentarily successful" and "however precariously" because

No regime lasts forever. Human mortality assures this even when the hazards and vicissitudes of political life do not. In this sense all political regimes are only temporary occupants of the heights of power to which they have climbed. None is entirely secure. None lives in a complete political vacuum. The heights each occupies always become, sooner or later, a besieged fortress. Every one of them is confronted by others anxious and striving to occupy those heights in its place. And awareness of this fact is what causes each of them, whether brought into power by democratic processes or by other ones, to constitute to some extent, psychologically, a conspiracy against all that lies outside its own ranks and presents a real or potential threat to its power.[55]

Power was the essence of past political structures such as the city-states, empires, and civilizations that have been eclipsed—at least for the moment in history—by the nation-state. No political structure has been able to sustain itself indefinitely, a stubborn fact that illustrates the elusiveness of power. Kennan's appreciation for this historical truth was influenced by Edward Gibbon. As Gaddis pointed out, Kennan gave more weight to the influence of Gibbon than to Burke on his understanding of international relations.[56] Gibbon observed that the Roman Empire's fall "was announced by a clearer omen than the flight of vultures: the Roman government appeared every day less formidable to its enemies, more odious and oppressive to its subjects."[57] He speculated that "If all the Barbarian conquerors had been annihilated in the same hour, their total destruction would not have restored the empire of the West: and if Rome still survived, she survived the loss of freedom, of virtue, and of honour."[58] Kennan's speculation in 1947 that the Soviet Union eventually would collapse undoubtedly was informed by his study of Gibbon and his appreciation for the momentary position of all regimes at the summit of power.[59]

MORALITY AND THE DEMANDS OF POWER POLITICS

Political realism often is criticized for purportedly advocating amoral aims—namely the accumulation of power as both a means and an end—in politics. These criticisms, however, are off the mark. American realists have devoted considerable attention to the study of morality, although they acknowledge that it cannot be divorced from the demands of power politics. Kennan wrote to Louis Halle in 1956, for example, "I am so glad you pointed out that there is no conflict between realism and morality. There could be no appreciation more helpful to the clarification of American thought on these matters."[60] Kennan presumably wanted to point out that realism does not preclude the pursuit of morality, although as will be discussed, there is a constant tension between morality and power in politics in general and in foreign policy in particular.

Practical morality, which balances the interests of politics against those of morality, is the goal for realists. Hans Morgenthau, in a reflection of this need for balance, judged that "A man who was nothing but 'political man' would be a beast, for he would be completely lacking in moral restraints. A man who was nothing but 'moral man' would be a fool, for he would be completely lacking in prudence."[61] Morgenthau's thoughts are the essence of practical morality. Joel Rosenthal, in tracing the roots of this realist thought, observed that the "realist concept of responsible power owed much to the world of Max Weber, one of the intellectual fathers of modern realism and a particular favorite of Morgenthau. It was Weber, in his essay 'Politics as a Vocation,' who outlined the central problem of political ethics that concerned the realists."[62]

Broadly speaking, there are two approaches to morality in politics. Weber set up the contrasting approaches when he wrote that "ethically oriented activity can follow two fundamentally different, irreconcilably opposed maxims. It can follow the 'ethic of principled conviction' or the 'ethic of responsibility' . . . acting by the maxim of the ethic of conviction (putting it in religious terms: 'The Christian does what is right and places the outcome in God's hands'), and acting by the maxim of the ethic of responsibility, which means that one must answer for the (foreseeable) *consequences* of one's actions."[63] Weber, in the realist tradition, argued that the latter approach was superior.

Although a significant amount of scholarship has identified Weber's work as the philosophic foundation for realist thought on morality in foreign policy, less attention has been devoted to Edmund Burke's influence on the American school of realism. Burke singled out prudence as the tool needed to balance the competing interests of power and morality. By his definition, "Prudence (in all things a virtue, in politics the first of virtues) will lead us rather to acquiesce in some qualified plan that does not come up to the full perfection of the abstract idea, than to push for the more perfect, which cannot be attained without tearing to pieces the whole contexture of the commonwealth."[64]

American realist thought on ethics and politics is steeped in Burke's philosophy. The similarities of Burke's philosophy with that of the American realists is striking. Morgenthau argued that "This being inherently a world of opposing interests and of conflict among them, moral principles can never be fully realized, but at best approximated through the ever temporary balancing of interests and the ever precarious settlement of conflicts."[65] Kenneth Thompson argued with a Burkean appreciation of politics that "Decisions in foreign policy seldom involve simple and tidy choices. Actions stem from on-balance judgments. What is usually called for is an evaluation of the elements involved in a decision and the consequences likely to flow from each alternative course of action. In choices that are made, the best may be the enemy of the good. Not absolute truth but practical morality must be the guide."[66] Political realists see the unceasing tension between the demands of power, political action, and ethics at play in the realm of politics and foreign policy. The successful statesman learns to cope with—but never to resolve—the competing demands of political action and morality.

The interplay between power and ethics is a constant preoccupation for realists. For them power sets the limits of morality in human affairs. Where there is no power, there is no morality. But where power is present, statesmen are more able to edge policy closer to the goals set by morality. In Thompson's words, "Power without justice within a state leads to tyranny, but justice without power means impotence."[67] Thompson captured the essence of ethical realism when he wrote that "the goal of politics is not the attainment of the higher values of religion or philosophy. It is not the realization of piety or pure virtue, although some statesmen exemplify these characteristics. The end of politics is justice. Justice means giving each person his due, taking into account individual and collective egoism. It seeks to balance and reconcile contending goals and interests. The realm of politics is the twilight zone in which moral principles and technical requirements merge and are ordered."[68] In Niebuhr's majestic prose, "Politics will, to the end of history, be an area where conscience and power meet, where the ethical and coercive factors of human life will interpenetrate and work out their tentative and uneasy compromises."[69] For the realists, political action requires an eye on Christian morality from within the bounds set by power and politics.

Kennan shared many of the perspectives of these realists—Weber, Burke, Morgenthau, Niebuhr, and Thompson—on the ethics of responsibility in politics, although his probing of this dimension of politics was limited. Kennan questioned the prospects for the existence of international standards or morality as a grand guiding concept for the ethical conduct of nation-states in international relations. He knew of "no international standards of morality which could be codified in a manner adequate as a guide for the behavior of all nations in their dealings with one another."[70] Instead, Kennan called for the exercise of prudence in the international realm for the advancement of morality. He doubted that "even for individuals there are any universally applicable standards of morality beyond those obvious rules of prudence, common to most of mankind, that flow from the necessity of the preservation of the family structure and the maintenance of good order in a society."[71]

In light of his skepticism that man could approximate universal law, Kennan cautioned Americans not to assume that their moral precepts were appropriate for all nation-states. He argued that Americans should not "assume that our moral values, based as they are on the specifics of our national tradition and the various religious outlooks represented in our country, necessarily have validity for people everywhere."[72] Kennan pointed out that many nation-states do not share American traditions or values: "what most of us would regard as ethically commendable values and virtues are culturally and sometimes religiously conditioned—culturally, even by those who are scarcely conscious of their own cultural inheritance; and religiously, even by those who would scoff at the mere suggestions that religion had anything to do with their reactions."[73]

Beyond these thoughts, however, Kennan was able to mine the dilemmas of politics and morality only at the margins. His thoughts on this score appear amorphous in comparison with those of the other realists discussed earlier. Kennan's mid-1980s article in *Foreign Affairs* in which he sought to put to rest questions about his position on morality and foreign policy illustrates this point.[74] In that article, Kennan gave a broad-brush treatment to a wide array of topics but avoided a head-on discussion of morality and failed to show the intellectual penetration that he so ably demonstrates in his treatments of other facets of international relations and foreign policy.

In fairness to Kennan, he had long recognized his shortcomings in this regard. In a 1956 letter to Louis Halle, Kennan admitted that he was uncomfortable with the topic of morality and foreign policy: "The subject of ethical obligation in the conduct of foreign affairs is one which I have always found it extremely hard to discuss in abstract terms. For this reason, probably, I have never succeeded in making myself fully understood about it."[75] Kennan argued for morality to be seen in context with concrete American interests rather than as commitments to morality in the abstract. For Kennan, the issue of morality in the abstract in politics proved to be an elusive animal that escaped his intellectual grasp. He grappled at the outer edges of the subject but failed to venture as deep into the dilemmas posed by ethics and politics as Niebuhr, Thompson, and Morgenthau. As Michael Smith lamented, "one might hope that Kennan would more openly acknowledge the considerable extent to which his policy recommendations flow not merely from Bismarckian Realpolitik but from his own deeply held moral convictions."[76]

DEMOCRATIC VERSUS NONDEMOCRATIC REGIMES

Kennan's writings on morality and foreign policy often drifted from discussions of ethics to examinations of forms of government, where Kennan was more intellectually comfortable. For Kennan, modern forms of government were institutional manifestations of the struggle for power. He viewed the structure of government—democratic or otherwise—as manifestations of the societies over which they preside. Kennan judged that on balance democratic forms of government are likely to produce a higher level of justice for their citizens than other types of regimes. Nevertheless, Kennan cautioned that democratic institutions are not applicable to all societies. Moreover, democratic forms of government suffer from weaknesses and vulnerabilities and are by no means a cure-all for man's dual nature and frailties. These views placed Kennan at odds with liberal political philosophy, which dominates the American political landscape and contends that a solution to political problems faced by nation-states everywhere is to replicate the American form of government.

In his discussions of forms of government, Kennan distinguished between "democratic" and "nondemocratic." Nondemocratic forms are not necessarily inferior to Western democratic forms of government. Kennan, in an echo of Burke, pointed out that some nondemocratic governments "no doubt, correspond closely to the customs, perceived requirements, degree of enlightenment, and expectations of the respective societies. In this sense they probably represent just about the best that circumstances will permit. And this I find neither distressing nor surprising. I know of no reason to suppose that 'democracy' along West European or American lines is necessarily, or even probably, the ultimate fate of all humanity."[77]

From the conservative perspective, man bases his political behavior on historical and cultural experience. Accordingly, Kennan held that man "is a creature of habit and tradition. Much of his ability to lead a civilized life has been the product of a long habit-forming process, closely linked to a respect for tradition, for ancient custom and outlook, for the accumulated wisdom of the past."[78] Kennan's words are reminiscent of those of Burke in *Reflections on the Revolution in France* which warned of the destabilizing effects of the radical break with tradition advocated by the philosophers of the French Enlightenment, particularly Rousseau.

Kennan viewed institutions as an important, but by no means exclusive, factor for preserving individual freedom. He stressed that institutions—designed to channel the struggle for power within societies—need to be buttressed by local culture, history, and heritage; otherwise they would have no ability to promote the freedom of the individual. Kennan remarked that

the preservation of freedom, where it already exists, is a moral and social rather than a political problem. To be sure, one can adopt constitutions and laws guaranteeing civil liberties; all this is useful and in the legal sense, no doubt, indispensable. But if freedom rests on institutional devices alone, it will never be safe. Unless the legal guarantees are anchored in the assumptions and the prejudices—if you will—of the average citizen, and unless they are associated with some subjective sense of moral duty and obligation to others, they will never suffice to protect mankind from that sizable portion of its own membership who seem to be by nature the enemies of freedom.[79]

The key to justice in a democratic state is the balancing of power. Kennan regarded

a proper system of self-government as one that embraced and respected what is in this country the traditional division of governmental powers into the executive, legislative, and judicial, with both the executive and the legislative branches being subject to some proper form of electoral control. Where such institutions are realities—where their integrity, that is, is not impaired or threatened by irregular bodies of armed men or by regular armed forces that step out of their normal constitutional role, or by some other irregular means—there we have before us, I would submit, a fundamental distinction, separating such systems from those that do not meet these criteria at all.[80]

Kennan shared with the Founding Fathers a concern about the potential for exploitation and corruption where political power is unconstrained. This concern drove the American Founding Fathers to create a system of divided powers. Powers within a democratic state are balanced to prevent one power from dominating the others to protect individual liberty. The American Founding Fathers—after a bitter struggle to escape the power of a tyrant—placed a high political premium on individual liberty. To preserve the freedom of the individual, they looked to Montesquieu's separation of powers and checks and balances to prevent the emergence of concentration of power capable of suppressing the freedom of citizens as the English throne had done in the colonies. James Madison wrote of this issue that "the great security against a gradual concentration of the several powers in the same department, consists in giving to those who administer each department, the necessary constitutional means, and personal motives, to resist encroachments of the others."[81] Kennan approached the problem as Madison had; if "one wishes to reform politics, one must not approach it by attempting to improve the motives. All that one can do is to place rules and restrictions upon it, to diffuse both power and rights, to narrow the area in which the most dangerous impulses are permitted to operate. This one can do by constitutional restrictions, by cultivation of traditional restraints, in the way of custom and habit; by fragmenting power as between executive and legislative and judicial branches; by separating economic, social and political power, etc."[82]

Kennan was not alone among the American realists in this appreciation of the need for balancing power to promote justice and liberty for the individual. Indeed, this appreciation is the centerpiece of a realist's political theory. Niebuhr argued that "All political justice is achieved by coercing the anarchy of collective self-interest into some kind of decent order by the most attainable balance of power. Such a balance, once achieved, can be stabilized, embellished, and even, on occasion, perfected by more purely moral considerations. But there has never been a scheme of justice in history which did not have a balance of power at its foundation."[83]

The horrors of unchecked power were evident in the rise of totalitarianism in the twentieth century. Kennan related this phenomenon to the inherent flaws in human nature and argued that "it is a disease to which all humanity is in some degree vulnerable. To live under such a regime is a misfortune that can befall a nation by virtue of reasons purely historic and not really traceable to any particular guilt on the part of the nation as a whole."[84] Kennan believed that "the decisive seat of evil in this world is not in social and political institutions, and not even, as a rule, in the will or iniquities of statesmen, but simply in the weakness and imperfection of the human soul itself, and by that I mean literally every soul, including my own and that of the student militant at the gates."[85]

Despite the power wielded by totalitarian states, Kennan viewed them as vulnerable to collapse in the long run. The repressive nature of totalitarian regimes fuels dissent, which erodes the legitimacy needed to retain the reins of power. Kennan argued that "There can be no genuine stability in any system which is based on the evil and weakness in man's nature—which attempts to live by man's degradation, feeding like a vulture on his anxieties, his capacity for hatred, his susceptibility to error, and his vulnerability to psychological manipulation. Such a system can represent no more than the particular frustrations and bitterness of the generation of men who created it, and the cold terror of those who have been weak or unwise enough to become its agents."[86] Kennan assessed that "Men of this sort can bequeath something of the passion of the struggle to those of their close associates who inherit their power. But the process of inheritance cannot be carried much further. People can move along, themselves, as by some force of habit, on the strength of an emotional drive acquired at second hand; but it is no longer theirs to transmit to others."[87] Kennan, who wrote these words in 1951, undoubtedly had Hitler and Stalin in the forefront of his mind. Kennan's assessment—although historically accurate—would bring little solace to those individuals who through the force of circumstance found themselves living under a totalitarian state.

The American democracy is not immune to the totalitarian dangers that have plagued Europe in this century. Kennan commented to a National War College audience in 1947:

I wish I could believe that the human impulses which give rise to the nightmares of totalitarianism were ones which Providence had allocated only to other peoples and to which the American people had been graciously left immune. Unfortunately, I know that is not true; and you know it is not true. After all, most of us are only Europeans once or twice removed; and some of us are less removed than that. There are openly totalitarian forces already working in our society . . . The fact of the matter is that there is a little bit of the totalitarian buried somewhere, way down deep, in each and every one of us. It is only the cheerful light of confidence and security which keeps this evil genius down at the usual helpless and invisible depth. If confidence and security were to disappear, don't think that the totalitarian impulse would not be waiting to take their place. Others may lull themselves to sleep with the pleasing assumption that the work of building freedom in this country was accomplished completely and for all time by our forefathers. I prefer to accept the word of a great European, the German poet, Goethe, that freedom is something that has to be reconquered every day.[88]

Kennan's views on the vulnerabilities of democracy were informed by his study of Tocqueville and Gibbon. Tocqueville's work underscored for Kennan the potential for a "tyranny of the majority," as evident in Kennan's address on Tocqueville at the University of Belgrade in October 1962. In his handwritten notes for the presentation, Kennan drew up a number of conclusions that highlighted the significance of *Democracy in America*: "What is the significance of T[ocqueville] today? His warnings against trying to solve all problems by institutional devices. His warning that majorities, as well as classes, can become tyrannical—which means that the liberality of democratic gov[ernmen]t is not to be taken for granted. His insistence that successful democracy is something that has to be worked at."[89] Gibbon's work also shed light on the vulnerabilities of democracy. Kennan observed that the possibility

of the consignment by a majority of the liberties of the population into the hands of some non-democratic force is also something I would not for a moment dispute. For years, Gibbon's dictum 'Under a democratic government the citizens exercise the powers of sovereignty; and those powers will be first abused, and afterwards lost, if they are committed to an unwieldy multitude' has lain at the heart of my political philosophy. But surely, the best sanctions against this eventuality will be found in the preservation of a strong and independent judiciary and in the vitality of the parliamentary process itself, and least of all in any direct interaction between the broad mass of the citizenry, or individual elements of it, and an all-powerful executive.[90]

The work of Tocqueville and Gibbon emphasized the importance of the balance of power as a check against democracy's fall into despotism.

This appreciation of the potential frailties of democracy led Kennan to view American democracy as a goal to be perpetually struggled for rather than as an absolute destined to govern the United States indefinitely. American citizens take our democratic form of government for granted, but Kennan viewed democracy in the United States as an experiment that had not assumed a permanency. He cited as evidence that "On every side of us we see proof of this thesis that our American civilization is still something experimental, unfinished, not fully tested . . . our society has not yet passed its final test, and . . . we cannot yet claim for it, whatever may be our hopes or our faith, any final validity as the answer to the problems of political organization here or elsewhere on this planet."[91]

Contemporary American political philosophy is seized with the goal of institution building to protect the freedom and equality of individuals, but it overlooks the underlying structures of power. Kennan was critical of the American philosophical disposition to dismiss the concept of power: "We Americans have a strange—and to me disturbing—attitude toward the subject of power. We don't like the word. We don't like the concept. We are suspicious of people who talk about it. We like to feel that the adjustment of conflicting interests is something that can be taken care of by juridical norms and institutional devices, voluntarily accepted and not involving violence to the feelings or interests of anyone."[92] For realists such as Kennan, institutions reflect power realities and do not exist independently of them. Institutions rely on power, but, where there is no power, they are but empty shells unable to affect the struggle for power between individuals and collectives within societies and to steer them from destructive to constructive paths to perpetuate civilization.

The preceding discussion with quotations from Kennan's work on political theory belies arguments that Kennan was antidemocratic and authoritarian. Kennan's willingness to question the universal applicability of democracy has fueled analysis that he was antidemocratic. Walter Hixson, for example, accused Kennan of adherence to "antidemocratic values throughout his career," with a preference for authoritarian rule to democracy.[93] Hixson argued that "Realism reinforced his anti-democratic values through its sanction of elite authority over foreign policy and its warnings about the dangers of succumbing to mass emotional compulsions."[94] Criticisms of democracy, however, do not directly translate into advocacy of authoritarian rule. Kennan did not juxtapose his criticisms of democracy against an overly rosy picture of authoritarian regimes. In fact, Kennan was harsher in his criticisms of authoritarian regimes than he was of democracies. One suspects that the philosophic position from which these critiques against Kennan are levied would overlook cases in recent memory in which democratic experiments for societies without political and cultural heritages conducive to democracy have collapsed into Hobbesian states of war, such as in Albania, the former Yugoslavia, and Somalia. Kennan's perspectives on democracy might more accurately be captured by Winston Churchill's quip that democracy is the worst possible form of government, except for all the rest.

POWER RIVALRIES AMONG NATION-STATES

These assumptions about the nature of man, power, morality, and government have important implications for the analysis of international politics. Kennan's views just discussed were integrally linked to his thoughts on American foreign policy. For him, foreign affairs were "inseparably connected with the fundamental human problem of power that lies at the heart of all politics: the problem of how the freedom of choice of the individual, or of the organized society, is to be limited in order to repress chaos and ensure the good order necessary to the continuation of civilization."[95]

Nation-states compete for power on the international scene much as individuals do with one another and for control of the reins of government. The struggle for power within a nation-state, however, often is constrained by norms, customs, history, laws, and institutions. These mechanisms are less effective in constraining the behavior of nation-states, which recognize no superior entity over their sovereignty. As Kennan described this stubborn fact, the "sovereign national state, this child of the modern age, notwithstanding the mantle of nebulous moral obligation in which it likes to wrap itself, still recognizes in the crucial moments of its own destiny no law but that of its own egoism—no higher focus of obligation, no overriding ethical code."[96] This view is consistent with that of Morgenthau, who saw international politics, like all politics, as the struggle for power.[97] For Kennan, as for the American realists in general, the international competition for power takes place in a Hobbesian state of nature with no overarching central authority to mitigate the struggle.

The struggle for power in international relations is ubiquitous. In Kennan's words,

Just as there is no uncomplicated personal relationship between individuals, so, I think, there is no international relationship between sovereign states which is without its elements of antagonism, its competitive aspects. Many of the present relationships of international life are only the eroded remnants of ones which, at one time, were relationships of most uncompromising hostility. Every government is in some respects a problem for every other government, and it will always be this way so long as the sovereign state, with its supremely self-centered rationale, remains the basis of international life. The variety of historical experience and geographic situation would assure the prevalence of this situation, even if such things as human error and ambition did not.[98]

The United States' current relations with Germany, Japan, and the United Kingdom, although characterized as good today, are examples of what Kennan might have meant by his reference to past relationships of hostility.

Nation-states struggle for power to achieve national interests. Each nation-state, regardless of the structure of its government, has a set of national interests to be pursued in the international arena. Nation-states have long-standing national interests born in geography and circumstance that remain constant regardless of the nature or character of the leadership in power at any given moment. As Kennan observed, "Anyone who has looked reasonably closely at political history will have had many occasions to observe that the very experience of holding and exercising supreme power in any country saddles any ruler, whatever his original ideological motives, with most of the traditional concerns of government in that country, subjects him to the customary compulsions of statesmanship within that framework, makes him the protagonist of the traditional interests and the guardian against the traditional dangers."[99] These thoughts mirror those of Hobbes's definition of the Leviathan: "*One Person, of whose Acts a great Multitude, by mutuall Convenants one with another, have made themselves every one the Author, to the end he may use the strength and means of them all, as he shall think expedient, for their Peace and Common Defence.*"[100] As alluded earlier, Kennan appears not to have made even a passing reference to Hobbes's work either in connection with the nature of international politics or in connection with the forces imposed on statesmen to pursue traditional national interests regardless of their style of rule or ideology. The absence of reference to Hobbes is particularly noteworthy in that scholarly literature on political realism commonly cites his political philosophy as a defining influence on the school.

Kennan linked the struggle for power within government to behavior in the international realm. In other words, the domestic struggle for power influences a nation-state's behavior in its relations with other nation-states. Kennan underscored that "what one is normally hearing, when one listens to the publicly expressed voice of government, particularly in matters of foreign affairs, is actually a mixture of two separate voices: on the one hand, the voice of the interests of the entire country, as the regime perceives them, and to the extent it chooses to defer to them; and on the other hand, the voice of a single political faction, deeply concerned to serve its own fortunes in the face of whatever domestic-political competition confronts it and threatens it."[101] Kennan concluded that "the experienced statesman or student of international affairs, in attempting to interpret the motives of a government on the basis of its various pronouncements, will always be on the lookout for both of these voices and will judge the significance of what is done or said by the probable predominance, at any point, of the one consideration or the other."[102] This insight distinguishes Kennan and the traditional realists from their neorealist successors, who view the struggle for power in international relations primarily as a function of the system of international anarchy, divorced from any manifestation of the internal struggle for power within nation-states.[103]

The international struggle for power is especially intense because of the power that nation-states possess, and modern nationalism acts to multiply the power assessable to nation-states. Nationalism has had a profound impact on the course of international politics since its inception in the French Revolution. It is the cohesive that holds a people together within a nation-state, and it enhances the strength of nation-states in the world competition for power. Clausewitz witnessed firsthand the dynamic forces injected into war with the advent of the modern nationalism that Napoleon had harnessed for his war machine, and his insight on the power of nationalism was not lost on Kennan, who studied *On War* closely while he was a professor at the National War College in 1946.[104] Kennan commented that "In the course of the two centuries that have passed since its emergence, nationalism has developed into the greatest emotional-political force of the age."[105]

Kennan distinguished between two types of nationalism. The first he called "natural and legitimate nationalism" or patriotism: "An outstanding feature of it is, together with the acceptance of a national framework as the definitive determinant of civil identity, a genuine affection for the country in question."[106] The other form of nationalism is "a pathological form of it—a mass emotional exaltation to which millions of people, particularly in democratic societies, appear to be highly susceptible. It could be called chauvinism, and this would not be wrong. But that term fails to bring out the full complexity of the state of mind in question. It has sometimes been referred to as romantic nationalism: and for this there is some reason, for it represents the carrying over into the collective national dimension of the self-idealization of the individual that was a striking feature of the philosophy of the romantic cultural movement of Europe in the early nineteenth century."[107] Kennan viewed the extreme form of nationalism as exaggerated pride. For the individual possessed of such nationalism, "It is not enough for him to affirm the superiority of his own nation; others must be brought to acknowledge it. The same sense of insecurity that prevents the individual romanticist from having confidence in himself, and compels him to rely on the outward deference of others to establish his personal self-regard, arises here once more to determine his attitude toward the collectivity; for it is in the membership in this collectivity, and here alone, that he finds reassurance as to his own worth."[108]

Militant nationalism, for Kennan and the realists, is a manifestation of the individual's drive to satisfy his lust for power vicariously through the nation-state. Niebuhr, who best defined the problem for the realists, observed that "The man in the street, with his lust for power and prestige thwarted by his own limitations and the necessities of social life, projects his *ego* upon his nation and indulges his anarchic lusts vicariously. So the nation is at one and the same time a check upon, and a final vent for, the expression of individual egoism."[109] Niebuhr, moreover, viewed the collective ego as more difficult to tame than the individual's self-regard. He attributed the inferiority of the morality of groups to that of individuals in part "to the difficulty of establishing a rational social force which is powerful enough to cope with the natural impulses by which society achieves its cohesion; but in part it is merely the revelation of a collective egoism, compounded of the egoistic impulses of individuals, which achieve a more vivid expression and a more cumulative effect when they express themselves separately and discreetly."[110]

Kennan echoed Niebuhr's assessment about the dangers posed by the collective ego of nationalism. Niebuhr warned that

Individual men may be moral in the sense that they are able to consider interests other than their own in determining problems of conduct, and are capable, on occasion, of preferring the advantages of others to their own. They are endowed by nature with a measure of sympathy and consideration for their kind, the breath of which may be extended by an astute social pedagogy. Their rational faculty prompts them to a sense of justice which educational discipline may refine and purge of egoistic elements until they are able to view a social situation, in which their own interests are involved, with a fair measure of objectivity. But all these achievements are more difficult, if not impossible, for human societies and social groups.[111]

Kennan similarly noted that "collective psychology, particularly in its exalted and demonstrational manifestations, is a much more dangerous phenomenon than individual psychology."[112]

Kennan, with his aristocratic tendencies, longed for the days of the ancient regime before the advent of nationalism. He suggested that "By and large, it seemed to me, only those people had been able to cope successfully with the emotional power of national feeling who had known national identity in the dynastic era—in the period before the Napoleonic wars—before the currency of the romantic linguistic nationalism of the nineteenth century. For those who acquired the sense of national identity after that time, for the Germans in particular, national feeling was a heady wine."[113] Kennan viewed international politics before the French Revolution as more temperate than that of today, inflamed as it is by passions of nationalism. Professor Gaddis pointed out that Kennan admired late-nineteenth-century German aristocratic society and culture.[114] His admiration of the Marquis de Custine and Tocqueville reflected this sentiment. Kennan observed that both men were "the products of a very similar family tradition and experience. Both were aristocrats. Both families had suffered severely in the Terror of the recent Revolution. Both men, perhaps partly by way of reaction to these injustices and atrocities, had taken particularly to heart the values of the *ancien regime* to which their fathers had been attached. Both were disgusted by the decline of aristocratic institutions, and the corresponding advance of social equality, as forces of the life in France."[115] Likewise, Burke, another of Kennan's intellectual mentors whom he occasionally quoted, abhorred the social and political consequences of nationalism born in the French Revolution.

Militant nationalism obstructed the rational assessment of national interests to undermine the stability of the ancient regime. Kennan's research into the antecedents of the First World War led him to argue that "the heady nationalism of the latter part of the nineteenth century seriously distorted Russian foreign policy, causing it to serve irrational, costly, and ultimately self-destructive purposes instead of those which a sober consideration of the highest interests of the Empire would have indicated."[116] Kennan cautioned that he "had seen more harm done in this world by those who tried to storm the bastions of society in the name of utopian beliefs, who were determined to achieve the elimination of all evil and the realization of the millennium within their own time, than by all the humble efforts of those who have tried to create a little order and civility and affection within their own intimate entourage, even at the cost of tolerating a great deal of evil in the public domain."[117] These words and ideas are more than a little reminiscent of those of Burke in his *Reflections on the Revolution in France.*

The destructive consequences of militant national egoism became even more pronounced in the course of international politics in the twentieth century. Reflecting on the period, Kennan recalled that militant nationalism

is a real and terrible disease of the human spirit. The damage it has done is appalling. It was one of the two fundamental causes of the First World War (the other being the failure of statesmen and of educated opinion generally to recognize how modern industry and technology were affecting the usefulness of war as an instrument of national policy). And the First World War was the great formative catastrophe of the European civilization of this century, not only impoverishing in the most serious way the societies of the principal participants but also becoming the true source of the two great totalitarian movements of midcentury—the Soviet Communist and the Nazi.[118]

CONCLUSION

Kennan's political theory held that the dual nature of man was central to the analysis of politics. He conceived of politics as the struggle for power that takes place between individuals and progressively larger collective units to include nation-states. Government, in his view, is a necessity to control and channel the struggle for power within political communities. Kennan looked to the balance of power to preserve the freedom and equality of individuals within a nation-state. American history and culture profoundly affected the creation of institutions needed to channel the struggle for power to constructive ends. Other nation-states, however, have experienced other sets of cultural and historical conditions, which, in turn, have influenced the formation of government differently from that in the United States. In the absence of world government, nation-states are left to their own devices to defend their interests in the international struggle for power.

The rise of modern nationalism is a manifestation at the collective level of the individual's will to power, which has been a violent undercurrent of international politics in this century. The drive for prestige and power leads to departures from rational, prudent behavior in politics—a phenomenon that escapes rational-actor models in political science. Rational-actor theories, such as neorealism, assume that nation-states seek only to ensure their survival and overlook the brutal behavior of nation-states as collectives in their drives to impose their will upon others in search of power and prestige. This vulgar lust for power—untempered by moral reasoning and prudence—has been witnessed in the reigns of Hitler and Stalin, and more recently in the conflict in the former Yugoslavia.[119] The neorealists neglect Niebuhr's wisdom to the detriment of their theories, while the traditional realists such as Kennan have had these thoughts in the forefront of their minds as they formed a more robust theory of politics.

These thoughts constitute the conservative philosophic foundation of Kennan's views on man and politics. Kennan's own brand of political theory informed and enriched his analysis of American foreign policy. Subsequent chapters will illuminate how Kennan's realist political theory provided the intellectual undergirding for the body of principles and concepts that comprise his worldview and, moreover, constitute a theory of American foreign policy.

NOTES

1. See Kenneth N. Waltz, *Man, the State and War* (New York, NY: Columbia University Press, 1959).

2. The term "man" is used throughout this study. Kennan was comfortable with the term and this study uses it for purposes of consistency.

3. George F. Kennan, "Training for Statesmanship," *Atlantic* 191, no. 5 (May 1953): 40.

4. Kennan, "Training for Statesmanship," 41.

5. Herbert Butterfield, *International Conflict in the Twentieth Century: A Christian View* (Westport, CT: Greenwood Press, 1960), 25.

6. Kennan, "Training for Statesmanship," 41.

7. See Hedley Bull, "International Theory: The Case for a Classical Approach," *World Politics*, Volume 18, Number 3, April 1966.

8. Kennan, "Training for Statesmanship," 42.

9. George F. Kennan, *Around the Cragged Hill: A Personal and Political Philosophy* (New York, NY: W.W. Norton & Company, 1993), 106.

10. Interview with John Lewis Gaddis, Woodrow Wilson International Center for Scholars, Washington, DC, 26 October 1995. Hereafter referred to as Gaddis Interview.

11. Edmund Burke, *Reflections on the Revolution in France*, J. G. A. Pocock (ed.) (Indianapolis, IN: Hackett Publishing Company, 1987), 162.

12. Kenneth W. Thompson, *Morality and Foreign Policy* (Baton Rouge, LA: Louisiana State University Press, 1980), 142.

13. George F. Kennan, "How New Are Our Problems?" *Illinois Law Review* 45, no. 6 (January–February 1951): 720.

14. "Correspondence to Louis J. Halle," 3 January 1956, George F. Kennan Papers, Box 31, Seeley G. Mudd Manuscript Library, Department of Rare Books and Special Collections, Princeton University Library.

15. Kennan, *Around the Cragged Hill*, 28.

16. George F. Kennan, "From Containment to . . . Self-Containment," in Mark F. Herz (ed.), *Decline of the West?: George Kennan and His Critics* (Washington, DC: Ethics and Public Policy Center of Georgetown University, 1978), 36.

17. Niccolo Machiavelli, *The Prince*, in Peter Bondandella and Mark Musa (eds.), *The Portable Machiavelli* (New York, NY: Penguin Books, 1979), 131. Kennan only makes a passing reference in *Around the Cragged Hill* to Machiavelli while commending Sebastian de Grazia's *Machiavelli in Hell* (Princeton, NJ: Princeton University Press, 1989). Kennan called attention to Grazia's observation that in *Discourses* Machiavelli wrote that "Men act either out of necessity or out of choice." Grazia went on to note that "Without pausing for nuances in such an assertion, we may simply recall that it fits the position of both Aristotle and Augustine that only with choice can an act be moral." See *Machiavelli in Hell*, 76. Kennan, in agreement with Machiavelli, Aristotle, and Augustine, wrote that "it is only where choice is involved that the question of morality enters into human action." See *Around the Cragged Hill*, 53.

18. Kennan, *Around the Cragged Hill*, 18.

19. See Reinhold Niebuhr, *Christian Realism and Political Problems* (Fairfield, NJ: Augustus M. Kelley Publishers, 1977), 120–124.

20. Reinhold Niebuhr, *The Irony of American History* (New York, NY: Charles Scribner's Sons, 1962), 17.

21. Kennan, *Around the Cragged Hill*, 17–18.

22. Kennan, *Around the Cragged Hill*, 27.

23. Kennan, *Around the Cragged Hill*, 17.

24. Kennan, *Around the Cragged Hill*, 36.

25. Kennan, *Around the Cragged Hill*, 27.

26. Kennan, *Around the Cragged Hill*, 17.

27. Kennan, *Around the Cragged Hill*, 27.

28. References to Kant and Hegel are absent from Kennan's work. He apparently devoted no special attention to these philosophers, according to Professor Gaddis. Gaddis Interview. For a contemporary version of the end of history philosophy in the Kant and Hegel tradition, see Francis Fukuyama's *The End of History and the Last Man* (New York, NY: Avon Books, 1992).

29. Hans J. Morgenthau and Kenneth W. Thompson, *Politics among Nations: The Struggle for Power and Peace*, Sixth Edition (New York, NY: McGraw-Hill Publishing Company, 1985), 32.

30. Kennan, *Around the Cragged Hill*, 25–26.

31. Kennan, *Around the Cragged Hill*, 26.

32. Kennan, *Around the Cragged Hill*, 26.

33. Thomas Hobbes, *Leviathan*, Edited by C. B. MacPherson (New York, NY: Penguin Books, 1985), 161.

34. Kennan, *Around the Cragged Hill*, 55.

35. Kennan, *Around the Cragged Hill*, 74.

36. Kennan, *Around the Cragged Hill*, 26.

37. Reinhold Niebuhr, *The Children of Light and the Children of Darkness: A Vindication of Democracy and a Critique of its Traditional Defense* (New York, NY: Charles Scribner's Sons, 1944), 20.

38. Kenneth W. Thompson, *Masters of International Thought* (Baton Rouge, LA: Louisiana State University Press, 1980), 31–32.

39. "Draft for a Possible Lecture Course on the Subject of Politics," 1964, George F. Kennan Papers, Box 27, Folder 24, Seeley G. Mudd Manuscript Library, Department of Rare Books and Special Collections, Princeton University Library.

40. Max Weber, "The Profession and Vocation of Politics," in Peter Lassman and Ronald Speirs (eds.), *Weber: Political Writings* (New York, NY: Cambridge University Press, 1994), 311.

41. Weber, "Profession and Vocation of Politics," 311.

42. Michael Joseph Smith, *Realist Thought from Weber to Kissinger* (Baton Rouge, LA: Louisiana State University Press, 1986), 15.

43. Kennan, *Around the Cragged Hill*, 74.

44. Kennan, *Around the Cragged Hill*, 55.

45. Kennan, "Draft for a Possible Lecture Course on the Subject of Politics."

46. Kennan, *Around the Cragged Hill*, 53.

47. Kennan, *Around the Cragged Hill*, 54.

48. George F. Kennan, "The Relation of Religion to Government," *The Princeton Seminary Bulletin* 62, no. 1 (Winter 1969): 43.

49. Butterfield, *International Conflict in the Twentieth Century*, 25.

50. Alexander Hamilton, *The Federalist XXXIV*, in Bernard Bailyn (ed.), *The Debate on the Constitution: Federalist and Antifederalist Speeches, Articles, and Letters during the Struggle over Ratification*, Part One (New York, NY: Literary Classics of the United States, 1993), 701.

51. James Madison, *The Federalist LI*, in Bailyn (ed.), *The Debate on the Constitution*, Part Two, 164.

52. Kennan, *Around the Cragged Hill*, 58.

53. Kennan, *Around the Cragged Hill*, 60.

54. Kennan, *Around the Cragged Hill*, 59.

55. Kennan, *Around the Cragged Hill*, 59.

56. Gaddis Interview.

57. Edward Gibbon, *The History of the Decline and Fall of the Roman Empire*, Volume II, Edited by David Womerly (New York, NY: Penguin Books, 1994), 355.

58. Gibbon, *Decline and Fall of the Roman Empire*, 356.

59. See X [George F. Kennan], "The Sources of Soviet Conduct," *Foreign Affairs* 25, no. 4 (July 1947).

60. "Correspondence to Louis J. Halle," 3 January 1956.

61. Morgenthau and Thompson, *Politics among Nations*, 16.

62. Joel H. Rosenthal, *Righteous Realists: Political Realism, Responsible Power, and American Culture in the Nuclear Age* (Baton Rouge, LA: Louisiana State University Press, 1991), 43.

63. Weber, "Profession and Vocation of Politics," 359–360.

64. Edmund Burke, "Letter to Mons. Dupont, October, 1789," in Louis I. Bredvold and Ralph G. Ross (eds.), *The Philosophy of Edmund Burke* (Ann Arbor, MI: University of Michigan Press, 1967), 38.

65. Hans J. Morgenthau, "Another 'Great Debate': The National Interest of the United States," *American Political Science Review* 66, no. 4 (December 1952): 962.

66. Kenneth W. Thompson, "Normative Theory in International Relations," *Journal of International Affairs* 21, no. 2 (1967): 281.

67. Thompson, *Morality and Foreign Policy*, 43.

68. Thompson, *Morality and Foreign Policy*, 143.

69. Reinhold Niebuhr, *Moral Man and Immoral Society: A Study in Ethics and Politics* (New York, NY: Charles Scribner's Sons, 1960), 4.

70. "Morality and Foreign Policy," Unused Lecture intended as Reith Lecture Number 3, Summer 1957, George F. Kennan Papers, Box 26, Seeley G. Mudd Manuscript Library, Department of Rare Books and Special Collections, Princeton University Library. Kennan did not use this draft lecture because the subject matter was not suitable for the final presentation in the Reith series.

71. George F. Kennan, *Realities of American Foreign Policy* (Princeton, NJ: Princeton University Press, 1954), 47–48.

72. Kennan, *Realities of American Foreign Policy*, 47.

73. Kennan, *Around the Cragged Hill*, 52.

74. See George F. Kennan, "Morality and Foreign Policy," *Foreign Affairs* 64, no. 2 (Winter 1985/86).

75. "Correspondence to Louis J. Halle," 3 January 1956.

76. Smith, *Realist Thought*, 189.

77. Kennan, *Around the Cragged Hill*, 64.

78. Kennan, *Realities of American Foreign Policy*, 34.

79. George F. Kennan, "The Challenge of Freedom," *The New Leader*, 26 December 1955, 11.

80. Kennan, *Around the Cragged Hill*, 64.

81. Madison, *Federalist LI*, 164.

82. "Notes on Politics Lectures," George F. Kennan Papers, Box 27, Seeley G. Mudd Manuscript Library, Department of Rare Books and Special Collections, Princeton University Library.

83. Reinhold Niebuhr, *Christianity and Power Politics* (New York, NY: Charles Scribner's Sons, 1940), 104.

84. George F. Kennan, "America and the Russian Future," *Foreign Affairs* 29, no. 3 (April 1951): 365.

85. George F. Kennan, *Democracy and the Student Left* (Boston, MA: Little, Brown and Company, 1968), 9–10.

86. Kennan, "America and the Russian Future," 366.

87. Kennan, "America and the Russian Future," 366.

88. George F. Kennan, "Comments on the National Security Problem," 27 March 1947, in Giles D. Harlow and George C. Maerz (eds.), *Measures Short of War: The George F. Kennan Lectures at the National War College, 1946–47* (Washington, DC: National Defense University Press, 1991), 168.

89. "Lecture on Tocqueville's *Democracy in America*," Delivered at the University of Belgrade, 31 October 1962, George F. Kennan Papers, Box 10, Seeley G. Mudd Manuscript Library, Department of Rare Books and Special Collections, Princeton University Library.

90. Kennan, *Democracy and the Student Left*, 206.

91. George F. Kennan, "The National Interest of the United States," *Illinois Law Review* 45, no. 6 (January-February 195): 734.

92. Kennan, "Training for Statesmanship," 41.

93. Walter L. Hixson, *George F. Kennan: Cold War Iconoclast* (New York, NY: Columbia University Press, 1989), 7.

94. Hixson, *Cold War Iconoclast*, 48.

95. Kennan, "Training for Statesmanship," 41.

96. George F. Kennan, "History and Diplomacy as Viewed by a Diplomatist," *Review of Politics* 18, no. 2 (April 1956): 171.

97. Morgenthau and Thompson, *Politics among Nations*, 31.

98. George F. Kennan, *Russia and the West under Lenin and Stalin* (New York, NY: Mentor, 1961), 367.

99. Kennan, *Russia and the West under Lenin and Stalin*, 367.

100. Hobbes, *Leviathan*, 228.

101. Kennan, *Around the Cragged Hill*, 60–61.

102. Kennan, *Around the Cragged Hill*, 61.

103. See Kenneth N. Waltz, *Theory of International Politics* (Reading, MA: Addison-Wesley Publishing Co., 1979).

104. Gaddis Interview.

105. Kennan, *Around the Cragged Hill*, 76–77.

106. Kennan, *Around the Cragged Hill*, 77.

107. Kennan, *Around the Cragged Hill*, 78.

108. Kennan, *Around the Cragged Hill*, 79.

109. Niebuhr, *Moral Man and Immoral Society*, 93.

110. Niebuhr, *Moral Man and Immoral Society*, xii.

111. Niebuhr, *Moral Man and Immoral Society*, xi.

112. Kennan, *Around the Cragged Hill*, 82.

113. George F. Kennan, *Memoirs, 1925–1950* (New York, NY: Pantheon Books, 1967), 416.

114. Gaddis Interview.

115. George F. Kennan, *The Marquis de Custine and His Russia in 1839* (Princeton, NJ: Princeton University Press, 1971), 19. Kennan, seemingly in envy of the aristocratic times of the Marquis and Tocqueville, lamented in his diary on 20 December 1927 that "I cannot help but regret that I did not live fifty or a hundred years sooner. Life is too full in these times to be comprehensible." See Kennan's *Sketches from a Life* (New York, NY: Pantheon Books, 1989), 7.

116. George F. Kennan, *The Decline of Bismarck's European Order: Franco-Russian Relations*, 1875-1890 (Princeton, NJ: Princeton University Press, 1979), 418.

117. Kennan, *Democracy and the Student Left*, 9.

118. Kennan, *Around the Cragged Hill*, 80.

119. Gordon A. Craig and Alexander L. George insightfully have referred to such individuals as "vulgar realists." See their *Force and Statecraft: Diplomatic Problems of Our Time*, Second Edition (New York, NY: Oxford University Press, 1990), 295.

3

AMERICAN NATIONAL INTEREST AND THE WORLD BALANCE OF POWER

Armed with Kennan's intellectual framework for understanding politics, we must now turn attention to his views on the role of the United States in the international arena. This chapter discusses Kennan's appreciation for the origins of American power or foreign policy means and the national interests or ends for which American power is exercised. In international politics the United States should recognize the need to equate means and ends within the geopolitical constraints and opportunities posed by the global balance of power. It was Kennan's appreciation for means and ends in foreign policy that most distinguished him as a strategist. As John Lewis Gaddis correctly pointed out, "there is in Kennan's approach a set of propositions so obvious that they often escape notice: that there are limits to power; that there are no commitments without costs; that there are risks in becoming so preoccupied with processes as to lose sight of objectives; that as strategy needs to be informed by policy, so policy needs to be informed by a clear vision of the national interest, framed with a keen sensitivity to both ideals and capabilities."[1] From Kennan's viewpoint, geopolitics formed the basis for American foreign policy.

NATIONAL INTEREST

Kennan throughout his career pleaded for an overarching framework to guide American foreign policy. He was dismayed at the haphazard fashion in which the United States emerged as a world power after the world wars. He suggested that "A policy might reasonably be expected to have a reason—or, since there can never be a single reason for something so complex as foreign policy, then a bundle of reasons, coherently inter-related, which we might call in their entirety a rationale."[2] The concept of the national interest fit Kennan's call for a guide for American foreign policy. Kennan advised that "Anyone who sets out to design or to conduct the foreign policy of a great country has to be clear as to the interests that policy is supposed to serve. Only if the image of these interests is clear in his mind can the policy he evolves have coherence and usefulness."[3] A clear articulation of American national interest is the starting point for the discussion, formulation, and implementation of foreign policy. National interest may be viewed as the strategic endgame and policy as the collection of tactics used to reach that objective. Without a clear articulation of national interest, policy debate is likely to be confused and risk leading the country on a path of open-ended commitments that drain national resources.

Kennan identified two broad sets of American national interests. "First, there are the parochial interests of the country itself, in the most narrow and traditional sense of that term. Second, there are the interests that engage this country as a participant in the affairs of the international community as a whole. Both of these sets of interests deserve our respect and attention. But it is those of our own country, in the narrower sense, that lie closest to our hearts; and they demand our first consideration."[4] As Kennan viewed them, "Within the first category lies the assurance of the security of the United States and the possibility for the United States people to go on with the development of their life without interference from outside. The second and the more constructive, the happier side of United States foreign policy, is the one that we can pursue only when and as security is restored. That is the task of trying to bring about conditions in the world under which this country can make the maximum contribution to advance civilization everywhere and derive the maximum contributions to other countries."[5] Kennan, however, was somewhat circumspect about the national interests in the second category out of fear that transcendent interests would risk moving the United States toward utopian goals that are beyond American means to achieve.

Kennan tried to narrow the field of vision regarding what constituted a national interest. He appreciated the difficulty in articulating the concept and referred to national interest as an elusive term that "is one of those things that you know must exist—you can demonstrate it by the process of exclusion—but it is too vast, too rich in meaning, too many-sided, for any positive definition."[6] He likened concepts such as national interest to "shy wild animals"—"You can never get near enough to touch them and make exact measurements of them, but you can round them up and gradually pen them in; you can mark out certain directions in which they are not permitted to move. In this way you can confine them from time to time and have some idea of what they are like."[7] In his struggle to illuminate the national interest, Kennan believed that, above all else, "The interest of the United States in international affairs is *not* a detached interest in our international environment *for its own sake*, independent of our own aspirations and problems here at home."[8] In other words, foreign policy in the first instance is a means to advance the domestic interests of the United States.

The interest that lies at the top of the hierarchy of any state's interests is the preservation of the state. Without preservation of the state, all other interests are moot. Kennan argued that "one ought to protect the physical intactness of our national life from any external military or political intrusion."[9] Kennan extended the need to protect the territorial integrity of the United States to its citizens abroad. He argued that consular services were needed: "in so far as the activities of our citizens in pursuit of their private interests spilled over beyond our borders and into the outside world, the best possible arrangements were made to promote and protect them."[10]

This conceptualization of the American national interest was a call for modest goals in international affairs. Kennan pointed out that "It is important to recognize that these two functions, the assurance of the national security and the promotion of private American activity abroad, were all that really did flow directly and logically from the original objects of American society. If you accepted them, and them alone, as valid points of departure in the conduct of our foreign affairs, you came up with a policy very modest and restrained."[11] Some observers would consider this hierarchy of national interests to be chauvinistic and fault it for failing to take into account more cosmopolitan foreign policy considerations that go beyond the bounds of protecting American sovereignty and citizens. Kennan, however, refused to apologize for what he argued should be the hierarchy of American national interests: "There is nothing wrong about this allotment of priorities. It is not the dictate of a national selfishness or disregard for others. This particular territory and these particular people, ourselves, are all that we, as a national state, have control over. The management of our society, and this in a credible way, is for us an unavoidable responsibility as well as a privilege. Unless we meet this responsibility, no one else will; for there is none who could. And unless we meet it creditably, there will be very little that we can do for others—very little that we can do even to serve global interests."[12] Kennan appreciated the difficulties in managing our own society and concluded that grappling with the problems of other societies was beyond our means; he thus freed American statesmen from such a responsibility.

Although the concept of national interest is analogous to a compass with which the United States can navigate the seas of foreign policy, it also is linked to the power of American society. Kennan was keenly aware that the roots of

American power lie at home. He commented that in his own professional activities he limited himself to foreign affairs "when it came to books, articles and other public statements on contemporary problems. But the exercise seemed increasingly, with the years, an empty one; for what use was there, I had to ask, in attempting to protect in its relations to others a society that was clearly failing in its relations to itself?"[13] He argued that "National strength is a question of political, economic, and moral strength. Above all it is a question of our internal strength; of the health and sanity of our own society."[14] Kennan observed that the "United States is not strong to the extent that its armed services are strong, or that its diplomacy is brilliant, but to the extent that strength goes beyond the armed services to the root of our society. For that reason, none of us can afford to be indifferent to internal disharmony, dissension, intolerance, and other things that break up the moral and political structure of our society at home."[15]

Kennan's remarks on the power of the United States illustrate a nuance in American realist thinking on the origins of power. Many critics of the school charge that the realists overemphasize the importance of military strength in international politics. Kennan was quick to point out that military power is but one of many measures of a nation-state's power. In fact, Kennan appeared to give greater weight to those intangibles that Hans Morgenthau called "national morale or character" and emphasized the importance of nurturing society at home as a prerequisite for a strong position abroad.[16]

The United States' pursuit of foreign policy as an extension of domestic needs is to be respected by other states. American policy makers should reciprocate and acknowledge the domestic interests inherent in the foreign policies of other nation-states. Kennan argued that "we are wholly entitled to approach other governments and to demand from them, without arrogance but without apology, respect for such of our interests as flow from a due regard to our security and are matched by a reciprocal readiness on our part to respect the similar interests of others."[17]

Although national interest is equated with ends in foreign policy, Kennan argued that it also is method. In his view, "national interest is not primarily a question of purpose or of objective; it is a question of method. It is a question of the 'how' rather than the 'what.'"[18] More specifically, Kennan distinguished between the purpose and form of national interest. He advised presidential hopeful Adlai Stevenson in 1956, for example, that "The conduct of foreign policy, first of all, is like tennis: primarily a matter of style rather than purpose."[19] Kennan's conceptualization of the American national interest as a method appears to have been influenced by John Quincy Adams. Greg Russell has drawn attention to the similarities of Adams's conceptualization of the national interest and that of his admirer Kennan. As Russell assessed Adams's view, "the national interest was not simply a question of purpose, objective, or doctrine; it also was a question of 'how' as much as 'what.' From this angle, Adams was preoccupied with the style or conduct of American foreign policy, rather than any hierarchy of predetermined goals."[20]

American realists called for adherence to foreign policy based on moderate conceptions of national interest as a means to ameliorate international conflict. Kennan made an appeal that "we will have the modesty to admit that our own national interest is all that we are really capable of knowing and understanding—and the courage to recognize that if our own purposes and undertakings here at home are decent ones, unsullied by arrogance or hostility toward other people or delusions of superiority, then the pursuit of our national interest can never fail to be conducive to a better world."[21] For realist thinkers, an appreciation for our own national interest as well as for the national interests of other nation-states would lessen the crusading spirit in international politics and serve as a basis for moderation and international stability. Unfortunately for the realist hope, emotional traits inherent in the human condition, particularly the power of collective egos, intervene in international politics and lead nation-states to deviate from the moderate policies dictated by prudent calculation of national interest.

BALANCE OF POWER IN THEORY

The American national interest for Kennan was integrally tied to the world balance of power. In the anarchical system of international relations, nation-states must rely on power to achieve national interests. From the realist perspective, the only mechanism for achieving international order under these conditions is the balance of power. A brief discussion of the theoretical conceptualization of the balance of power is in order before turning to an examination of Kennan's practical and concrete views of the United States position.

The use of the term "balance" has caused confusion in international relations literature because it is used in a variety of ways. As Inis Claude has observed, the balance of power sometimes means equilibrium or equivalent power, at other times its means not balanced or disequilibrium, and at still other times it refers to the distribution of power.[22] The debate is a complicated one and cannot be fully treated here. For purposes of this discussion, the balance of power was best defined by Morgenthau and Thompson: "the attempt on the part of one nation to counteract the power of another nation by increasing its strength to a point where it is at least equal, if not superior, to the other nation's strength."[23] In a more recent study of the balance of power, Stephen Walt argued that "states ally to balance against threats rather than against power alone. Although the distribution of power is an extremely important factor, the level of threat is also affected by geographic proximity, offensive capabilities, and perceived intentions."[24]   In contrast to Walt's conceptualization, traditional realists generally would argue that the existence of a preponderance of power alone presents a potential threat even if a hostile intention is not immediately present.[25]

Detractors of the balance of power have often blamed it—and foreign policies informed by the concept—as a cause of war. Such criticism does not do justice to the complexities of international politics. Morgenthau and Thompson more accurately captured the relationship between the balance of power and war:

As a method to maintain international order, the balance of power has been eminently successful throughout long stages of history; for it has prevented the rise of any one nation to such power as would have enabled it to destroy the independence of all the others. As a method to preserve international peace, the balance of power has met with indifferent success. It has been spectacularly successful in preventing threatening wars, especially in the nineteenth century, but the enormous number of wars known to history are a monument to its failure as an instrument of peace. The balance of power so often failed to preserve peace because either its principles were disregarded, or, more frequently, a nation erred in comparing its strength with that of another.[26]

The balance of power is fluid, dynamic, and ever-changing. Statesmen must be alert to fluxes in the balance of power to nurture international order. In Kennan's appraisal, "International political life is something organic, not something mechanical. Its essence is change; and the only systems for the regulation of international life which can be effective over long periods of time are ones sufficiently subtle, sufficiently pliable, to adjust themselves to constant change in the interests and power of the various countries involved."[27] It is in this context that the balance of power must be viewed—as part of the ebbs and flows of international politics throughout the ages.

Kennan's conceptualization of the balance of power is reflected in his historical analysis of Bismarck's geopolitical strategy. As Kennan viewed German diplomatic strategy, "Bismarck set about, quietly and with great skill, to create a situation in which, even if the Russians and the French were to combine against Germany, they would not find support anywhere else. Bearing in mind his principle that in a company of five great European Powers, it was essential always to be one of a grouping of at least three, he skillfully manipulated international events in such a way as to assure that the French and Russians remained, at the most, two."[28] Kennan judged that "Bismarck's entire European policy was predicated on the preservation of a reasonable balance of power between Austria and Russia and the avoidance of any major conflict between those two Powers."[29]

Kennan's study and admiration for Gibbon also instilled in him an appreciation of the importance of the balance of power for maintaining political autonomy and international order. Gibbon had observed that "The division of Europe into a number of independent states, connected, however, with each other, by the general resemblance of religion, language, and manners, is productive of the most beneficial consequences to the liberty of mankind. A modern tyrant, who should find no resistance either in his own breast, or in his people, would soon experience a gentle restraint from the example of his equals, the dread of present censure, the advice of his allies, and the apprehension of his enemies."[30] Gibbon's work probably had the greatest impact on Kennan's intellectual development during his time as a Foreign Service officer; Kennan read Gibbon while traveling abroad.[31]

Conversely, neglect of the balance of power and its disequilibrium results in a tragic loss of national autonomy. This phenomenon was painfully evident to Kennan in his experience as a diplomat during World War II. The collapse of the balance of power in Europe during the Second World War ended the autonomy of numerous nation-states in the region. Kennan witnessed the dilemmas posed to defeated peoples in Czechoslovakia and The Netherlands. Kennan hoped that his wartime diplomatic dispatches from Prague while under Nazi occupation would "at least serve to shed some light on one of humanity's oldest and most recalcitrant dilemmas: the dilemma of a limited collaboration with evil, in the interests of its ultimate mitigation, as opposed to an uncompromising, heroic but suicidal resistance to it, at the expense of the ultimate weakening of the forces capable of acting against it."[32] Kennan also surveyed Nazi-occupied Holland, and his diary notes taken then reflect the tragedy of a people's loss of autonomy to a superior power. "One could only expect that to the spiritual misery attendant upon the destruction of a great culture and a great tradition there would be added the misery of foreign exploitation and economic decline, and that some day large parts of these Dutch cities, sinking back into the swamps from which they had been so proudly and so competently erected, would become merely a curiosity for the edification of future generations of German tourists and would perhaps help to give the latter a sense of appreciation—tardy and helpless appreciation—for the values their forefathers had so lightheartedly destroyed."[33]

Restoring the balance of power with military force requires a steady hand at the helm of state. Despite the emotional urge for retribution, the interests of the balance of power often necessitate the restoration of defeated aggressor powers, albeit with reduced levels of power. Kennan noted from history, for example, that Bismarck viewed as a basic requirement of German security the preservation of the Austro-Hungarian Empire as one of the great powers of Europe because the disappearance of Austria "would not only be profoundly unsettling in its effect upon internal conditions within the new and as yet not fully consolidated German Reich but it would leave Germany isolated in the face of a Franco-Russian combination."[34]

AMERICA'S POSITION IN THE WORLD BALANCE OF POWER

Kennan's understandings of American national interest and the balance of power were intertwined to form his geopolitical worldview. The crux of the problem of achieving the American national interest was to prevent the consolidation of sufficient power to pose a threat to the autonomy of the United States.   As Kennan assessed this American foreign policy challenge in the twentieth century, "military strength on a major scale, and particularly strength of an amphibious nature, capable of reaching our homeland and disputing our power within it, can be produced only in a limited number of parts of the globe: in those regions where major industrial power, enjoying adequate access to raw materials, is combined with large reserves of educated and technically skilled manpower."[35]   Kennan recognized other sources of national power, but he was most articulate in identifying the military-industrial capability as the cornerstone for power among nation-states with the greatest potential impact on international order.

Only a handful of regions in the world could harness such potential sources of power.   Kennan assessed that centers of military-industrial strength lay in North America, Japan, England, Germany, and the former Soviet Union and emphasized that "nowhere outside these five areas can military-industrial strength be produced in this world today on what we might call a grand scale."[36] The distribution of power needed to be manipulated to prevent a concentration of power among the regions that present a threat to the autonomies of the remaining regions.

The Eurasian land mass was the central focus of Kennan's analysis.   In his global calculus, "the heart of our problem is to prevent the gathering together of the military-industrial potential of the entire Eurasian land mass under a single power threatening to the interests of the insular and maritime portions of the globe."[37]   He commented that "We can see that our security has been dependent throughout much of our history on the position of Britain; that Canada, in particular, has been a useful and indispensable hostage to good relations between our country and the British Empire; and that Britain's position, in turn, has depended on the maintenance of a balance of power on the European Continent.   Thus it was essential to us, as it was to Britain, that no single Continental land power should come to dominate the entire Eurasian land mass."[38]

The consolidation of continental power would invariably threaten maritime powers.   In Kennan's judgment, "Our interest has lain rather in the maintenance of some sort of stable balance among the powers of the interior, in order that none of them should effect the subjugation of the others, conquer the seafaring fringes of the land mass, become a great sea power as well as land power, shatter the position of England, and enter—as in these circumstances it certainly would—on an overseas expansion hostile to ourselves and supported by the immense resources of the interior of Europe and Asia."[39]   Kennan appeared to use the term "balance" to refer to a rough parity of power between nation-states.

Kennan's view of the United States position within the world distribution of power was consistent with that of Hans Morgenthau.   Morgenthau judged that "Since a threat to our national interest in the Western Hemisphere can only come from outside it—historically, from Europe—we have always striven to prevent the development of conditions in Europe which would be conducive to a European nation's interfering in the affairs of the Western Hemisphere or contemplating a direct attack upon the United States. These conditions would be most likely to arise if a European nation, its predominance unchallenged within Europe, could look across the sea for conquest without fear of being menaced at the center of its power; that is, in Europe itself."[40] Both Kennan and Morgenthau feared that a concentration of power in Europe would lead to a direct threat to American territory. Inis Claude has best summed up the views of Kennan and Morgenthau on this issue: both argued for a global distribution of power that included an equilibrium in Europe so that the United States could maintain a disequilibrium of power in the Western Hemisphere.[41]

The geopolitical worldviews of both Kennan and Morgenthau contain traces of that of Sir Halford MacKinder. MacKinder called the "joint continent of Europe, Asia, and Africa" the "World-Island."[42] The "Heartland," which consisted "of Arctic and Continental drainage, includes most of the Great Lowland and most of the Iranian Upland; it extends therefore to the long, height, curving brink of the Persian Mountains, beyond which is the depression occupied by the Euphrates Valley and the Persian Gulf."[43] As he viewed the globe, MacKinder concluded that "*Who rules East Europe commands the Heartland: Who rules the Heartland commands the World-Island: Who rules the World-Island commands the World.*"[44]

Kennan assessed that modern technology enabled powers to more easily threaten the heartland, although he did not specifically use this terminology. In his assessment, with "the aid of modern technology it is now possible to move and supply land forces over a greater distance from their industrial-political base than was the case in past centuries."[45] The implication of this analysis would be an increased potential for the projection of continental land power to threaten the heartland, the world island, and, in turn, the world at large. MacKinder's thoughts—filtered through the writings Nicholas Spykman—probably found their way into Kennan's readings while he was assigned to the National War College in the mid-1940s, although Kennan never acknowledged any such debt in his published work.[46]

Regardless of its origins, Kennan recognized that his geopolitical worldview was a broad generalization that needed refinements for purposes of policy making. It was in this context that Kennan identified key nation-states with which the United States needed strong security ties to hold the fabric of the world balance of power together. He identified the major maritime powers as the linchpins for American security policy. Kennan wrote that "with any reasonable degree of good will and understanding, we need never fear that Britain will be our enemy. I earnestly hope that a similar situation now prevails with respect to the Japanese, whose geographic situation in the Pacific is analogous to that of the British in the Atlantic."[47] These relationships were necessary to balance the power in the fulcrum of the world balance of power—the keys to which were Germany and Russia. As Kennan succinctly put it; the relationship between Germany and Russia is "at the heart of our security problem in the physical sense."[48]

Kennan's geopolitical worldview comes into sharper focus with an examination of his views on American foreign policy in the world wars and the Cold War. The United States failed to take a balance of power assessment into account after World War I. The United States slept while Germany and Japan emerged as major powers in the global balance of power. The power of the United States fell short of that required to defeat the aligned Axis powers of Germany and Japan in the Second World War and forced the United States to compensate with an alliance with the Soviet Union. In Kennan's framework, the global balance of power during World War II was in disequilibrium. He observed that

Before the war began the overwhelming portion of the world's armed strength in land forces and air forces has accumulated in the hands of three political entities—Nazi Germany, Soviet Russia, and Imperial Japan. All these entities were deeply and dangerously hostile to the Western democracies. As things stood in the late thirties, if these three powers were to combine their efforts and stick together in a military enterprise, the remaining Western nations plainly had no hope of defeating them on the land mass of Europe and Asia, with the armaments at hand or even those in prospect. In Europe and Asia, Western democracy had become militarily outclassed. The world balance of power had turned decisively against it.[49]

Kennan viewed the Cold War between the United States and the Soviet Union through this geopolitical prism. Kennan drew on his study of Gibbon to put the Cold War rivalry in historical context as yet another manifestation of competition in the balance of power: "he was pointing out the diversity of Europe and the improbability that anyone could come to control the whole place....That was the problem of security in the western Europe of the 18th century which Gibbon knew, and I would like to submit that that is basically the problem of security which this country now faces."[50] An elaboration of Kennan's conceptualization of the balance of power was expressed in a discussion about the American-Soviet Cold War rivalry. As Kennan responded to a question posed by an interviewer, "If a 'balance of power policy' means using American influence, wherever possible, to assure that the ability to develop military power on the grand scale is divided among several governmental entities and not concentrated entirely in any one of them, then I think that I favor it," although Kennan caveated this view by stating that such a policy should not mean pushing other people into conflict with each other and that the United States should not overestimate its power to affect these relationships.[51] Kennan's Cold War analysis, therefore, was predicated on the need to preserve the autonomy of nation-states in Europe through the adroit manipulation of the balance of power to hold in check the power of the Soviet Union.

Kennan's conceptualization of geopolitics had policy implications in the initial stages of the Cold War. For Kennan, Germany and Japan were key cornerstones to holding Soviet power in check; they "were the centers, respectively, of the two greatest industrial complexes of East and West. Their recovery was essential to the restoration of stability in Europe and East Asia. It was essential, if any sort of a tolerable balance of power was to be established in the postwar world, that they be kept out of Communist hands and that their great resources be utilized to the full for constructive purposes."[52] Kennan held in the forefront of his mind the tenet that defeated powers should be restored to maintain the balance of power in his post–World War II policy recommendations, particularly in his role in the formulation of the Marshall Plan, which significantly helped to restore the political and economic integrity of Western Europe to include West Germany.

Kennan assessed Soviet moves in peripheral geographic areas by gauging their potential impact on key positions for controlling the Heartland. He viewed the potential for Russian military penetration of Greece as a "serious complicating factor for the Western world in the event of any military conflict. And with time, the Russian position in the Eastern Mediterranean might grow, like that of the Germans in the last war, into one that could not be assailed with reasonable chance of success except by a major military effort."[53] As for the Middle East, Kennan speculated that Russia "might be able to garrison key points even though she had failed in her efforts to police the area as a whole. Supplemented by the control of Greece, Russia's control of the Eastern Mediterranean, of the Suez Canal, and the Persian Gulf would then be complete. Russia's strategic position for the contingency of a possible major conflict would be so improved that the Kremlin would be able to pursue aggressive and expansive policies elsewhere with far greater impunity and self-assurance than would otherwise be the case."[54]

These comments belie criticisms leveled against Kennan's policy of containment for failing to prioritize regions of importance for the competition with the Soviet Union. Notwithstanding such criticisms, Kennan had a hierarchy of geopolitical interests in his own mind's eye, although he neglected to spell them out in his famous X article.[55] The ambiguity of Kennan's words in the article made him vulnerable to criticism—most notably by his contemporary Walter Lippmann—that the policy of containment committed the United States to a military strategy it did not have the means to fulfill.[56] Such criticism, however, focused exclusively on Kennan's X article and failed to give adequate treatment to a broader sample of his work, which clearly shows that Kennan was primarily concerned about Soviet political expansion into strategic regions of the globe.[57]

Kennan's vision for a stable post–War World II international balance of power substantially differed from the power alignments that emerged during the Cold War. Instead of a two-alliance division of Europe manifested in NATO and the Warsaw Pact, Kennan advocated in his Reith lectures in 1957 demilitarization with a negotiated withdrawal of American and Soviet forces from the heart of Europe to create a large neutral zone with a unified Germany. He judged that such a system would have been inherently more stable than the Cold War division of Europe. In Kennan's assessment, "if Germany could not be broken up—if the problem of German nationalism could not be solved by thrusting Germany farther into the past—then the only thing to do was to thrust both Germany and Europe farther into the future: to create, that is, some sort of a united federal Europe into which the united Germany could be imbedded, and in this way to widen the horizon of aspiration and loyalty which, at its purely linguistic and national limits, had proven too narrow for the safety of Europe, too narrow for Germany herself."[58] He advised a similar approach for the Asian theater. Kennan wanted to facilitate the emergence of large areas in Europe and Asia—with a unified Germany and a demilitarized Japan, respectively—that would be militarily uncommitted: "In each case, I was prepared to see us withdraw our military forces if Soviet power would be equivalently withdrawn and if we could look forward to the rise, in the areas thus thrown open, of political authority independent of Soviet domination."[59] From Kennan's perspective, Tito's Yugoslavia "suited my book perfectly, as did Sweden and the neutralized Austria. I would have liked to see this uncommitted area increased until it came to constitute a large part of the European continent. I believed that a readiness on our side to withdraw would eventually stimulate a disposition on the Soviet side to do likewise. Only in this way, as I saw it, could one bring about the withdrawal of the lines of Soviet power to limits more compatible with the stability of Europe and thus make a beginning, at least, at the correction of the great geopolitical disbalance to which the outcome of World War II had led."[60]

Kennan viewed the Cold War division of Europe as "unnatural" because of its heavy reliance on American power to maintain the balance of power. Kennan thought that the United States was "not fitted, either institutionally or temperamentally, to be an imperial power in the grand manner, and particularly not one holding the great peoples of Western Europe indefinitely in some sort of paternal tutelage. Some day, it appeared to me, this divided Europe, dominated by the military presences of ourselves and the Russians, would have to yield to something more natural—something that did more justice to the true strength and interests of the intermediate European peoples themselves."[61] As Kennan wrote to scholar and former British diplomat Adam Watson in 1967, "As I look back now on the developments of the years, and on the evolution of my own thoughts, I realize that what I have really been pressing for, all this time, has been the earliest possible break up of the excessive bipolarity that marked the continental scene in the 1940's and '50's, and the creation in its place of some sort of balanced multiplicity of forces, by virtue of which the main European countries could shoulder a larger share of their traditional burden of providing a balance to Russian power on that part of the land mass."[62] Kennan, in other words, envisioned a return to a multipolar Europe reminiscent of Gibbon's time, away from a bipolar balance of power, in the belief that the former would be more sustainable and provide for greater stability than the latter.

In retrospect, Kennan's analysis of the balance of power in Europe suffered from several weaknesses. First, Kennan underestimated the stability of the bipolar division of Europe from 1945 to 1989. This division provided a clear demarcation of spheres of influence, which reduced ambiguities that could have nurtured conflicts between the superpowers.[63] Kennan's policy recommendations for neutralization of Europe were more than thirty years premature. With the collapse of the Soviet Union and the independence of Central and East European states in 1989, Europe began to move toward the geopolitical situation that Kennan had envisioned in 1957 in his Reith lectures. The contemporary situation is far from settled, and it remains to be seen whether Europe in the future will be more or less stable than it was during the Cold War.[64] Second, Kennan grossly underestimated the American ability to sustain its forces in Europe. The United States commitment to NATO proved to be remarkably constant for a period of more than forty years. Third, Kennan minimized the United States role as a balancing force within the Western alliance. In this regard, Josef Joffe accurately characterized the United States as "Europe's American pacifier" in that it provided a cushion of security to the major Western powers of West Germany, France, and the United Kingdom and dampened the historic security rivalries between these states.[65] Had Kennan been more concerned with the United States' stabilizing influence within Western Europe, he probably would not have been such a strong advocate of withdrawing American forces from Europe as a means to induce the Soviet Union to reciprocate.

ALLIANCES AND THE BALANCE OF POWER

The preceding discussion of the Second World War and the Cold War underscores the importance of alliances in statecraft. The United States alone lacked the power to manage the global balance of power and had to look to allies to augment American power to maintain a global equilibrium. For Kennan, alliances were a product of confluences of national interest in the global balance of power, but they also reflected in some instances historical and cultural affinities between nation-states. This view is a marked contrast with contemporary neorealists, who argue that alliance formation primarily is the result of external factors.[66]

Kennan was skeptical of the efficacy of alliances unless they were founded on geopolitical realities that formed a confluence of national interests. He cautioned that "There is something basically unsound about the alliance concept, as it is usually applied. No great nation is going to do anything in the military field—anything, that is, which has an important bearing on its security—merely because it has at some past time set its signature to some document, and if in the

existing circumstances that action would be contrary to its national security."[67]
Kennan distinguished between alliances forged in the heat of battle and those
formal treaties signed in periods of tranquility. He was skeptical that the latter
would withstand the pressure of concrete realities. The former, on the other
hand, were manifestations of concrete interests and more likely to endure.

Conversely, Kennan noted from his study of history that states have come
to the aid of other states in conflict despite the absence of treaties at the outset
of hostilities. He remarked that "It is surprising when you look back over the
annals of European history to see how little military alliances have meant, unless
there were realities behind them which would have obliged the countries to go
to war anyway. I think in moments of great decision in national affairs it is
very, very seldom that governments operate really in accordance with a piece
of paper; unless that piece of paper is backed up by certain real pressures that
work upon them, it wouldn't amount to much."[68] In other words, for Kennan,
treaties could not be used to forge common interests among signatories. To be
effective, treaties must reflect—rather than define—the interests of states.

NATO represented an alliance based on concrete interests. Kennan wrote
that "It cannot be stressed too often that NATO's real strength does not lie in
the paper undertakings which underpin it; it lies—and will continue in any
circumstances to lie—in the appreciation of the member nations for the identity
of their real interests, as members of the Western spiritual and cultural
community."[69] The signing of the NATO treaty reflected the national interests
of all signatories to counterbalance the power of the Soviet Union in Europe and
to preserve the political autonomy of each NATO member. The American
alliance with European states also was based, in part, on cultural identification.
The Europeans "are our good friends as are the inhabitants of no other
continent—not because they love us (words of that sort are misplaced when one
is talking about great peoples) but because they recognize both the common
traditions that unite us and the importance of our attitudes and our disposition
for their own security."[70] Kennan argued that "The British Isles and parts
(particularly the northwestern part) of the European mainland are still the source
of a major portion of our cultural and political heritage" and that the "best we
can hope for from other peoples is that they should be aware of having a stake
in our survival as a great power and of the value to themselves of a relationship
of mutual confidence with us."[71]

These internal cultural similarities are decreasing as the multicultural
composition of the United States changes. Kennan acknowledged this trend
when he wrote that "It is true that the focus on Europe that predominated in
American opinion and policy from the time of the foundation of the republic
down into the first half of this century is now being relatively weakened by
changes in the ethnic and national composition of the American populace and by
the growing importance for this country of Latin America and the Far East."[72]
Nevertheless, Kennan argued that the United States "governmental tradition and
its political culture generally have been largely derived from that side of the

ocean, particularly, though not exclusively, from the British Isles. And the close relationship between the security of Western Europe and that of this country has not only been recognized in two great wars but has been sealed, in a sense, by those many Americans who laid down their lives in the service of it."[73] Despite the decreasing cultural similarities, Kennan saw geopolitical circumstances as the strongest justification for a U.S. alliance in Europe.

Kennan, therefore, had moved intellectually from a position in 1957 of trying to divest the United States of involvement in NATO as a centerpiece of European security to accepting it as such in 1993. Kennan during the intervening years had come—in Burkean fashion—to see NATO as a tradition, custom, or matter of habit ingrained in societies on both sides of the Atlantic. NATO became a means for promoting international order and continuity as well as for perpetuating American involvement in Europe where geopolitical interests remained, despite the absence of a readily apparent threat after the collapse of the Soviet Union.

In stark contrast to the American alliance with West European states, the alignment with the Soviet Union during World War II was based solely on a calculus of power. Without the alliance, the national identities of both states were gravely threatened by a preponderance of German power. Kennan concisely summed up the situation when he reflected in 1951 that "There was no prospect for victory over Germany, unless it were with the help of Russia."[74] During the collaboration, the United States and the Soviet Union were able to put their political differences aside. After the defeat of Nazi Germany, these differences became abundantly apparent with the birth of the Cold War. Few if any cultural links between the great states existed to bind them into a continuing alliance beyond the defeat of their mutual foe.

Kennan also took note of other relationships that would not be conducive for alliance formation. For example, he saw poor prospects for an alliance between China and the United States, primarily on the basis of his assessment of China's cultural character. Kennan wrote in 1972 that "the Chinese were, as a people, intensely xenophobic and arrogant" and "despite the highly civilized nature of their normal outward behavior, were capable of great ruthlessness when they considered themselves to be crossed. Admirable as were many of their qualities—their industriousness, their business honesty, their practical astuteness, and their political acumen—they seemed to me to be lacking in two attributes of the Western-Christian mentality: the capacity for pity and the sense of sin."[75] China, moreover, played little role in Kennan's geopolitical worldview. It will be recalled that Kennan did not identify China as one of the five major centers of global power. He was skeptical of China's capabilities to emerge within the global balance of power as a major power. In 1967 congressional hearings, he stated that "I do not see China entering the ranks of the great powers by the 1980s. As a matter of fact, Japan potentially far outranks her today. We have had a tendency in this country ever since World War II to underrate greatly the potential importance of Japan and to overrate the importance of China."[76]

China's geopolitical position, in Kennan's analysis, was not a requisite to fulfill the American national interest of maintaining the global balance of power.

Paradoxically, Japan was an essential power in the United States strategy to maintain the balance of power. Kennan observed that Japan's industrial power "is so tremendous a factor in world affairs that it can hardly help constituting a force either for great good or for great bad."[77] Because of Japan's geopolitical significance, Kennan apparently was willing to overlook the cultural barriers that inhibit a closer relationship such as the one that the United States enjoys with Great Britain, the world's other major maritime power. Kennan, however, was not willing to make a similar allowance for internal cultural characteristics for the Chinese. In contrast to Kennan, Morgenthau had a firmer grasp of the importance of China in the global balance of power: "However unsure the United States has been in its Asiatic policy, it has always assumed that the domination of China by another nation would lead to so great an accumulation of power as to threaten the security of the United States."[78] This inconsistency in Kennan's thought and his underestimation of the role and influence of China in the world balance of power probably is attributable to what Professor Gaddis has identified as Kennan's rudimentary understanding of Asia in comparison to the expertise he had achieved on European affairs.[79]

CONCLUSION

The interrelationships between national interest and the global balance of power emerge in Kennan's analysis of United States participation in international relations in this century. An examination of his assessments of American policy brings to the fore concrete illustrations of theoretical geopolitical conceptualizations. These concepts are the measuring sticks by which Kennan judged American foreign policy. What Kennan tried to do was to make explicit the American national interest in order to equate ends and means for more effective and prudent foreign policy. The undertaking of commitments in areas beyond the core areas of power threatens to reduce American resources available to defend critical interests. Kennan counseled restraint in foreign affairs while paying close attention to the world balance of power. In the final analysis, Kennan—armed with a complex web of geopolitical thought—was concerned that U.S. foreign policy was bound to fail if it neglected the equation of ends and means or national interest and power. These concepts represent the core of his strategic thought on American foreign policy.

NOTES

1. John Lewis Gaddis, "Containment: A Reassessment," *Foreign Affairs* 55, no. 4 (July 1977): 886.

2. George F. Kennan, "The Quest for Concept," *Harvard Today*, Autumn 1967, 15.

3. George F. Kennan, *Around the Cragged Hill: A Personal and Political Philosophy* (New York, NY: W.W. Norton & Company, 1993), 181.

4. Kennan, *Around the Cragged Hill*, 181.

5. "United States Foreign Policy," Lecture Delivered to the Naval War College, 11 October 1948, George F. Kennan Papers, Box 17, File 14, Seeley G. Mudd Manuscript Library, Department of Rare Books and Special Collections, Princeton University Library.

6. George F. Kennan, "The National Interest of the United States," *Illinois Law Review* 45, no. 6 (January–February 1951): 730.

7. Kennan, "The National Interest of the United States," 730.

8. Kennan, "The National Interest of the United States," 730.

9. George F. Kennan, *Realities of American Foreign Policy* (Princeton, NJ: Princeton University Press, 1954), 11.

10. Kennan, *Realities of American Foreign Policy*, 11.

11. Kennan, *Realities of American Foreign Policy*, 12.

12. Kennan, *Around the Cragged Hill*, 181–182.

13. George F. Kennan, *Memoirs, 1950–1963* (New York, NY: Pantheon Books, 1972), 88.

14. George F. Kennan, "Measures Short of War," 16 September 1946, in Giles D. Harlow and George C. Maerz (eds.), *Measures Short of War: The George F. Kennan Lectures at the National War College, 1946–47* (Washington, DC: National Defense University Press, 1991), 14.

15. Kennan, "Measures Short of War," 15.

16. See Hans J. Morgenthau and Kenneth W. Thompson, "Elements of National Power," in their *Politics among Nations: The Struggle for Power and Peace*, Sixth Edition (New York, NY: McGraw-Hill Publishing Company, 1985), 146–158, for a discussion of national character and morale as sources of power for nation-states.

17. "Correspondence to Louis J. Halle," 3 January 1956, George F. Kennan Papers, Box 31, Seeley G. Mudd Manuscript Library, Department of Rare Books and Special Collections, Princeton University Library.

18. Kennan, "The National Interest of the United States," 738.

19. "Correspondence to Adlai Stevenson," 28 March 1956, George F. Kennan Papers, Box 31, Seeley G. Mudd Manuscript Library, Department of Rare Books and Special Collections, Princeton University Library.

20. Greg Russell, *John Quincy Adams and the Public Virtues of Diplomacy* (Columbia, MO: University of Missouri Press, 1995), 134.

21. George F. Kennan, *American Diplomacy*, Expanded Edition (Chicago, IL: University of Chicago Press, 1984), 102.

22. See Inis L. Claude, Jr., "Balance of Power: An Ambiguous Concept," in his *Power and International Relations* (New York, NY: Random House, 1962), 11–39, for a discussion of the multiple meanings given to the concept.

23. Hans J. Morgenthau and Kenneth W. Thompson (eds.), *Principles and Problems of International Politics* (Washington, DC: University Press of America, 1950), 103.

24. Stephen M. Walt, *The Origins of Alliances* (Ithaca, NY: Cornell University Press, 1987), 5.

25. Henry Kissinger probably best captured for the traditional realists the relationship between power and threat in the balance of power. Kissinger wrote that "The domination by a single power of either of Eurasia's two principal spheres—Europe or Asia—remains a good definition of strategic danger for America, Cold War or no Cold War. For such a grouping would have the capacity to outstrip America economically and, in the end, militarily. The danger would have to be resisted even were the dominant power apparently benevolent, for if the intentions ever changed, America would find itself with a grossly diminished capacity for effective resistance and a growing inability to shape events." See Henry A. Kissinger, *Diplomacy* (New York, NY: Simon & Schuster, 1994), 813.

26. Morgenthau and Thompson, *Principles and Problems of International Politics*, 103.

27. George F. Kennan, *Memoirs, 1925–1950* (New York, NY: Pantheon Books, 1967), 218.

28. George F. Kennan, *The Decline of Bismarck's European Order: Franco-Russian Relations, 1875-1890* (Princeton, NJ: Princeton University Press, 1979), 249.

29. Kennan, *The Decline of Bismarck's European Order*, 277.

30. Edward Gibbon, *The History of the Decline and Fall of the Roman Empire*, Volume I, Edited by David Womerly (New York, NY: Penguin Books, 1994), 106.

31. Interview with John Lewis Gaddis, Woodrow Wilson International Center for Scholars, Washington, DC, 26 October 1995. Hereafter referred to as Gaddis Interview.

32. George F. Kennan, *From Prague after Munich: Diplomatic Papers, 1938–1940* (Princeton, NJ: Princeton University Press, 1968), x.

33. George F. Kennan, Diary Entry, 15 June 1940, The Hague, in *Sketches from a Life* (New York, NY: Pantheon Books, 1989), 67–68.

34. Kennan, *The Decline of Bismarck's European Order*, 277.

35. Kennan, *Realities of American Foreign Policy*, 63–64.

36. Kennan, *Realities of American Foreign Policy*, 64.

37. Kennan, *Realities of American Foreign Policy*, 65.

38. Kennan, *American Diplomacy*, 4–5.

39. Kennan, *American Diplomacy*, 5.

40. Hans J. Morgenthau, *In Defense of the National Interest: A Critical Examination of American Foreign Policy* (Lanham, MD: University Press of America, 1982), 5.

41. Inis L. Claude, Jr., Comments to the Author, 17 February 1997, Miller Center of Public Affairs, University of Virginia, Charlottesville, VA.

42. Halford J. MacKinder, *Democratic Ideals and Reality* (New York, NY: Henry Holt and Company, 1942), 62.

43. MacKinder, *Democratic Ideals and Reality*, 74.

44. MacKinder, *Democratic Ideals and Reality*, 150.

45. George F. Kennan, "How New Are Our Problems?" *Illinois Law Review* 45, no. 6 (January–February 1951): 725.

46. Kennan probably looked at Spykman's work while Kennan was at the National War College in 1946. Professor Gaddis suspects that MacKinder most heavily influenced Kennan through the work of Spykman, who gained many of his ideals from MacKinder. See Nicholas John Spykman, *America's Strategy in World Politics: The United States and the Balance of Power* (New York, NY: Harcourt, Brace and Company, 1942). Another academic influence on Kennan and his strategic thought was a collection of essays

published in *Makers of Modern Strategy*, edited by Edward Mead Earle in 1943, which was required reading at the War College, according to Gaddis. Gaddis Interview. Interestingly, Earle wrote the introduction for MacKinder's 1942 edition of *Democratic Ideals and Reality* and was a confidant of Kennan at the Institute for Advanced Study at Princeton. For an updated version of Earle's volume, see Peter Paret (ed.), *Makers of Modern Strategy: From Machiavelli to the Nuclear Age* (Princeton, NJ: Princeton University Press, 1986).

47. Kennan, *Realities of American Foreign Policy*, 65.

48. Kennan, *Realities of American Foreign Policy*, 65.

49. Kennan, *American Diplomacy*, 74–75.

50. "Contemporary Problems of Foreign Policy," National War College Lecture, 17 September 1948, George F. Kennan Papers, Box 17, Folder 11, Seeley G. Mudd Manuscript Library, Department of Rare Books and Special Collections, Princeton University Library.

51. "Interview with George F. Kennan," *Foreign Policy* 7 (Summer 1972): 17.

52. Kennan, *Memoirs, 1925–1950*, 368.

53. George F. Kennan, "Comments on the National Security Problem," 28 March 1947, in Harlow and Maerz (eds.), *Measures Short of War*, 161. Kennan later commented that these thoughts presented at the National War College reflected his concentration on the Greek-Turkish crisis as then head of the Policy Planning Staff and that these considerations went into the Marshall Plan.

54. Kennan, "Comments on the National Security Problem," 164–165.

55. Kennan's policy of containment was publicly articulated in the article written under the pseudonym Mr. X, "The Sources of Soviet Conduct," *Foreign Affairs* 25, no. 4 (July 1947).

56. See Walter Lippmann, *The Cold War: A Study in U.S. Foreign Policy* (New York, NY: Harper & Brothers Publishers, 1947).

57. For the most authoritative treatment of this controversy, see Gaddis, "Containment: A Reassessment."

58. Kennan, *Memoirs, 1925–1950*, 416–417.

59. Kennan, *Memoirs, 1925–1950*, 463.

60. Kennan, *Memoirs, 1925–1950*, 463.

61. Kennan, *Memoirs, 1925–1950*, 464.

62. "Correspondence to Adam Watson," 7 December 1967, George F. Kennan Papers, Box 31, Seeley G. Mudd Manuscript Library, Department of Rare Books and Special Collections, Princeton University Library.

63. The author is indebted to John Lewis Gaddis, "The Long Peace," *International Security*, Volume 10, Number 4, Spring 1986, 112, for this important point.

64. For an optimistic assessment of the prospects for stability in post–Cold War Europe, see Stephen Van Evera, "Primed for Peace: Europe after the Cold War," *International Security* 15, no. 3 (Winter 1990/91). For an opposing view, see John Mearsheimer, "Back to the Future: Instability in Europe after the Cold War," *International Security* 15, no. 1 (Summer 1990).

65. See Josef Joffe, "Europe's American Pacifier," *Foreign Policy* 54 (Spring 1984).

66. See Kenneth N. Waltz, *Theory of International Politics* (Reading, MA: Addison-Wesley Publishing Co., 1979).

67. "Diary Notes," 30 September 1950, George F. Kennan Papers, Box 26, Folder 2, Seeley G. Mudd Manuscript Library, Department of Rare Books and Special Collections, Princeton University Library.

68. George F. Kennan, "What Is Policy?" 18 December 1947, in Harlow and Maerz (eds.), *Measures Short of War*, 310.

69. George F. Kennan, *Russia, the Atom and the West* (New York, NY: Harper & Brothers Publishers, 1958), 46.

70. Kennan, *Around the Cragged Hill*, 205.

71. Kennan, *Around the Cragged Hill*, 196.

72. Kennan, *Around the Cragged Hill*, 196.

73. Kennan, *Around the Cragged Hill*, 205.

74. Kennan, *American Diplomacy*, 77.

75. Kennan, *Memoirs, 1950–1963*, 55–56.

76. George F. Kennan, "The Communist World in 1967," Hearing before the Committee on Foreign Relations, United States Senate, Ninetieth Congress, First Session, 30 January 1967 (Washington, DC: U.S. Government Printing Office, 1967), 27.

77. George F. Kennan, *The Cloud of Danger: Current Realities of American Foreign Policy* (Boston, MA: Little, Brown and Company, 1977), 108.

78. Morgenthau, *In Defense of the National Interest*, 7.

79. Gaddis Interview.

4

THE DOMESTIC STRUGGLE FOR POWER

American statesmen cannot frame policy exclusively on the basis of a realist's geopolitical calculus. They are forced to operate in realms other than those of power, national interest, and the balance of power in the international realm. The internal power struggle to control the government also shapes the course of American behavior abroad. The competition for power between the executive and the legislative branches as well as within each of these branches, coupled by the lobbying efforts of interest groups, has a profound impact on American foreign policy. The traditional realists, including Kennan, had a keen appreciation for the effects of the domestic struggle for power on foreign policy. They judged that foreign policies for all nation-states—including the United States—to varying degrees are manifestations of internal struggles for power and not merely reactions to events in the international realm. Such a dimension is absent in the literature of neorealists, who argue that the external structure of the international system is the critical defining variable for foreign policy behavior.

The separation of powers in American democracy presents unique problems to policy makers and diplomats alike who must try to craft and implement foreign policy within the context of the domestic competition for power. If the United States is to deal effectively in the realm of foreign policy, these traits must be recognized and addressed. Kennan argued that, to overcome these obstacles, responsibility for the direction of foreign policy needs to be taken by the executive branch. The chief executive is best able to articulate governing principles for foreign policy and meet the demands of policy implementation. Conversely, Kennan argued that the diffusion of power in the legislature and submission to whims of the mood swings in public opinion was a prescription for floundering in foreign policy. His criticisms about democracy and foreign policy were in no sense a rejection of democracy. At a time when American foreign policy is increasingly influenced by the legislature and public opinion, an examination of Kennan's views warns us of the potential pitfalls of this trend.

THE CONTEST FOR POWER AT HOME

Alexis de Tocqueville stands out as one of the most perceptive observers of the relationship between American democracy and foreign policy. Kennan took Tocqueville's philosophy as the basis for his analysis of the impact of domestic politics on foreign policy. Louis Halle observed that like Kennan, Tocqueville "saw how great were the disadvantages of a democracy when it came to the conduct of foreign relations."[1] Tocqueville wrote: "I do not hesitate to say that it is especially in the conduct of their foreign relations that democracies appear to me decidedly inferior to other governments."[2] Kennan clearly saw problems inherent in a democratic form of government and noted that "many wise observers beside Tocqueville have drawn attention, that our political system is in many ways poorly designed for the conduct of the foreign policies of a great power aspiring to world leadership."[3]

American democracy faces unique challenges in foreign policy because of the institutions that channel and control the domestic struggle for power and the political culture that is the foundation for these institutions. Kennan related that "The peculiar impediments that rest upon the United States government in the conduct of foreign policy are ones that flow partly from institutions, imbedded as these are in the revered and almost ancient Constitution, but partly also from deeply ingrained traditions, customs, and habits of thought—all those things that Tocqueville referred to as *les manieres* and to which, incidentally, he attributed greater importance, as determinants of national behavior, than to institutions."[4] These characteristics impede the achievement of the theoretical requirements for effective statecraft and diplomacy. Tocqueville observed that foreign policy demands qualities that a democracy generally does not possess: "It cannot combine its measures with secrecy or await their consequences with patience. These are qualities which more especially belong to an individual or an aristocracy; and they are precisely the qualities by which a nation, like an individual, attains a dominant position."[5] In the same vein, Kennan argued that the separation of powers in American government "goes far to rule out the privacy, the flexibility, and the promptness and incisiveness of decision and action, which have marked the great imperial powers of the past and which are generally considered necessary to the conduct of an effective world policy by the rulers of a great state."[6] The United States is blessed with checks and balances to stem the abuse of power that would be inevitable if it rested exclusively in the hands of the executive, but these internal checks and balances of power are cumbersome for the formulation and implementation of foreign policy.

There has been a seepage of power from the executive to the legislature in foreign policy, particularly since the Vietnam War. The Congress, however, is poorly suited as an institution for the demands of statecraft. Kennan argued that Congress can "act upon foreign policy only fitfully, in great ponderous lurches which establish its direction, and the limits within which it can vary, for often prolonged periods into the future."[7]

Special interests bring a disproportionately heavy weight to bear on Congress to influence the executive's conduct of foreign policy and obscure the articulation of the national interest as the method or end for diplomatic initiatives. Kennan argued that American diplomacy is helpless "before the pressures of various highly organized lobbies and interest groups, which intimidate the legislators and cause American foreign policy to be conducted in the interests of minorities rather than of the population at large."[8] Kennan observed in 1977, moreover, that lobbying undermines executive control over foreign policy because it invites "foreign statesmen and their representatives to gain concessions from the United States not by a reasoned approach through the constituted channels of the President or the Secretary of State but by going through the back door and enlisting the support of particular American lobbies and persons in Congress whose purposes happen to coincide with their own."[9]

The Congress's function as designed by the Founding Fathers was to do precisely this—represent the views and needs of their constituents. The views of constituents, however, may be at odds with the larger strategic foreign policy interests of the collective state. Fear of the loss of constituent backing and reelection is a powerful disincentive to those elected representatives that would try to take a step back from local politics to see the larger national interests at stake in foreign policy endeavors.

Kennan was quick to identify domestic pressures on congressmen but neglected to address similar pressures coming from political parties on their president or the president's use of foreign policy endeavors to garner domestic political support from particular interest groups. One might cite President Nixon's historic trip to China, in part, to the need to divert domestic attention from the Watergate scandal. Alternatively, one might view President Clinton's refusal to veto legislation that enables American legal action against European businesses involved in Cuba as an effort to win domestic political support from expatriate Cuban-Americans. These pressures are becoming more pronounced as the financial demands of presidential election campaigns become increasingly high.

Kennan believed that the ability of our diplomatic corps to carry out traditional tasks has seriously declined, in part due to its disadvantages in the domestic competition for power. On the domestic scene, the Foreign Service

tends to become an object of bewilderment and suspicion in the eyes of Congress, the political parties, and of much of the press. And yet the legislators and the party politicians, in particular, are precisely the people on whom the Service is of course dependent for its appropriation of its salaries, and the physical premises and facilities with which it has to work. Underlying this organizational isolation, and in part explaining and reinforcing it, the Foreign Service is encumbered with an even more widespread and serious burden—namely, a deeply ingrained prejudice against people who give their lives professionally to diplomatic work—prejudice on the part of the political establishment in the first instance but also on the part of much of the press and portions of the public as well.[10]

The State Department, moreover, traditionally has not fared well in the competition with other executive departments, particularly the Department of Defense, for budget resources, given the lack of a strong domestic constituency. Consequently, the State Department is no longer the principal actor in the foreign policy decision-making process. Instead, it is but one of numerous bureaucracies competing for control over foreign policy. Indeed, many observers including Kennan have argued that the executive's foreign policy apparatus has become too bureaucratized and unmanageable since the Second World War: "The governmental machinery is simply too unwieldy, too cumbersome, too unknown, and too deflated of meaning by its own vastness to be useful as an instrument of policy."[11]

Multilayered bureaucracies are bogged down in prolonged policy processes that cause delays and dim the prospects for effective implementation. Kennan, as head of the State Department's Policy Planning Staff in 1947, gained a firsthand appreciation of the time lags between policy conceptualization and implementation due to bureaucratic hurdles that policy proposals must clear.[12] Not only do bureaucracies cause delays, but they hamper other key requisites for effective diplomacy—flexibility and creativity. Adroit diplomacy "cannot emanate from the workings of a great bureaucratic apparatus. It requires, necessarily and properly, too much of the personal, too much of the private, too much—if you will—of the conspiratorial to be conceived and implemented in this way. The chief executive is faced today with the choice of bypassing the regular apparatus both as a source of information and inspiration and as a channel of execution, or of forgoing effective diplomacy altogether and contenting himself with the monumental inflexibility, the philosophical shallowness, the ideological obscurity, and the unimaginative execution which the great organization ensures."[13] Henry Kissinger similarly observed that, because foreign policy bureaucracies are so absorbed with internal problems, "Decisions are reached so painfully that the very anguish of decision-making acts as a brake on the give-and-take of traditional diplomacy."[14]

Public opinion also exerts a heavy influence on the executive's conduct of foreign policy. Kennan, with his aristocratic leanings, was critical of the tendency for public opinion to drive American policy and diplomacy. He thought public opinion was best suited to inform longer-run objectives while leaving tactical navigation in the short run to diplomats: "I do not consider public reaction to foreign-policy questions to be erratic and undependable over the long term; but I think the record indicates that in the short term our public opinion, or what passes for our public opinion in the thinking of official Washington, can be easily led astray into areas of emotionalism and subjectivity which make it a poor and inadequate guide for national action."[15] Diplomatic historian Norman Graebner shared this view but stressed the importance of public opinion in the struggle over the direction of foreign policy—to a degree to which Kennan had not—when he wrote that "In any executive-congressional contest over specific foreign policy issues, public opinion, the ultimate sources of power in a democratic order, determines the winner."[16]

The American public at large generally does not have command—nor should it be expected to—of the international complexities and ambiguities to be gauged in crafting foreign policy. In Kennan's view, most great problems of foreign affairs "usually involved a bewildering welter of conflicting considerations requiring, for their understanding, much historical background and much detailed study."[17] Sound judgment in foreign policy takes years of study to nurture, and most working men and women—preoccupied with supporting themselves and their families in their own chosen occupations—should not be expected to accumulate sufficient knowledge to make informed foreign policy decisions. After all, no one should expect a diplomat to become expert in fields beyond his or her expertise, such as medicine or computer science.

The public is more likely to support slogans and simplifications than sophisticated foreign policy analysis. As Kennan described the phenomenon, "These people take refuge in the pat and chauvinistic slogans because they are incapable of understanding any others, because these slogans are safer from the stand-point of short-term gain, because the truth is sometimes a poor competitor in the market place of ideas—complicated, unsatisfying, full of dilemmas, always vulnerable to misinterpretation and abuse. The counsels of impatience and hatred can always be supported by the crudest and cheapest symbols; for the counsels of moderation, the reasons are often intricate, rather than emotional, and difficult to explain."[18] Kennan believed, to his dismay, that "the chauvinists of all times and places go their appointed way: plucking the easy fruits, reaping the little triumphs of the day at the expense of someone else tomorrow, deluging in noise and filth anyone who gets in their way, dancing their reckless dance on the prospects for human progress, drawing the shadow of a great doubt over the validity of democratic institutions."[19]

The media, in turn, inform public opinion, which magnifies the former's impact on diplomacy and foreign policy. Kennan held out little prospect for informed discourse on foreign policy when the discussion was driven by the media: "The American mass media produce upon any given event an effect analogous to that produced on a man's shadow by the angle of the sun—causing it normally to be either much greater or much less than life-size."[20] The media's portrayal of international events can drive policy along avenues beyond the moderate definition of national interest. Kennan, for example, attributed U.S. military intervention in Somalia in 1992 to American media coverage. He wrote in his diary that "The reaction was an emotional one, occasioned by the sight of the suffering of the starving people in question . . . But if American policy from here on out, particularly policy involving the uses of our armed forces abroad, is to be controlled by popular emotional impulses, and particularly ones provoked by the commercial television industry, then there is no place—not only for myself, but for what have traditionally been regarded as the responsible deliberative organs of our government, in both the executive and legislative branches."[21] In Kennan's view, "Fleeting, disjointed, visual glimpses of reality, flickering on and off the screen, here today and gone tomorrow, are not the 'information' on which sound judgments on complicated international problems are to be formed. Television cannot consult the rich voice of prior experience, nor can it outline probable consequences, or define alternatives, or express the nuances of the arguments pro and con."[22]

Nor is the American public or the media well suited for the patience required of effective diplomacy. Diplomatic efforts more often than not are slow to come to fruition. Kennan noted that "It seems to me that in the field of foreign affairs there is generally a great time lag—as much as 5 or 10 years on the average—between cause and effect in major developments. This is something that few people in this country are aware of. Their unawareness expresses itself in a demand for quick results, where such results often simply cannot be obtained. It also expresses itself in a tendency to lay the blame or credit for current developments on people who happen to bear public responsibility at the moment, even though the real causes of these developments may go much deeper in time and in complexity."[23] Kennan lamented the public's inadequate grasp of diplomacy when he wrote to Walter Lippmann, "To me, the saddest part of this year's experience with the high affairs of state is not the realization of how hard it is for a democracy to conduct a successful foreign policy—although that *is* sad. It is the realization that if it did conduct a successful foreign policy, so few people would recognize it for what it was."[24] One example of the slow maturation time between policy implementation and achievement of desired results in which Kennan was intimately involved was the Marshall Plan. Only many years after the plan's birth was it apparent that it had successfully contributed to the rebuilding of war-devastated Europe to place it on sound footing to resist Soviet encroachment throughout the Cold War.

The domestic struggle for power obfuscates the clear articulation of national interest needed to guide diplomacy and foreign policy. Much to Kennan's chagrin, "American diplomacy is seldom conducted solely for what appear to be its ostensible ends. It is often so conducted when the questions at issue are ones in which no strong domestic-political issue is visible. It is also so conducted, within reasonable limits, in time of war or great national danger. But for the remainder, official Washington is inclined to view whatever happens in its own internal relationships as much more important than whatever is happening elsewhere in the world, or indeed in its relations with the rest of the world."[25] Consequently, American statesmanship is "ineffective in the pursuit of real objectives in the national interest, allowing it to degenerate into a mere striking of attitudes before the mirror of domestic political opinion."[26] In the aftermath of the Cold War and the absence of any readily apparent near-term threat to American security to the extent that the former Soviet Union had been, this trait may be becoming increasingly pronounced in American foreign policy.

Statesmen and diplomats need to have the long-term horizon in sight in foreign policy and diplomacy despite the day-to-day pressures exerted by public opinion, special interest groups, the media, and Congress. Kennan warned that the apparent lulls in significant events in the international realm belie stormy political undercurrents. The task of diplomacy is to prevent them from coming to the surface in a violent torrent. He wrote in 1956 that "in the long dull intervals between these dramatic moments, in those prosaic reaches of everyday life where the element of danger is more remote and more subtle and often not entirely external—in these times the primacy of domestic policy comes into its own and the voices that resound on the forums of international intercourse are more apt to be the voices of internal factions, intent on their competition with other factions within the given country, saying and doing on the international plane those things which, in their judgment, are most likely to promote their political prospects at home."[27] Ironically, "it is precisely in these long, dull periods of peace that the most decisive things really happen. It is in these times that the predicaments and dilemmas are created, from which the wars and catastrophes then flow."[28] Kennan undoubtedly arrived at this view through his study of history. He particularly was struck by the historical antecedents of World War I, which developed during a period of international stability. That war laid the foundation for World War II, which, in turn, gave rise to the Cold War that lasted for more than forty years.

THE CASE FOR A STRONG EXECUTIVE HAND

Power has become so dispersed within the government that it cannot be harnessed effectively for the conduct of foreign policy. Kennan observed that "The President and the Secretary of State are expected to communicate with other governments concerning those aspects of American behavior which affect them; but it is a behavior they do not, and in many instances cannot, control. They find themselves forced, in many instances, into the position of helpless intermediaries between internal and external forces both of which lie beyond their effective power of influence."[29] This tendency, in part, reflects contemporary American opinion that emphasizes the Founding Fathers' concern about a concentration of power in executive hands. "There is a feeling that concentration of authority is in some way 'undemocratic,' that the allotment to a single individual of the power to decide something is in some way incompatible with the spirit of the American political system."[30]

Contrary to the popular perception, a heavy dose of power in the hands of the executive for foreign policy was consistent with the ideas of the Founding Fathers, and Kennan wanted to swing the pendulum of power back to the executive in foreign policy. He repudiated "the suggestion that to advocate such concentration constitutes fascism and in this I find myself in agreement with one of the greatest of the early Americans, with Alexander Hamilton."[31] Hamilton was indeed a guiding light for Kennan. It was Hamilton who most eloquently articulated the case for a strong executive, particularly in times of war: "Of all the cares or concerns of government, the direction of war most peculiarly demands those qualities which distinguish the exercise of power by a single hand. The direction of war implies the direction of the common strength; and the power of direction and employing the common strength, forms an usual and essential part in the definition of the executive authority."[32] Hamilton's words stand as elegant testimony to the benefits of the concentration of power in the executive as commander in chief.

Kennan's interpretation of the Constitution in regard to foreign policy is somewhat at odds with mainstream interpretations. As Norman Graebner has pointed out, the Constitution grants power to the president as commander in chief, but that does not directly translate into control over foreign policy.[33] Indeed, the Founding Fathers gave a strong role to Congress in foreign policy. As Graebner has noted, "For the framers the Congress, not the President, was the true representative of the people. They placed in Congress the powers to tax, control commerce, raise armies, and provide for their use through a declaration of war. The President shared none of these powers."[34] Nevertheless, what Kennan had in mind was not altering the Constitution, but the full exercise of the powers granted under it to the president. The practice of foreign policy in recent memory has evolved into a routine in which Congress not only exercises its important oversight role but is involved in day-to-day management of operations policy, which encumbers foreign policy. Kennan looked to the president to take the reins of responsibility for leading a more coherent course in foreign policy.

GOVERNING PRINCIPLES OF STATECRAFT

The most demanding role for the executive is the articulation of principles and national interest upon which to base the country's foreign policy. In Kennan's view, principle cannot be "the product of the normal workings of the political process in any democratic country."[35] The tendency in debates over foreign policy in democracies is to arrive at consensus or the lowest-common-denominator rather than a clear articulation of interest and policy.

To avoid the lowest-common-denominator phenomenon, Kennan looked to enlightened statesmanship to formulate American foreign policy principles. In his judgment, "A principle is something that can only be declared, and then only by a political leader. It represents, of necessity, his own view of what sort of a country his is, and how it should conduct itself in the international arena. But the principle finds its reality, if it finds it at all, in the degree of acceptance, tacit or otherwise, that its proclamation ultimately receives from the remainder of the political establishment and from the populace at large."[36] Although statesmen articulate the governing principles, these principles must be backed by public support to be sustained and effective.

This task may appear at first glance to be unrealistic, but it is not without historical precedent. Kennan cited, for example, President Adams's formulation of principle that received broad popular support as did the principles in Washington's Farewell Address, Jefferson's prose in the Declaration of Independence, and Lincoln's Gettysburg Address.[37] In each of these cases, American statesmen put forward their idea of principle based on their own well-informed estimates of what would find "sufficient response on the part of a large body, and not just a partisan body, of American opinion."[38] To take one example of a president articulating a guiding principle, Professor Graebner assessed Washington's Farewell Address as "the culminating declaration of diplomatic independence from Europe. Its accent was less on isolationism than on the flexibility which would permit the nation to pursue its interests whenever and wherever it saw them challenged."[39]

For Kennan, Washington, Jefferson, and Lincoln bore traits of statesmanship in that they defined principles and only then turned to rally public opinion to support their views. In contrast, an increasingly common tendency today is for American statesmen to put "the cart before the horse," turning to public opinion first and then fashioning policies that accord with public sentiment. Kennan acknowledged that in a democracy the formulation and implementation of foreign policy must take into account public opinion, but he believed public opinion needed to be subordinate to statesmanship, not the other way around. Effective leadership shapes public opinion toward the national interest instead of articulating the national interest by gauging the winds of public opinion.

Statesmanship to steer the ship of state through the turbulent waters of foreign affairs requires a steady hand, and Kennan questioned American democracy's ability to meet this challenge. International crises have long incubation periods that need to be anticipated. American foreign policy has frequently failed to measure up to that challenge. Kennan criticized, for example, American foreign policy after the First World War and observed that

Had Wilson been able to survey the scene of 1918 as we are able to survey it today, he would have had to recognize that when great forces have come into motion in world affairs, either in war or in developing crisis, no government, however great its prestige or its military power, can hope to keep them under control and then to direct their motion by months of silence, followed by a single vague and cryptic declaration. It takes a different order of statesmanship—one marked by the most anxious and careful following of events and by a determination to act upon the situation unintermittently by every conceivable means—to shape to one's own purpose the mighty and incessant process of change that forms the relationships between nations in troubled times.[40]

Although Kennan never mentioned him in this context, Franklin D. Roosevelt is an example of a president who worked diligently to move public opinion to where he wanted policy to go. Roosevelt saw the threat posed to the United States by Nazi Germany and buttressed British means to withstand the German challenge long before the American public would have supported direct American military intervention in "Europe's war."

Kennan hoped for enlightened American statesmen, with the unique set of political skills needed, to see the national interest and to rally the populace behind policies designed to achieve it. He lamented in a personal letter in 1951 that "I know of no instance in which political leaders in our country have endeavored to explain clearly and honestly to the people at large why they should follow the restrained and unexciting course rather than the other one, and I am not ready to conclude that people would not respond to such an appeal. Lincoln, it seems to me, did this with respect to the Civil War in our own country and managed, as long as he was alive, to keep the image of the war effort in the minds of his constituents from assuming fantastic and ruinous emotional proportions."[41]   Hans Morgenthau, too, admired Lincoln's sober approach to balancing the demands of national interest and public opinion, and for this reason Lincoln is seen as a model of statesmanship by the traditional realists.[42]

CONCLUSION

The preceding discussion reveals Kennan's remarkable ability to view American democracy and the mechanics of its foreign policy process with clear-eyed detachment. Foreign policy scholars and observers often gloss over the realities of the struggle for power among the competing institutions of the executive and legislative branches of government and derive a sterile conception of how the United States formulates and implements foreign policy. American statesmen must gauge the dynamics of the international struggle for power to advance our interests abroad, but an assessment of the international geopolitical situation is only a first step. The second step for American statesmen is to navigate the difficult terrain of domestic politics and competing centers of power and interests to fashion policies that will advance the national interest abroad. Geopolitical analysis, in other words, must pass through the filter of domestic politics to arrive at foreign policies that can be sustained within the domestic political atmosphere.

Kennan's analysis calls attention to the fact that there is a cost to the excessive diffusion of power in foreign policy from executive to legislative hands. To be sure, the contemporary swing of the pendulum of power from the executive toward the legislature was instigated by the Vietnam War and increased concern about the ability of the executive branch to manage foreign policy. Although the pendulum swung back toward executive hands during the Reagan and Bush administrations, it has more recently tilted again toward the Congress under the Clinton presidency.

A glaring shortcoming in Kennan's analysis was that he was inclined to point out the deficiencies of the Congress in foreign policy while predisposed to see the strengths in the executive. And yet, in private life, Kennan himself looked to the Congress to salvage American foreign policy during the Vietnam War. His testimony in 1967 to Congress was his own contribution to redressing what he viewed as executive branch folly. Kennan, in other words, was inclined to see the strengths of the balance of power in international politics and to see its disadvantages in domestic politics.

Although the Founding Fathers created an ingenious system of government based on checks and balances of power to curb the abuse of power by the executive, Kennan argued that, when power tilts in practice too far toward the legislature, our overall effectiveness in foreign policy is diminished. There is no foolproof means to ensure that the executive is run by statesmen of sufficient capabilities to fully exploit the potential advantages inherent in the branch and to clearly articulate governing principles for foreign policy. Past experience with weak American presidents in the foreign policy realm testifies to this stubborn fact. Nevertheless, Kennan's analysis would lead us to believe that, on balance, the prospects for the executive articulation of such principles are much higher if power is exercised more fully by the executive than by the legislature. At a time in which legislative micromanagement of foreign policy is increasingly evident, reflection on Kennan's thoughts introduces a cautionary note.

NOTES

1. Louis J. Halle, "George Kennan and the Common Mind," *Virginia Quarterly* 45, no. 1 (Winter 1969): 51.

2. Alexis de Tocqueville, *Democracy in America*, Volume I (New York, NY: Vintage Books, 1990), 234.

3. George F. Kennan, *American Diplomacy*, Expanded Edition (Chicago, IL: University of Chicago Press, 1984), 177.

4. George F. Kennan, "Foreign Policy and the Professional Diplomat," in Louis J. Halle and Kenneth W. Thompson (eds.), the Geneva Papers, *Foreign Policy and the Democratic Process* (Washington, DC: University Press of America, 1978), 15.

5. Tocqueville, *Democracy in America*, 235.

6. George F. Kennan, *The Cloud of Danger: Current Realities of American Foreign Policy* (Boston, MA: Little, Brown and Company, 1977), 4.

7. Kennan, *The Cloud of Danger*, 5–6.

8. Kennan, "Foreign Policy and the Professional Diplomat," 17.

9. Kennan, *The Cloud of Danger*, 7.

10. Kennan, "Foreign Policy and the Professional Diplomat," 18.

11. George F. Kennan, "America's Administrative Response to Its World Problems," *Daedalus* 87, no. 2 (Spring 1958): 20.

12. George F. Kennan, "Planning of Foreign Policy," 18 June 1947, in Giles D. Harlow and George C. Maerz (eds.), *Measures Short of War: The George F. Kennan Lectures at the National War College, 1946–47* (Washington, DC: National Defense University Press, 1991), 208.

13. Kennan, "America's Administrative Response to Its World Problems," 20–21.

14. Henry A. Kissinger, *American Foreign Policy* (New York, NY: W.W. Norton & Company, 1969), 24.

15. Kennan, *American Diplomacy*, 93.

16. Norman A. Graebner, "The President as Commander in Chief: A Study in Power," *Journal of Military History* 57, no. 1 (January 1993): 132.

17. Kennan, *American Diplomacy*, 167.

18. Kennan, *American Diplomacy*, 62.

19. Kennan, *American Diplomacy*, 62.

20. George F. Kennan, "Interview with George F. Kennan," *Foreign Policy* 7 (Summer 1972): 20.

21. George F. Kennan, "Somalia, Through a Glass Darkly," *New York Times*, 30 September 1993, A25.

22. George F. Kennan, "If TV Drives Foreign Policy, We're in Trouble," Letter to the Editor, *New York Times*, 24 October 1993, A14.

23. George F. Kennan, "Current Problems in the Conduct of Foreign Policy," *Department of State Bulletin*, 15 May 1950, 3.

24. "Correspondence to Walter Lippmann," 6 April 1948, George F. Kennan Papers, Box 17, Seeley G. Mudd Manuscript Library, Department of Rare Books and Special Collections, Princeton University Library.

25. George F. Kennan, *Memoirs, 1950–1963* (New York, NY: Pantheon Books, 1972), 320.

26. George F. Kennan, *Memoirs, 1925–1950* (New York, NY: Pantheon Books, 1967), 54.

27. George F. Kennan, "History and Diplomacy as Viewed by a Diplomatist," *Review of Politics* 18, no. 2 (April 1956): 174.

28. Kennan, "History and Diplomacy as Viewed by a Diplomatist," 174.

29. Kennan, "Foreign Policy and the Professional Diplomat," 16.

30. Kennan, "America's Administrative Response to Its World Problems," 17.

31. Kennan, "Planning of Foreign Policy," 18 June 1947, in Harlow and Maerz (eds.), *Measures Short of War*, 215.

32. Alexander Hamilton, *The Federalist LXXIV*, in Bernard Bailyn (ed.), *The Debate on the Constitution: Federalist and Antifederalist Speeches, Articles, and Letters during the Struggle over Ratification,* Part II (New York, NY: Literary Classics of the United States, 1993), 379.

33. Norman Graebner, Correspondence to the Author, 8 October 1996.

34. Graebner, "The President as Commander in Chief," 115.

35. George F. Kennan, "On American Principles," *Foreign Affairs* 74, no. 2, (March/April 1995): 121.

36. Kennan, "On American Principles," 121.

37. Kennan, "On American Principles," 121.

38. Kennan, "On American Principles," 121–122.

39. Norman A. Graebner (ed.), *Ideas and Diplomacy: Readings in the Intellectual Tradition of American Foreign Policy* (New York, NY: Oxford University Press, 1964), 17.

40. George F. Kennan, *Soviet-American Relations, 1917–1920: Volume II: The Decision to Intervene* (Princeton, NJ: Princeton University Press, 1958), 428–429.

41. "Correspondence to Percy W. Bidwell," 17 October 1951, George F. Kennan Papers, Box 29, Seeley G. Mudd Manuscript Library, Department of Rare Books and Special Collections, Princeton University Library.

42. See Hans J. Morgenthau, "The Mind of Abraham Lincoln: A Study in Detachment and Practicality," in Kenneth W. Thompson (ed.), *Essays on Lincoln's Faith and Politics* (Lanham, MD: University Press of America, 1983), 3–101.

5

THE FORGOTTEN AMERICAN ART OF DIPLOMACY

Diplomacy is a critical tool used by American statesmen to influence the course of events abroad toward circumstances amenable to the national interest. Kennan devoted considerable study to the contemporary American philosophy of diplomacy and contrasted it to the diplomacy exercised by the Founding Fathers, who, for Kennan, had a fine grasp of the art that eludes many contemporary statesmen. American diplomatic thought in this century has been seized with international law and organizations as the primary means to mitigate the circumstances conducive to the outbreak of violence and war. International law and organizations, however, to the extent that they have any efficacy in world politics, are shadows of power realities—the real substance of diplomacy.

American statesmen and diplomats are prone to deal with law and organizations to the neglect of power realities and thereby decrease the prospects for achieving the national interest. Kennan questioned the related tendency for Americans to promote democracy abroad as a means to strengthen the role and impact of law and institutions in international relations. Kennan's sober assessment of the strengths and weaknesses of American democracy tempered his enthusiasm for placing the promotion of democracy abroad as a centerpiece for American foreign policy. Kennan's views on traditional diplomacy constitute a normative framework that can be used to critically examine commonly held assumptions that have taken root in the American approach to foreign policy.

DIPLOMACY IN THEORY

A discussion of the theory of diplomacy is in order to provide a measuring stick or benchmark for evaluating American diplomacy. What is diplomacy's role as a tool of statecraft? What are its goals, and what factors contribute to diplomatic success or failure? A key task of diplomacy is to mitigate conflicts of national interest between nation-states struggling for power in international politics. Hans Morgenthau concisely summed up the primary purpose of diplomacy as the "promotion of the national interest by peaceful means."[1] The achievement of the national interest without resort to war requires compromise. In Kennan's words, "One can remember that *some degree* of conflict and antagonism is present in every international relationship; *some* measure of compromise is necessary everywhere, if political societies are to live together on the same planet."[2] This more often than not is a painstaking task. As Kennan viewed the process, the task of diplomacy is

essentially a menial one, consisting of hovering around the fringes of a process one is powerless to control, tidying up the messes other people have made, attempting to keep small disasters from turning into big ones, moderating the passions of governments and of opinionated individuals, and attempting to transmit to one's own government the unwelcome image of the outside world—but always, mark you, only in discreet, moderate doses, bearing in mind the lowliness of the diplomatic estate in the general governmental order—bearing in mind that the truth about external reality will never be wholly compatible with those internal ideological fictions which the national state engenders and by which it lives.[3]

Skilled diplomats can place themselves in the position of an adversary to work toward compromise. Kennan emphasized the importance of knowing "one's own country, its capabilities, and its natural role in the world" and "the psychology, the political personality, the intentions, and the likely behavior of an adversary."[4] He affirmed that most of a diplomat's "usefulness consists precisely in his ability to put himself in the position of the other man."[5] The diplomat's career abroad helps him to overcome deeply rooted American political assumptions to more readily come to appreciate the positions of other states, whether friend or foe. Diplomats, however, must guard themselves against identifying and sympathizing with the interests of host countries more than they do with the interests of the United States.

Compromise is not tidy and neat, and diplomacy, therefore, is inherently laden with ambiguity. Kennan argued that "What must be sought is not the perfect and not the best, but the acceptable. We may have our indignation and our sense of righteousness but we will do well to rule it out of our diplomatic dealings. It is not intimate understanding that we must cultivate with the nations of other climes and continents, it is merely tolerable arrangements which will make it possible for us both to live."[6] Kennan elsewhere elaborated that the most hopeful diplomatic approaches "have always to be dialectical ones, embracing contradictory elements, embracing both repulsion and attraction, pressure and conciliation, the readiness to defend where defense is the only answer, but also the readiness to receive, to listen, to concede, to be generous, to take chances, and to give confidence, even while defending."[7] Edmund Burke held the same appreciation of the ambiguities in politics and diplomacy: "No lines can be laid down for civil or political wisdom. They are a matter incapable of exact definition. But, though no man can draw a stroke between the confines of day and night, yet light and darkness are upon the whole tolerably distinguishable."[8]

The meticulous process of diplomacy often is unable to keep pace with rapidly changing situations. This stubborn reality underscored for Kennan the need for flexibility and the avoidance of overly restrictive arrangements that are prone to become overtaken by events. He observed that "wise and experienced statesmen usually shy away from commitments likely to constitute limitations on a government's behavior at an unknown date in the future in the face of unpredictable situations. This is also a reason why agreements long in process of negotiation, particularly when negotiated in great secrecy, run the risk of being somewhat out of date before they are ever completed."[9] In Kennan's view, "The function of a system of international relationships is not to inhibit this process of change by imposing a legal strait jacket upon it but rather to facilitate it: to ease its transitions, to temper the asperities to which it often leads, to isolate and moderate the conflicts to which it gives rise, and to see that these conflicts do not assume forms too unsettling for international life in general."[10]

The severance of relations is one such rigid commitment that may work against the interests of a nation-state that employs this tactical diplomatic tool. Kennan was leery of the practice, as it "has the direct disadvantage of sometimes redounding to your own discomfort, because the maintenance of relations between governments has been found to be generally advantageous to both parties. If you break off relations with another government, the chances are, over the next few years, you are going to find you need relations with that country."[11] The United States, for example, does not have ambassadors in Cuba or North Korea. And yet, ambassadors in these countries would be useful for direct and formal communication when Cuban and North Korean policies encroach on American interests. Only recently has the United States been able to overcome domestic political resistance to reestablishing diplomatic ties to Vietnam, given the legacy of the war there, a development that will facilitate the advancement of our interests.

Power is the ingredient critical to diplomacy for obtaining national interests while mitigating conflicts of interest with other nation-states. In other words, diplomacy without power is an empty shell. Kennan remarked in private correspondence to Walt Rostow in 1956 that, when "the military used to say to us: this or that must be obtained by 'diplomatic means,' they were using an empty term. Strictly speaking, there are no diplomatic means, divorced from the real elements of national power and influence, which are all—in the U.S.—remote from diplomatic control."[12]   Along similar lines, scholar and former British diplomat Adam Watson observed that "The extent to which one state can persuade another to act or refrain from acting in a certain way depends on the power which each of them commands, including the will to use it, and the extent to which other states support them—that is, lend their power to one side or the other."[13]

LEGALISTIC MORALISM VERSUS POWER POLITICS

American foreign policy in this century generally has neglected these traditional theoretical foundations of diplomacy. Kennan was one of the sharpest critics of the United States' neglect of diplomacy as a tool to obtain national interests by measures short of war.   Contemporary American political philosophy tends to reject the wisdom of the Founding Fathers in favor of excessively moralistic and legalistic notions of diplomacy, which undermine its overall effectiveness. The dominant American mind-set places heavy weight on the importance of international law, institutions, and democracy to produce a more peaceful international realm. Kennan did not dismiss international law and institutions, but he strenuously argued against lofty expectations for their efficacy in stemming international conflict.

The American Founding Fathers had an impressive grasp of diplomacy. Kennan remarked that "In such casual reading on American diplomatic history as I had had occasion to do while in government, I had been struck by the contrast between the lucid and realist thinking of early American statesmen of the Federalist period and the cloudy bombast of their successors of later decades."[14]   Kennan recalled that his postgovernment historical research while resident at the Institute for Advanced Study in Princeton revealed "how much of our stock equipment, in the way of the rationale and rhetoric of foreign policy, was what we had inherited from the statesmen of the period from the Civil War to World War II, and how much of this equipment was utopian in its expectation, legalistic in its concept of methodology, moralistic in the demands its seemed to place on others, and self-righteous in the degree of high-mindedness and rectitude it imputed to ourselves."[15]

Specifically, American diplomacy, particularly after World War I, had lost the Founding Fathers' understanding of the ubiquity of power in politics. As Kennan observed, "American statesmen in the early part of the nineteenth century dealt frankly and very confidently with power realities."[16] He lamented that "with the advance of the nineteenth century, the consciousness of the power factor in the scheme of our foreign relations seemed to pass gradually out of the American mind."[17]   Ironically, this trend occurred just as American power in international affairs grew to substantial proportions.

American diplomacy has become enchanted with international law and institutions as mechanisms for overcoming international conflict, to the neglect of fundamental power realities. American statesmen came to believe that the world could be reshaped and modeled after the domestic structures of the United States. Kennan observed that "American statesmen came to devote themselves increasingly to the cultivation of what I might call, for the sake of convenience, the American dream . . . [T]he main problem of world peace, as it appeared to us, was plainly the arrangement of a suitable framework of contractual engagements in which this happy *status quo*, the final fruit of human progress, could be sealed and perpetuated. If such a framework could be provided, then, it seemed, the ugly conflicts of international politics would cease to threaten world peace."[18]

Our unique experience nurturing a state based on the rule of law has substantially influenced the contemporary American philosophy of diplomacy. Americans habitually assume that our respect for law can be replicated throughout the world regardless of the cultural, historical, economic, and political conditions within other nation-states. Kennan referred to this philosophic mind-set as the "legalistic-moralistic" approach to international politics. As Kennan characterized this mind-set; "It has in it something of the old emphasis on arbitration treaties, something of the Hague Conferences and schemes for universal disarmament, something of the more ambitious American concepts of the role of international law, something of the League of Nations and the United Nations, something of the Kellogg Pact, something of the idea of a universal 'Article 51' pact, something of the belief in World Law and World Government. But it is none of these entirely."[19] Kennan faulted the prevalence of this legalistic-moralistic mind-set toward international relations as a major cause for the deterioration in the quality of American diplomacy.

THE FALLACIES OF INTERNATIONAL LAW

The legalistic-moralistic approach to international politics relies on international law as the chief mechanism for promoting order. Kennan defined the approach as "the belief that it should be possible to suppress the chaotic and dangerous aspirations of governments in the international field by the acceptance of some system of legal rules and restraints. This belief undoubtedly represents in part an attempt to transpose the Anglo-Saxon concept of individual law into the international field and to make it applicable to governments as it is applicable here at home to individuals."[20] He continued that "It must also stem in part from the memory of the origin of our own political system—from the recollection that we were able, through acceptance of a common institutional and juridical framework, to reduce to harmless dimensions the conflicts of interest and aspiration among the original thirteen colonies and to bring them all into an ordered and peaceful relationship with one another."[21]

Although the legalistic-moralist approach stresses the rule of law in the conduct of relations between nation-states, it rejects the operation of power politics. The approach, "instead of taking the awkward conflicts of national interest and dealing with them on their merits with a view to finding the solutions least unsettling to the stability of international life," holds that "it would be better to find some formal criteria of a juridical nature by which the permissible behavior of states could be defined. There would then be judicial entities competent to measure the actions of governments against these criteria and to decide when their behavior was acceptable and when unacceptable."[22] This approach minimizes or ignores the fact that there is no enforcement mechanism—analogous to law enforcement present within nation-states—to impose the law on conflicting nation-states.

The legalistic-moralistic approach assumes that all peoples everywhere place order above all other values. As Kennan observed, "To the American mind, it is implausible that people should have positive aspirations, and ones that they regard as legitimate, more important to them than the peacefulness and orderliness of international life. From this standpoint, it is not apparent why other peoples should not join us in accepting the rules of the game in international politics, just as we accept such rules in the competition of sport in order that the game may not become too cruel and too destructive and may not assume an importance we did not mean it to have."[23]

International law and institutions take this mind-set a step further and rest on the assumption of the desirability of maintaining the status quo in the international realm. Kennan noted that

the idea of the subordination of a large number of states to an international juridical regime, limiting their possibilities for aggression and injury to other states, implies that these are all states like our own, reasonably content with their international borders and status, at least to the extent that they would be willing to refrain from pressing for change without international agreement. Actually, this has generally been true only of a portion of international society. We tend to underestimate the violence of national maladjustments and discontents elsewhere in the world if we think that they would always appear to other people as less important than the preservation of the juridical tidiness of international life.[24]

In other words, circumstances often dictate to other peoples that the potential benefits derived from disrupting the status quo outweigh the merits of living under it. American political philosophy minimizes the possibilities of legitimate causes for challenging the status quo of international politics. This contemporary American perspective is ironic, in that our own Founding Fathers preferred to take up arms to fight for independence than accept a peaceful status quo under British rule.

International law grows out of custom and practice among states and cannot be imposed on nation-states if it conflicts with their vital interests. Kennan observed that "What people call international law is a useful codification of standards of international behavior generally accepted between certain governments and in certain conditions. But it represents a body of understanding which, so long as sovereignty remains what it is, must of necessity grow out of the conduct of governments rather than determining that conduct; and it cannot hope to limit their behavior where vital interests are at stake."[25] International law, therefore, cannot be divorced from power realities. Kennan strenuously argued that international law "cannot yet replace power as the vital force for a large part of the world. And the realities of power will soon seep into any legalistic structure which we erect to govern international life. They will permeate it. They will become the content of it; and the structure will remain only the form. International security will depend on *them*: on the realities of power—not on the structure in which they are clothed."[26] Kennan's comments imply that international law has diminishing influence the closer it approaches the core interests of nation-states, such as their autonomies and survival.

Despite his recognition of the limitations of international law, Kennan saw its utility within limited bounds in his personal experience as a diplomat. He noted that "No one who has spent many years of his life in practical contact with the workings of international affairs can fail to appreciate the immense and vital value of international law in assuring the smooth functioning of that part of international life that is not concerned with such things as vital interest and military security."[27] His views were shaped by his experience of internment by Nazi Germany during the Second World War. International law then afforded Kennan and his colleagues some protection against execution by German authorities.[28] To argue that Kennan entirely dismissed international law, therefore, would overstate his position. What Kennan warned against was overly high expectations of international law to the neglect of the power realities that underlie it.

INTERNATIONAL INSTITUTIONS: CONFUSING CAUSE AND EFFECT

The American legalistic-moralist approach stresses the importance of international law while it views international institutions as mechanisms for overcoming power politics. Kennan was a harsh critic of the international legal and organizational efforts to restore peace in the aftermath of the world wars. In August 1944, Kennan wrote some thoughts in reaction to the Dumbarton Oaks discussions that laid the framework for the United Nations: "Underlying the whole conception of an organization for international security is the simple reasoning that if only the status quo could be rigidly preserved, there could be no further wars in Europe, and the European problem, as far as our country is concerned, would be solved. This reasoning, which mistakes the symptoms for the disease, is not new. It underlay the Holy Alliance, the League of Nations, and numerous other political structures set up by nations which were, for the moment, satisfied with the international setup and did not wish to see it changed."[29]

The view that international institutions are the primary instruments for promoting international order suffers from several shortcomings from Kennan's perspective. First and foremost, international institutions in many cases are not conducive to diplomatic compromise. They are public forums that often create rather than reduce obstacles to compromise. Diplomacy requires privacy to increase the ability and flexibility for opposing parties to compromise. Public negotiations, on the other hand, create difficult conditions for diplomats to compromise, given the fear of a loss of prestige. Kennan argued that "The treatment of questions in multilateral bodies is no doubt justified in many instances; but there are times when the requirement for privacy and secrecy is absolutely vital to success, where two governments have need to talk to each other tete a tete, and where the multilateral forum is most unsuitable."[30]

Proponents of international institutions overlook the realities of power of member nation-states and assume that all member states have an equal say on issues at hand. The philosophy underlying international organizations "envisages a world composed exclusively of sovereign national states with a full equality of status. In doing this, it ignores the tremendous variations in the firmness and soundness of national divisions: the fact that the origins of state borders and national personalities were in many instances fortuitous or at least poorly related to realities. It also ignores the law of change. The national state pattern is not, should not be, and cannot be a fixed and static thing. By nature, it is an unstable phenomenon in a constant state of change and flux."[31] Kennan's profound understanding of changes over long periods in history gave him a greater intellectual breadth than those advocates of international organization who take as their departure point of analysis only the politics of the day.

International institutions tend to turn a blind eye to the power realities of member states. In Kennan's view, "No international organization can be stronger than the structure of the relationships among the Great Powers that underlies it; and to look to such an organization to resolve deep-seated conflicts of interest among those Great Powers is to ignore its limitations and to jeopardize its usefulness in other fields."[32] In other words, the efficiency of these organizations rests upon underlying power relationships of major member powers. In Kennan's judgment, "These structures have always served the purpose for which they were designed just so long as the interests of the great powers gave substance and reality to their existence. The moment this situation changed, the moment it became in the interests of one or the other of the great powers to alter the status quo, none of these treaty structures ever stood in the way of such alteration."[33] International organizations are reflections of the power of nation-states rather than autonomous entities operating beyond the control of nation-states.

International institutions such as the League of Nations and the United Nations have stressed the importance of collective action to maintain international stability. They have also looked to the concept of collective security and the notion of "all for one and one for all" to enforce the status quo. International institutions—explicitly in the League of Nations and implicitly in the United Nations—aim at the deterrence of threats to the rule of international law by threatening to harness a preponderance of power against a would-be aggressor state or states and thereby escaping from the balance of power politics that had been faulted for the outbreaks of both world wars.[34] From the realist perspective, however, a strict application of adherence to the status quo could in fact fuel incentives for the outbreak of violence, contrary to the goals set for international institutions.

The ability of an international organization and its members to single out an aggressor state or states for punitive collective action to enforce the international status quo is not a foregone conclusion, contrary to the theory of collective security. This fact is evident, for example, in the unsettled debate over responsibility for the start of World War I some eighty years after the event. Even if a belligerent could be readily identified, marshaling military power against the aggressor would be problematic, not automatic as advocates of collective security hope. As Kennan argued, an international institution designed to promote peaceful relations among nation-states "looks to collective action to provide such sanction against the bad behavior of states. In doing so, it forgets the limitations on the effectiveness of military coalition. It forgets that, as a circle of military associates widens in any conceivable political-military venture, the theoretical total of available military strength may increase, but only at the cost of compactness and ease of control. And the wider a coalition becomes, the more difficult it becomes to retain political unity and general agreements on the purposes and effects of what is being done."[35]

Despite these deficiencies, Kennan did not overlook the potential contributions of international organization to international society. As was the case in respect to international law, Kennan held a modest view of the potential contribution of international organizations. For example, they might be used diplomatically to address global problems that transcend the authority and capability of individual nation-states. Kennan in 1970 even proposed the establishment of an international organization to address transnational environmental issues such as overpopulation and resource depletion.[36]

Somewhat ironically, Kennan was a temperate defender of the United Nations. He criticized the hostility voiced against the United Nations by segments of the American public and dismissed "the alarmed emotionalism with which a portion of our people have turned against the United Nations as though it were some menacing external force that had tried to do something evil to us."[37] In Kennan's view, "As interdependence and mutual responsibility grow among nations, as we may hope that they will, the United Nations will provide one of the most important channels through which these changes can find practical expression. But it cannot in itself bring about the growth of these tendencies, nor can it at once abolish or restrain the deepest and most dangerous sources of international tension."[38] He hoped, moreover, that the United Nations represented "the germ of something immensely necessary and immensely hopeful for this endangered world: namely, a sense of conscience higher than the national one, a sense of fellowship of fate by which we are increasingly bound together. I cannot conceive of a satisfactory future for humanity that does not embrace, and draw its strength from, the growth of this consciousness."[39] In other words, the United Nations can play an important role in international relations—albeit a more modest one than that envisioned by the adherents of the legalist-moralistic school of American thought—as a forum for diplomatic discourse to promote mutual interests as long as it does not excessively infringe on the sovereignty of nation-states.

MORALISM AND THE CRUSADE FOR DEMOCRACY

Beyond its heavy emphasis on international law and institutions, Kennan's major criticism of American diplomacy was its moralism. Although Kennan used the term loosely, Kenneth Thompson explicitly defined the concept: "Moralism is the tendency to make one moral value supreme and to apply it indiscriminately without regard to time and place; morality, by comparison, is the endless quest for what is right amidst the complexity of competing and sometimes conflicting, sometimes compatible, moral ends."[40] The United States in recent times has been prone to the former in its foreign policy.

American moralism in diplomacy is manifested in the call for other nation-states to abide by rules of international law and conform to the rules of international organizations. Kennan wrote that "The tendency to achieve our foreign policy objectives by inducing other governments to sign up to professions of high moral and legal principle appears to have a great and enduring vitality in our diplomatic practice. It is linked, certainly, with the strong American belief in the power of public opinion to overrule governments. It is also linked, no doubt, with the pronounced American tendency to transplant legal concepts from the domestic to the international field: to believe that international society could—and should—operate on the basis of general contractual obligation, and hence to lay stress on verbal undertaking rather than on the concrete manifestations of political interest."[41]

Moralism is particularly evident in holding the universal promotion of human rights as a central goal in American foreign policy. Kennan lamented American sanctimoniousness in holding human rights up as a guiding objective of foreign policy: "I sense here the same implied assumption of superior understanding and superior virtue on our part. I sense it in the anxious inquiries as to whether the 'human rights record' of this or that government is found, upon lofty inquiry, to be adequate or inadequate from our standpoint. I sense it in our inclination to rate other governments, independently of their remaining practices, outstandingly on the basis of our judgment of their performance in this one particular field."[42]

Despite his criticisms of a foreign policy based on the promotion of human rights, Kennan gave credit for the amelioration of human rights abuses to increased attention to human rights. He confessed in 1993 that

I must now do penance by recognizing that the world wide effects of the human rights movement in which both the United Nations and the U.S. government have invested so much of their energies and enthusiasm have been in a number of respects beneficial. A useful influence seems at least to have been exerted from time to time on regimes whose practices are far from lending themselves to classification as 'democratic.' Even where these regimes have by no means been able to show a perfect human rights record, there has at least been inflicted upon some of them a certain self-consciousness before world opinion--a certain reluctance to be caught out in the more flagrant abuses of human freedom and dignity--which otherwise would have been lacking.[43]

The apparent need for nation-states to pay at least lipservice to the promotion of human rights is evidence that international efforts can have an impact on domestic behaviors. Kennan noted, for example, that "Numbers of nondemocratic regimes, including those of Russia (in the pre-Gorbachevian era) but right-wing dictatorships as well, have put forward patently specious claims that they were extending human rights to their peoples; but I do not recall instances where they denied the obligation to extend them. This would suggest that in certain circumstances there may be greater value in these human rights demands than I have been inclined to attribute to them."[44]

Although Kennan did not object to human rights as one modest facet of foreign policy, he rejected holding them up as the primary objective to the neglect of other interests. Kennan undoubtedly was personally sympathetic to the promotion of civil liberties for all peoples in principle because of his own Christian beliefs. Nevertheless, what Kennan objected to was the holding of this sentiment—which was beyond the U.S. means to directly achieve—as the supreme objective of American foreign policy to the detriment of national interests abroad that have a more direct impact on the well-being of American citizens.

Kennan rejected an American foreign policy predicated on the assumption of universally applicable laws, but argued that American policy in its objectives and methods should be consistent with our own moral precepts. Americans ought to conduct ourselves "in such a manner as to meet our own standards and satisfy our own conscience—in such a manner as to make it possible for us to live with ourselves without embarrassment. But what we have no right to do, and this is the essence of my feeling on this subject, is to hold standards of morality up as models for the world at large and to claim a special virtue to the extent that we ourselves contrive to live up to them."[45] Elsewhere Kennan elaborated that "If the policies and actions of the U.S. government are to be made to conform to moral standards, those standards are going to have to be America's own, founded on traditional American principles of justice and propriety. When others fail to conform to those principles, and when their failure to conform has an adverse effect on American *interests*, as distinct from political tastes, we have every right to complain and, if necessary, to take retaliatory action. What we cannot do is to assume that our moral standards are theirs as well, and to appeal to those standards as the source of our grievances. "[46] These comments reflect Kennan's belief that the national interest is as much a matter of method as it is of objective.

Moralism also is reflected in contemporary policy devotion to the promotion of democracy abroad. This trait is intertwined with the American push for international laws, institutions, and human rights. Kennan—with his recognition of democracy's shortcomings—was critical of the American philosophy typified by President Woodrow Wilson, who advocated the spread of democracy as the centerpiece of foreign policy.

The role of American democracy—whether as a model or as a system of government to be exported—has been perpetually in or near the center of our foreign policy debates. The competing perspectives are debated by two schools of thought. As Henry Kissinger defined these two attitudes toward foreign policy, "The first is that America serves its values best by perfecting democracy at home, thereby acting as a beacon for the rest of mankind; the second, that America's values impose on it an obligation to crusade for them around the world. "[47] The intensity of this debate has increased after the collapse of the Soviet Union and the end of the Cold War.

Kennan criticized the urge in contemporary diplomacy to try to reshape the world in America's self-image. He questioned from a conservative philosophic disposition the universal applicability of American democracy. In Kennan's words, "Frankly, I do not discern any special universal virtues in our political system or our way of life. Both, it seems to me, are very largely conditioned, and made possible, by the unique circumstances in which our nation has developed; and I think they have little relevance to the problems of other people elsewhere. "[48] Kennan's philosophy was rooted in traditional conservative thought, which holds that political institutions are grounded in the history, culture, and society of a people. Clinton Rossiter attributed to traditional conservative thinkers the belief that "Society is a living organism with roots deep in the past. "[49] And Kennan was quick to point out that the polity of the United States was born in a unique set of circumstances: "Our national experience was never shared by any country and will never be shared by any country in the future. Never again will it be given to a national society to develop a vast, unpopulated area in the northern, temperate zone of the world. "[50]

Those nation-states that have a tradition of democratic government tend to share common cultural heritages. Kennan wrote that

I know of no evidence that "democracy," or what we picture to ourselves under that word, is the natural state of most of mankind. It seems rather to be a form of government (and a difficult one, with many drawbacks, at that) which evolved in the eighteenth and nineteenth centuries in northwestern Europe, primarily among those countries that border on the English Channel and the North Sea (but with a certain extension into Central Europe), and which was then carried into other parts of the world, including North America, where peoples from that northwestern European area appeared as original settlers, or as colonialists, and had laid down the prevailing patterns of civil government.[51]

Americans, moreover, often overlook the fact that democracy is a broad term and that many forms of government loosely fall within this characterization. Many democracies in Europe, for instance, are monarchies, unlike the American democratic tradition.

Political institutions that are rooted in American habit may not take hold and operate as effectively in other political societies. Institutions, if they are to have any longevity in a society, must be rooted and integrated into the politics, history, and culture of the people over which they preside. Institutions, in other words, reflect rather than create a society's heritage. Kennan believed that "Democracy is a matter of tradition, of custom, of what people are used to, of what they understand and expect. It is not something that can be suddenly grafted onto an unprepared people—particularly not from outside, and particularly not by precept, preaching, and pressure rather than by example."[52] He argued, moreover, that it behooves Americans "to recognize that our institutions may not have relevance for people living in other climes and conditions and that there can be social structures and forms of government in no way resembling our own and yet not deserving of censure."[53]

The assumption that American-style democracy is well suited for all nation-states entailed more than a whiff of arrogance for Kennan. "I am wholly and emphatically rejecting any and all messianic concepts of America's role in the world: rejecting, that is, the image of ourselves as teachers and redeemers to the rest of humanity, rejecting the illusions of unique and superior virtue on our part, the prattle about Manifest Destiny or the 'American Century'—all those visions that have so richly commended themselves to Americans of all generations since, and even before, the foundation of our country."[54] Kennan suggested that Americans "would do well to ask themselves whether they are not actually attempting to impose their own values, traditions, and habits of thought on peoples for whom these things have no validity and no usefulness."[55]

Americans are accustomed to democracy, and this familiarity makes it difficult for us to comprehend the potential benefits of alternative forms of government for other political societies. It is plausible to argue that in some societies political stability is strengthened by authoritarian rule. In reflecting on the downfall of the Russian tsar, for example, Kennan observed that there "was nothing in the traditional American political philosophy to make Americans aware of such virtues as the Tsarist system may have had or to cause them to doubt that the removal of this system would be followed by rapid progress in the direction of parliamentary democracy."[56] The tsar's replacement by an even more authoritarian communist rule belies the common American assumption that the fall of authoritarian regimes is inherently in the interests of citizens over which they rule and in the interests of international society at large. That a successor regime in Moscow was authoritarian was not a surprise to Kennan, with his Burkean view of politics. "By and large, successive governments in a given society tend to resemble each other in methodology if not in professed ideology. Particularly in a society accustomed to brutal or authoritarian rule, it is hard for anyone to govern, however lofty his original intentions, by methods strikingly different from those to which people have become accustomed by long experience and tradition."[57] Americans—with our historical experience under British rule, which compelled the Founding Fathers to take up arms in revolution—are ingrained with a contempt for authoritarian rule. In other societies, however, such rule may be more conducive than democracy to political order.

Professions of the desire or aspiration to create democracy may also be misleading. Kennan cautioned against assuming that oppressed peoples everywhere are committed to the liberty and the tenets of Western liberalism. In contrast to most Americans, who tend to assume that those citizens suffering under an authoritarian regime are committed to the principles of democracy, Kennan was skeptical. "Too often, the highest hope of political dissidents in an authoritarian society is the dream of someday treating their tormentors as their tormentors have treated them—an objective not likely to have anything to do with the principles of democracy."[58]

The United States is under no moral obligation to transform the political institutions of states independent of our own national interests. "Despite frequent assertions to the contrary, not everyone in this world is responsible, after all, for the actions of everyone else, everywhere. Without the power to compel change, there is no responsibility for its absence."[59] From Kennan's viewpoint, the transformation of the political institutions of other states to those resembling the institutions in Western liberal democracies was simply beyond the means of the United States. "The great mass of humanity, beyond our borders, does not lie on our conscience. We have no reason to pass moral judgment on its undertakings; and we will do well to reserve judgment, in fact, about them all, except insofar as they infringe on our own interests."[60] Kennan concluded that "We have to confess that we have not got the answers to the problems of human society in the modern age. Moreover, every society has specific qualities of its own that we in America do not understand very well; therefore I don't want to see us put in a position of taking responsibility for the affairs of people we do not comprehend."[61]

Democratic forms of government do not necessarily further American national interests. Kennan cautioned that "The mere fact that a country acquires the trappings of self-government does not automatically mean that the interests of the United States are thereby furthered. There are forms of plebiscitary 'democracy' that may well prove less favorable to American interests than a wise and benevolent authoritarianism. There can be tyrannies of a majority as well as tyrannies of a minority, with the one hardly less odious than the other. Hitler came to power (albeit under highly unusual circumstances) with an electoral mandate, and there is scarcely a dictatorship of this age that would not claim the legitimacy of mass support."[62]

Democratic states, moreover, are not precluded from having mutual conflicts of interest. Kennan probably would have been skeptical of the growing body of political science literature—if he had paid attention to it—which argues that democracies do not go to war against other democracies, an assumption that undergirds contemporary American foreign policy. This body of literature, grounded in the Kantian philosophic tradition, argues that the proliferation of democracies in the world increases the prospects for cooperation in international relations, reduces political conflict, and consequently advances the American national interest by promoting international order. In an oblique criticism of this school of thought, Kennan wrote that, if one held "no high hopes for the development of a world consisting only of democracies, perhaps reason could be seen for addressing the plea for greater humanity to all governments alike, ignoring the degree of their commitment to popular representation."[63] Although Kennan acknowledged that "It may be true, and I suspect that it is, that the mass of people everywhere are normally peace-loving and would accept many restraints and sacrifices in preference to the monstrous calamities of war,"[64] he was too aware of the influences of the collective ego of nation-states to believe that this sentiment could be strengthened sufficiently to lead to a perpetual peace. Today the United States has conflicts of interest with other democracies, such as trade issues with Japan and NATO reform issues with France. None of these conflicts of interest are of the severity to threaten war, but they are illustrative of conflicts of interest that will always exist, even between democracies.

Although we have no right to insist that the political institutions of other nation-states are similar to those in the United States, American statesmen must gauge how the internal political structures of other nation-states affect their foreign policies, which, in turn, affect American national interests. Kennan's analysis on this score was contained in his policy recommendations during the Cold War vis-à-vis the Soviet Union. He cautioned that totalitarian regimes have a "tendency to justify internal oppression by pointing to the menacing iniquity of the outside world" and "In this way, excess of internal authority leads inevitably to unsocial and aggressive conduct as a government among governments, and is a matter of concern to the international community."[65] For Kennan, the internal polity of the Soviet Union in and of itself was not the concern of the United States. America should not have taken on the responsibility—even if it had the power to do so—for pressing for the transformation of the Soviet empire into a democracy. Instead, what was a legitimate concern for American statesmen was the impact of the Soviet polity on its foreign policy. To the extent that the totalitarian state drove a belligerent foreign policy against the United States and the West, American diplomats were prudent in expressing concerns about the internal composition of the Soviet state. Kennan's perspective reflected the traditional conception of diplomacy and its primary focus on the foreign policy of states, with a secondary emphasis on their internal politics, but only to the extent to which such politics affect international behavior and, in turn, the American national interest.

For all of these reasons, Kennan argued that the United States should act as a model to the world rather than attempt to transplant its own form of polity to other states. The United States would best envision itself as a role model for other nation-states to emulate should they so elect rather than as a form of government that provides a ready-made solution to the political shortcomings of all societies abroad. In Kennan's final analysis, "I would like to see us influence the world, if we can, by the power of our example to the extent that other people wish to follow it and find it applicable to themselves."[66] Kennan's preference for American democracy serving as a model for those nation-states that decide to study it for possible applications within their own historical and cultural circumstances follows the approach Tocqueville took to the study of American democracy. Tocqueville wrote from the French perspective, "I am very far from thinking that we ought to follow the example of the American democracy and copy the means that it has employed to attain this end; for I am well aware of the influence which the nature of a country and its political antecedents exercise upon its political constitution; and I should regard it as a great misfortune for mankind if liberty were to exist all over the world under the same features."[67] In agreement with Kennan and Tocqueville, Hans Morgenthau argued that "the very uniqueness of the American purpose and its achievement—that is, the establishment of freedom conceived as equality of opportunity and minimization of political control—brings into being another purpose that does not by itself require additional action but endows the action required by the fundamental purpose with a special dignity and responsibility: to maintain equality in freedom in America as an example for other nations to emulate."[68]

The United States' foremost responsibility as a model is to strengthen our democracy at home instead of launching a crusade to promote democracy abroad. Kennan suggested that "It is because no country can hope to be, over the long run, much more to others than it is to itself that we have a moral duty to put our own house in order, if we are to take our proper part in the affairs of the rest of the world."[69] Late in his life he remarked that America leads in the world "primarily by example, never by precept, that a country such as ours exerts the most useful influence beyond its borders, but remembering, too, that there are limits to what any one sovereign country can do to help another, and that unless we preserve the quality, the vigor and the morale of or own society, we will be of little use to anyone at all."[70] Kennan throughout his life quoted from President John Quincy Adams's 1821 Fourth of July address as a paradigm delineation of this school of thought:

America goes not abroad in search of monsters to destroy. She is the well-wisher to the freedom and independence of all. She is the champion and vindicator only of her own. She will recommend the general cause by the countenance of her voice, and the benignant sympathy of her example. She well knows that by once enlisting under other banners than her own, were they even the banners of foreign independence, she would involve herself beyond the power of extrication, in all the wars of interest and intrigue, of individual avarice, envy, and ambition, which assumed the colors and usurped the standards of freedom . . . She might become the dictatress of the world. She would be no longer the ruler of her own spirit.[71]

CONCLUSION

Traditional diplomacy recognized demands that many American statesmen and diplomats today appear ill prepared to meet. It requires subtlety, patience, and consistency coupled with an appreciation of power relationships. The diplomatic process is inherently laden with ambiguity, and its response to challenges rarely if ever comes to complete closure. Instead, diplomacy is the constant task of trying to limit and constrain tensions and to mitigate the prospects for armed conflict. For Americans accustomed to thinking in stark terms of good versus evil or right versus wrong and holding a presumption that every problem can be solved if only statesmen are clever enough to craft the appropriate policy, diplomacy is not a satisfying endeavor. The challenge from Kennan's perspective was to harness and channel international politics toward more peaceful directions rather than to seek a fundamental reversal of historical patterns as sought by the legalistic-moralistic American approach to diplomacy. For Kennan, the task, although difficult, was within the grasp of wise statesmen such as the American Founding Fathers who understood the demands, limitations, and possibilities of diplomacy. The Founding Fathers sought to use diplomacy to achieve the national interest by means—including compromise—short of war and set the model for Kennan's conceptualization of American diplomacy.

American statesmen, particularly since President Wilson, have in many instances mistakenly viewed international law and organizations as the substance of international politics and have neglected power realities. Law and organizations, however, as Kennan pointed out, have no enforcement means independent of the major powers. The power relationships between major powers, therefore, are the real subject of diplomacy, not the facades of law and organization. Kennan cautioned that setting moral aims as the guiding star of American foreign policy without regard to the realities of power and the national interest was self-defeating. The United States lacked the power to achieve far-reaching, unrealistic objectives, and in the end such moralism would lead to the erosion of American strength.

Kennan's warnings about moralism and crusades in American foreign policy have taken on increased importance in the post–Cold War period. As American statesman and diplomats scurry to find centerpieces for foreign policy to fill the void created by the end of the Cold War, many have latched on to the promotion of democracy abroad to fill the gap. Kennan's sober assessment of inconsistencies in such an approach can be used to critically examine commonly held assumptions in the debate. The appreciation for the cultural foundations of democracy, its strengths as well as weaknesses, led Kennan to call for a modest assessment of our democracy and for humility in dealing with other nation-states struggling with their own unique problems and political challenges. American democracy might offer other states clues to more effective governance, but it is not the master key. Any lessons to be learned by other nation-states from the American experience need to be accommodated with their own circumstances.

Attempts either to impose or to establish democratic government upon a society may even destroy a social fabric and promote disorder and chaos. Numerous test cases of this potential are spread throughout the world as nation-states strive to move toward democracy. The political tradition in Russia today, for example, is unsettled, and it is unclear if Russia will manage to make a transition to practice government as is done in Western democracies. One wonders whether the peoples of the newly independent states of the former Yugoslavia or Somalia prefer their tragic current circumstances of civil war to their lack of civil liberties under past authoritarian rule. No adequate answers could ever be found for these difficult questions, but they illustrate the dilemmas posed by attempts to achieve democratic rule in countries without the prerequisite social conditions. These problems underscore the complexities of politics that belie the simple notion that the promotion of democracy in all instances offers the best prospects for the promotion of international order and the American national interest.

NOTES

1. Hans J. Morgenthau and Kenneth W. Thompson, *Politics among Nations: The Struggle for Power and Peace*, Sixth Edition (New York, NY: McGraw-Hill Publishing Company, 1985), 563.

2. George F. Kennan, *Russia and the West under Lenin and Stalin* (New York, NY: Mentor, 1961), 245.

3. George F. Kennan, "History and Diplomacy as Viewed by a Diplomatist," *Review of Politics* 18, no. 2 (April 1956): 176.

4. George F. Kennan, *Memoirs, 1925–1950* (New York, NY: Pantheon Books, 1967), 465.

5. George F. Kennan, "The Future of Our Professional Diplomacy," *Foreign Affairs* 33, no. 4 (July 1955): 574.

6. "Morality and Foreign Policy," Unused Lecture, Intended for Reith Lecture #3, Summer 1957, George F. Kennan Papers, Box 26, Folder 14, Seeley G. Mudd Manuscript Library, Department of Rare Books and Special Collections, Princeton University Library.

7. George F. Kennan, *On Dealing with the Communist World* (New York, NY: Harper & Row Publishers Inc., 1964), 18-19.

8. Edmund Burke, "Thoughts on the Cause of the Present Discontents," in Burke, *Pre-Revolutionary Writings*, Edited by Ian Harris (New York, NY: Cambridge University Press, 1993), 149.

9. George F. Kennan, *The Fateful Alliance: France, Russia, and the Coming of the First World War* (New York, NY: Pantheon Books, 1984), 238.

10. George F. Kennan, *American Diplomacy*, Expanded Edition (Chicago, IL: University of Chicago Press, 1984), 98.

11. George F. Kennan, "Measures Short of War," 16 September 1946, in Giles D. Harlow and George C. Maerz (eds.), *Measures Short of War: The George F. Kennan Lectures at the National War College, 1946–47* (Washington, DC: National Defense University Press, 1991), 12–13.

12. "Correspondence to Walt W. Rostow," 29 May 1956, George F. Kennan Papers, Box 31, Seeley G. Mudd Manuscript Library, Department of Rare Books and Special Collections, Princeton University Library.

13. Adam Watson, *Diplomacy: The Dialogue Between States* (New York, NY: Routledge, 1991), 52.

14. George F. Kennan, *Memoirs, 1950–1963* (New York, NY: Pantheon Books, 1972), 71.

15. Kennan, *Memoirs, 1950–1963*, 71.

16. George F. Kennan, *Realities of American Foreign Policy* (Princeton, NJ: Princeton University Press, 1954), 13.

17. Kennan, *Realities of American Foreign Policy*, 14.

18. Kennan, *Realities of American Foreign Policy*, 16.

19. Kennan, *American Diplomacy*, 95.

20. Kennan, *American Diplomacy*, 95.

21. Kennan, *American Diplomacy*, 96.

22. Kennan, *American Diplomacy*, 96.

23. Kennan, *American Diplomacy*, 96.

24. Kennan, *American Diplomacy*, 97.

25. "Morality and Foreign Policy," Kennan Papers.

26. Kennan, *Memoirs, 1925–1950*, 218–219.

27. Kennan, *Realities of American Foreign Policy*, 38.

28. Kennan was detained by the Nazis for five and a half months in 1942–43 while he was a diplomat assigned to Berlin. For his account of the episode, see *Memoirs, 1925–1950*, 134–141.

29. Kennan, *Memoirs, 1925–1950*, 218.

30. "Morality and Foreign Policy," Kennan Papers.

31. Kennan, *American Diplomacy*, 97–98.

32. George F. Kennan, *Russia, the Atom and the West* (New York, NY: Harper & Brothers Publishers, 1958), 27.

33. Kennan, *Memoirs, 1925–1950*, 218.

34. For a more rigorous and systematic treatment of the concept of collective security in international relations theory literature, see Inis L. Claude, Jr., *Swords into Plowshares*, Fourth Edition (New York, NY: Random House, 1971).

35. Kennan, *American Diplomacy*, 99.

36. See George F. Kennan, "To Prevent a World Wasteland: A Proposal," *Foreign Affairs* 48, no. 3 (April 1970).

37. Kennan, *Realities of American Foreign Policy*, 46.

38. Kennan, *Realities of American Foreign Policy*, 46.

39. George F. Kennan, "Foreign Policy and Christian Conscience," *Atlantic* 203, no. 5 (May 1959): 47.

40. Kenneth W. Thompson, *Morality and Foreign Policy* (Baton Rouge, LA: Louisiana State University Press, 1980), 75.

41. Kennan, *American Diplomacy*, 46.

42. George F. Kennan, *Around the Cragged Hill: A Personal and Political Philosophy* (New York, NY: W.W. Norton & Company, 1993), 72.

43. Kennan, *Around the Cragged Hill*, 72.

44. Kennan, *Around the Cragged Hill*, 72–73.

45. "Morality and Foreign Policy," Kennan Papers.

46. George F. Kennan, "Morality and Foreign Policy," *Foreign Affairs* 64, no. 2 (Winter 1985/86): 208.

47. Henry A. Kissinger, *Diplomacy* (New York, NY: Simon & Schuster, 1994), 18.

48. "Correspondence to Louis J. Halle," 3 January 1956, George F. Kennan Papers, Box 31, Seeley G. Mudd Manuscript Library, Department of Rare Books and Special Collections, Princeton University Library.

49. Clinton Rossiter, *Conservatism in America*, Second Edition (Cambridge, MA: Harvard University Press, 1982), 27.

50. George F. Kennan, "From Containment to . . . Self-Containment," in Martin F. Herz (ed.), *Decline of the West? George Kennan and His Critics* (Washington, DC: Ethics and Public Policy Center of Georgetown University, 1978), 18.

51. George F. Kennan, *The Cloud of Danger: Current Realities of American Foreign Policy* (Boston, MA: Little, Brown and Company, 1977), 41–42.

52. George F. Kennan, "Breaking the Spell," *The New Yorker*, 3 October 1983, 53.

53. George F. Kennan, "America and the Russian Future," *Foreign Affairs* 29, no. 3 (April 1951): 356.

54. Kennan, *Around the Cragged Hill*, 182–183.

55. Kennan, *The Cloud of Danger*, 43. Samuel Huntington has cited Kennan as one of the most explicit in making the argument that "the world's great historic cultural traditions vary significantly in the extent to which their attitudes, values, beliefs, and related behavior patterns are conducive to the development of democracy." See Huntington's *The Third Wave: Democratization in the Late Twentieth Century* (Norman, OK: University of Oklahoma Press, 1991), 298. Huntington notes, however, that great cultural traditions are highly complex and are bound to have some elements that are compatible with democracy, while dominant beliefs and attitudes in a society are subject to change. See pages 310–311. One might, as John Lewis Gaddis has in an interview with the author, note that the Allied occupations of Germany and Japan in the aftermath of World War II facilitated the transitions from authoritarian rule to democracy. These accomplishments were achieved at enormous cost to the United States. This debate is complex and lies beyond the scope of this study to resolve.

56. George F. Kennan, *Soviet-American Relations, 1917-1920: Volume I: Russia Leaves the War* (Princeton, NJ: Princeton University Press, 1956), 12.

57. Kennan, *The Cloud of Danger*, 45.

58. Kennan, *The Cloud of Danger*, 45.

59. Kennan, "Morality and Foreign Policy," *Foreign Affairs*, 212.

60. "Correspondence to Louis J. Halle," 3 January 1956.

61. Kennan, "From Containment to . . . Self Containment," 18.

62. Kennan, "Morality and Foreign Policy," *Foreign Affairs*, 209.

63. Kennan, *Around the Cragged Hill*, 71.

64. Kennan, *American Diplomacy*, 61.

65. Kennan, "America and the Russian Future," 358–359.

66. Kennan, "From Containment to . . . Self-Containment," 18.

67. Alexis de Tocqueville, *Democracy in America*, Volume I, Henry Reeve Text, Revised by Francis Bowen, Further Corrected and Edited by Phillips Bradley (New York, NY: Vintage Books, 1990), 329–330.

68. Hans J. Morgenthau, *The Purpose of American Politics* (Lanham, MD: University Press of America, 1982), 34.

69. Kennan, *Around the Cragged Hill*, 182.

70. George F. Kennan, "The Failure in Our Success," *New York Times*, 14 March 1994, A17.

71. George F. Kennan, "On American Principles," *Foreign Affairs* 74, no. 2 (March/April 1995): 118.

6

FORCE AND WAR AS
FOREIGN POLICY INSTRUMENTS

The efficacy of American diplomacy is integrally linked to our country's ability to use force and wage war. A principle of force and war as instruments of foreign policy runs like a thread through the fabric of Kennan's writings. His principle is consistent with that of the great Prussian strategist Carl von Clausewitz, who viewed war as a continuation of politics by other means. For Kennan, this principle was a guide for the formulation and implementation of policy as well as a measuring stick for evaluating its effectiveness. This chapter distills Kennan's principle by examining his writings on the general ubiquity of force and war in international politics. It then examines his views of conflict along Clausewitz's spectrum of war. Within this framework, American policy in the world wars, the Korean War, the Vietnam War, the Soviet-American nuclear stalemate, and post–Cold War interventions are examined.

THE UBIQUITY OF FORCE AND WAR

Kennan's principle rests on assumptions about force, war, and politics which must be explored in general before a more detailed discussion about their relationship to American foreign policy. Kennan viewed force as ubiquitous in human affairs. It is a central feature, for instance, in the creation and perpetuation of all nation-states. "Force is, and always will be, an indispensable ingredient in human affairs."[1] Kennan observed that "There is hardly a national state in this world community, including our own, whose ultimate origins did not lie in acts of violence. The source of every governmental claim to legitimacy will be found to rest in some situation created originally by the arbitrary exertion of armed might. There is hardly a constitution that does not trace its origin to some act which was formally one of insurrection or of usurpation."[2] The United States' own revolution and civil war bear testimony to the ubiquity of violence in politics.

Although the internal structures of nation-states are based on force, they also rely on force in their relations with other nation-states. Without an overarching authority in the international realm, nation-states resort to war as the final arbiter of conflicts of interest. Wars often erupt, however, due to ambiguity and unsettled circumstances instead of from rational calculation of political objectives and interests. Kennan wrote that wars "do not always arise from acts of outright aggression; they are more apt to proceed, as history shows, from confused situations arising against a background of extreme political tension."[3] In his judgment, "Wars can arise by accident, even though none of the parties really wants them. Considerations of prestige, and the natural nervousness which surrounds the use of armed forces anywhere, mean that nations can become involved in wars accidentally."[4] War can also occur because states mistakenly believe that opposing states are poised to attack based on a lack of objective and reliable information or faulty analysis.

Kennan drew from his study of history—most notably of World War I—evidence of the unpredictable consequences of war. "History reveals that every one of the warring powers would have been better off to have concluded peace in the early stages of the war *on the adversary's terms* rather than to accept the loss of life attendant on continuation of the war to 1918."[5] Kennan continued that "The war, as it turned out, produced the destruction of all three of the great empires so prominently involved in its outbreak: the Austro-Hungarian, the Russian, and the German. This was something which no one—not even the French and the British, but least of all the statesmen of those three empires themselves—wished or expected to achieve when they went to war in 1914, and from which no one really profited."[6] The resort to war creates new circumstances that will always lie beyond the means of statesmen to fully control.

Moral ambiguity is a frequent characteristic of conflict between nation-states, a fact that conflicts with mainstream American political philosophy. War more often than not is characterized by rights and wrongs by some or all participants. Americans generally have an expectation that one of the belligerents in a conflict will be readily identifiable as the party most responsible for the outbreak of war. From Kennan's perspective, "We Americans like our adversaries wholly inhuman: all powerful, omniscient, monstrously efficient, unhampered by any serious problems of their own, and bent only on schemes for our destruction. Whatever their real nature, we will always persist in seeing them this way. It is the reflection of a philosophic weakness—of an inability to recognize any relativity in matters of friendship and enmity."[7] Kennan highlighted the element of ambiguity in war when he wrote, "Let us face it: in most international differences elements of right or wrong, comparable to those that prevail in personal relationships, are—if they exist at all, which is a question—simply not discernible to the outsider."[8] Americans would be well served to take into account the circumstances in which violence and force are used in politics. A blanket rejection of the ubiquity of force may overlook political subtleties and the injustices suffered by those compelled to resort to force.

War is an instrument for advancing political objectives, not for asserting moral principles. The main lesson carried away by a reader of Clausewitz's *On War* is that war is a reflection of political interest. If diplomacy fails to achieve the national interest, war steps in to fill the breach. Clausewitz elegantly captured the essence of war: "The political object is the goal, war is the means of reaching it, and means can never be considered in isolation from their purpose."[9] This wisdom was not lost on Kennan, who, as John Lewis Gaddis has pointed out, read Clausewitz while he was assigned to the National War College during his Foreign Service career.[10]

War's rational aim is to compel change in the psychological and political calculus of an adversary. The purpose of warfare should be "not just to work maximum destruction on the chosen enemy but rather to produce a useful effect on his understanding and his disposition—to convert him, if there seems to be no other way of doing it, to a more useful and more acceptable frame of mind than that which forced you to resort to arms against him in the first place, and to do this with the minimum, not the maximum, of destruction."[11] A change in the psychological relationship amenable to one's own interest with the least amount of violence is the ideal purpose of war.

Other realist thinkers also pointed to the importance of the psychological purpose of war. Hans Morgenthau and Kenneth Thompson asserted that "The actual exercise of physical violence substitutes for the psychological relation between two minds, which is of the essence of political power, the physical relation between two bodies, one of which is strong enough to dominate the other's movements. It is for this reason that in the exercise of physical violence the psychological element of the political relationship is lost, and that we must distinguish between military and political power."[12] As Thompson elaborated, "Once war has ceased, nations resume their psychological relationship. Political power determines territorial changes which have resulted from warfare and are determined by residual military and political strength. Power expresses itself in peace settlements or agreements and its instrument is effective diplomacy, not the continued employment of force."[13] For the realists, then, the aim of war is to reestablish the psychological, political relationship between belligerents severed at the onset of combat.

Statesmen need to have full control over their military establishments to ensure that war is subordinate to political objectives. Kennan's research as a diplomatic historian drew his attention to the dangers posed by the subordination of civilians to military establishments. The Franco-Russian Alliance forged in the early 1890s, which was "destined to play an important part in determining the alignment of forces in the First World War" was based on military considerations apart from political objectives.[14] Specifically, Kennan found that the agreement between France and Russia "prescribed the circumstances in which military operations were to be put in hand and placed certain strictures on the manner in which they were to be conducted; but it did not treat the question of *why* they were to be conducted in the first place, or to what end."[15] Under these circumstances, it "was largely inconsequential whether civilian statesmen came or went, whether changes occurred in the moods of public opinion, whether new diplomatic problems did or did not emerge on the horizons of the various foreign offices."[16] For Kennan, as for Edmund Burke, therefore, "*The nature of things requires* that the army should never act but as *an instrument.*"[17] Military leaders—unless constrained by civilian statesmen—are prone to see war as an end in and of itself rather than as a means to reestablish a psychological relationship and obtain political objectives.

THE LIMITED WAR MODEL: EQUATING MEANS AND ENDS

Rational calculation of political interest and the use of force to alter the psychological disposition of an adversary to attain those interests is the essence of limited war. The military instrument is subordinate to political objectives in limited war. Military operations are restrained to reduce the destructiveness and the unintended consequences of conflict. The limited war model, for the realists, is the standard with which to evaluate war as a foreign policy instrument. The realist hope is that adherence to the principle of limited war would ameliorate the excesses in combat witnessed in the twentieth century.

The model of limited war as a moderating influence in international politics stems from its operation in the eighteenth century. Kennan urged that "we would have to recognize the wisdom shown by Gibbon when he listed among the elements of strength in the European civilization of the eighteenth century the fact that the armies of the European powers were 'exercised in temperate and indecisive conflicts.' Man would have to recognize, in short, that the device of military coercion could have, in the future, only a relative—never an absolute—value in the pursuit of political objectives."[18] Kennan noted that wars then "were generally fought for specific limited purposes. The amount of force was made, if possible, commensurate to the purpose at hand—no more, no less. When the immediate objective had been obtained, or had proven unobtainable, one desisted. One did not try to carry hostilities to the point of the total destruction of the adversary's armed power and his complete humiliation and political emasculation. For that, there was too keen an awareness of the ultimate community of fate of all dynasties, even those with which one might, at the moment, be contending."[19]

The practice of limited war eroded in the nineteenth century. Kennan laid the blame for the disrepute of limited warfare to two factors. First, the "industrial revolution and the rapid rise in populations that accompanied it had played a major part in making possible the maintenance in peacetime of great standing armies. These armies were not only numerically greater than anything known in the preindustrial era, but they were rapidly acquiring technological capabilities, particularly in point of firepower and mobility, that gave them the possibility not just of inflicting massive and devastating damage on the armed forces of another country but also of threatening the integrity of its political system, and sometimes even its very identity as a sovereign member of the family of nations."[20] The second factor was the growing power of modern nationalism, which, in part, "could be seen as a product of democracy—of a spreading of the decision-taking power from crowned heads and their personal aides to parliamentary bodies and the constituencies they represented."[21]

Despite the advent of industrialization and nationalism, war under some circumstances could still serve constructive purposes in international politics. As Kennan acknowledged, war "can be the regrettable alternative to similar destruction in our own country or the killing of our own people. It can conceivably protect values which it is necessary to protect and which can be protected in no other way. Occasionally, if used with forethought and circumspection and restraint, it may trade the lesser violence for the greater and impel the stream of human events into channels which will be more hopeful ones than it would otherwise have taken."[22] Kennan viewed war as a necessary evil. "Major war can be at best the lesser of two evils, a terrible and heavy price paid in order to avoid the necessity of paying one still more terrible and still more heavy; but then it must be a defensive war, forced upon us, accepted reluctantly and with heavy hearts."[23]

Limited war, for Kennan and other realists, was the model for the conduct of war. Kennan argued that "Limited war—war for limited objectives—might still have a rational purpose, provided the actual military effort could be held to modest dimensions and provided one could be sure of stopping in time."[24] Henry Kissinger similarly viewed limited war as "fought for specific political objectives which, by their very existence, tend to establish a relationship between the force employed and the goal to be attained. It reflects an attempt to *affect* the opponent's will, not to *crush* it, to make the conditions to be imposed seem more attractive than continued resistance, to strive for specific goals and not for complete annihilation."[25] Kennan's thinking on limited war may have been stimulated by his colleague at the National War College, Bernard Brodie, who judged that "limited war involves an important kind and degree of restraint—deliberate restraint."[26]

The costs of waging limited war as a means in foreign policy should be commensurate with political ends. Kennan, however, was critical of the United States' ability to perform such a calculus and viewed it as a pronounced problem in the conduct of American foreign policy in this century. In his words, "the effort to evolve a sound theory of military strategy and to relate it to the other concerns of the national state has been, I believe, a difficult problem for most great countries; but it is hard to believe that any country has ever been farther from finding satisfactory solutions to it than our own."[27]   It is to Kennan's evaluation of the United States' use of force and war as an instrument of foreign policy to which we now must turn attention.

The United States has used force and war as an instrument of policy on numerous occasions this century. The rationale for the reliance on these tools in each instance has varied, but the United States generally has stumbled into war instead of clearly articulating the national interest at stake in each conflict. This tendency was evident in American participation in the world wars, Korea, Vietnam, and in the Cold War nuclear stalemate with the Soviet Union. More recent uses of American military force in Haiti, Somalia, and the Persian Gulf also raise questions about the use of force as an extension of foreign policy. War in each of these instances may be characterized as points along Clausewitz's spectrum of limited to absolute war.[28] Kennan's principle of war and foreign policy suggests that U.S. foreign policy is better served when war is waged as a means to achieve clearly articulated national interests than when it is waged with a blurred vision of political objectives.

TOTAL WORLD WAR

The United States mobilized its full military power twice to participate in total war in this century. The United States lurched into both world wars with less than a clear-cut view of national interest.   Kennan criticized the sophistication of the American understanding of war as not commensurate with United States power and influence in world politics. For Kennan, the policy priority and aim of each of the world wars should have been reestablishment of a global balance of power. He worried in particular that a hostile power in control of Europe would move to directly threaten the United States in the Western Hemisphere.

American utopianism, instead of balance of power calculations, guided rhetoric and policy in both the First and Second World Wars.   Americans viewed the conflicts as aberrations of human nature rather than as reflections of egoistic nationalism rooted in the capacity of man to be both good and evil. In Kennan's words, "These enemies appeared to us in the aspect of monsters that had arisen from nowhere, as by some black magic. We deluded ourselves with the belief that if they could be in some way exorcised, like evil spirits, through the process of military defeat, then nothing would remain of them and our world would be restored to us as though they had never existed."[29] War in both world wars was viewed as a means to achieve the moral end of purging the world of evil.

Such a view contributed to war aims that went well beyond those called for by the limited war model. Political objectives were not effectively articulated:

"The commitment to total defeat of the enemy, followed by unconditional surrender, had served for us as an excuse for not giving serious thought to political objectives while the war was on."[30] "The result was that we had ended these contests with very little in the way of realistic ideas as to where we wanted to go—what political objectives we wished to pursue with relation to our ex-enemy, once his capitulation had been obtained."[31] Both world wars, moreover, set into the American psyche the belief that all wars should set unconditional surrender as the goal of conflict regardless of the political interests at stake. Each "ended in unconditional surrender, encouraging us in the view that the purpose of war was not to bring about a mutually advantageous compromise with an external adversary seen as totally evil and inhuman, but to destroy completely the power and the will of that adversary."[32] The commitment to the total defeat of the enemy may have prolonged the duration and increased the destructiveness of each conflict, contrary to the goals of the limited war model.

Although the advancement of weapons technology had a significant hand in the increased destructiveness of the world wars as compared to previous conflicts, the excessive war aims also contributed to a level of destructiveness that went well beyond that experienced in wars fought for limited political objectives. The scale of destruction, particularly civilian casualties, in the world wars was a break from traditionally limited forms of warfare. Kennan remarked from his study of history that "In the old days, wartime objectives were generally limited and practical ones, and it was common to measure the success of your military operations by the extent to which they brought you closer to your objectives. But where your objectives are moral and ideological ones and run to changing attitudes and traditions of an entire people or the personality of a regime, then victory is probably something not to be achieved entirely by military means or indeed in any short space of time at all; and perhaps that is the source of our confusion."[33] In sharp contrast to past epochs in warfare, in both world wars, "but particularly the second, we departed increasingly from the principle, embodied in the earlier rules of warfare, that war should be waged only against the armed forces of an enemy, not against the helpless civilian population. And it was by our wholehearted acceptance of the practice of waging war against civilians as well as against soldiers, and especially by our commitment to the so-called area bombings of World War II, that we were led into the terrible bewilderments we are confronting today."[34]

Some of Kennan's most critical analysis was aimed at the military conduct of the Second World War. He argued that the Allied strategic bombing campaign was militarily ineffective as well as morally unacceptable. Kennan's judgment on this score was profoundly influenced by his visit to Hamburg in 1949, six years after it experienced severe Allied bombing. Kennan observed "sweeping devastation, down to the ground, mile after mile. It had all been done in three days and nights in 1943, my host told me. Seventy-five thousand persons had perished in the process . . . And here, for the first time, I felt an unshakable conviction that no momentary military advantage—even if such could have been calculated to exist—could have justified this stupendous, careless destruction of civilian life and of material values, built up laboriously by human hands over the course of centuries for purposes having nothing to do with this war."[35]   Kennan's concern for stopping wanton military violence against unarmed civilians resembles that in just war theory, as David Mayers has perceptively noted.[36] One gets glimpses of just war theory in many of Kennan's passages.   For example, as he described his experience surveying the damage on the ground in Germany after World War II, "it suddenly appeared to me that in these ruins there was an unanswerable symbolism which we in the West could not afford to ignore. If the Western world was really going to make valid the pretense of a higher moral departure point—of greater sympathy and understanding for the human being as God made him, as expressed not only in himself but in the things he had wrought and cared about—then it had to learn to fight its wars morally as well as militarily, or not fight them at all; for moral principles were a part of its strength."[37]

There is little evidence to suggest that Kennan devoted substantial attention to the just war theory literature. In his personal papers, Kennan left only one clue of his familiarity with just war theory. In a 1959 letter to the chairman of the department of religion at Princeton University, Kennan remarked, "I do not think that the killing of innocent non-combatants should be made an *instrument* through which to try to damage the enemy. I think one should make every effort to confine the injuries of war to those who bear weapons."[38] This passage suggests that Kennan accepted the tenets of just war theory, which allow for civilian deaths only as a secondary effect of operations designed first and foremost to reduce an aggressor's means for waging war.[39] Although Kennan argued against morality setting the objectives of war, he believed that morality should shape the method or conduct of war to obtain political objectives.

The American desire to achieve moral objectives in war is buttressed by public opinion and contributes to the waging of total war. Kennan commented that "public opinion, or what passes for public opinion, is not invariably a moderating force in the jungle of politics."[40] He recalled, for example, that "In 1916 people in Europe had not yet learned this, any more than many people in the United States have learned it today; and, by consequence, the progress of World War I did not bring reasonableness, or humility, or the spirit of compromise to the warring peoples. As hostilities ran their course, hatreds congealed, one's own propaganda came to be believed, moderate people were shouted down and brought into disrepute, and war aims hardened and became more extreme all around. The Allies came to be interested only in a total victory over Germany: a victory of national humiliation, of annexations, of crushing reparations."[41]

United States behavior in the two world wars reflected a broader characteristic of democratic government. For Kennan, democracies show a propensity to resist the initiation of conflict but, once engaged, aggressively wage war. "Democracy fights in anger—it fights for the very reason that it was forced to go to war. It fights to punish the power that was rash enough and hostile enough to provoke it—to teach that power a lesson it will not forget, to prevent the thing from happening again."[42] Similarly, Reinhold Niebuhr noted that "Democracies are indeed slow to make war, but once they embarked upon a martial venture are equally slow to make peace and reluctant to make a tolerable, rather than a vindictive, peace."[43] Sir Herbert Butterfield also observed this tendency when he wrote that "Democracies sometimes hate to have to think of war; but when they do turn to the idea they have shown more than once in the twentieth century that they quickly become headstrong, forgetting the limits of what power can actually achieve."[44]

Kennan's experience with the Allied bombings of Germany was to heavily influence his policy recommendations for the use of force in post–World War II American foreign policy. He noted that "These were thoughts that were to pursue me into the trials and problems of future years: into arguments in Washington as to whether we should commit ourselves to the development of the hydrogen bomb, into the BBC [British Broadcasting Corporation] Reith Lectures of 1957 in which I inveighed against basing the defense of the continental NATO members on nuclear missiles, and in senatorial hearings of 1966 and 1967 where talk turned on the bombing of North Vietnam."[45] Kennan's principle of war and foreign policy must now be addressed in connection with American military campaigns in Korea and Vietnam.

LIMITED WAR IN KOREA AND VIETNAM

The wars in Korea and Vietnam were short of total war because in both conflicts the United States limited its means for waging war. It refrained from full mobilization of military resources as well as from the use of nuclear weapons. Both wars also had limited ends: the restoration of the status quo ante in Korea—at least at the war's conclusion—and the territorial integrity of South Vietnam. Both wars were viewed as bricks in the edifice of the American policy of containment, which sought to stem the spread of communism. Kennan was critical of United States conduct in both wars. Although he supported a military response to the North Korean attack on South Korea, he worried that United States' movement north of the 38th parallel threatened to transform a limited war into total war. As for the conflict between North and South Vietnam, Kennan saw insufficient national interest at stake to warrant a major commitment of American military power.

The Korean War was a limited conflict, although it risked crossing the threshold to total war between the superpowers. Kennan initially approved of the use of force to resist North Korea's June 1950 invasion of South Korea "on the assumption and understanding that our action was only for a limited purpose: namely, the restoration of the *status quo ante* on the Korean peninsula, and that our force would not, even if military success permitted, advance beyond the former demarcation line along the 38th parallel."[46] Kennan's primary concern was to prevent actions that would expand a limited war on the Korean peninsula to a conflict between major powers. He "saw in the North Korean attack adequate reason for us to undertake military operations for this limited purpose; I did not see in it justification for involving ourselves in another world war."[47]

None of the major powers—the United States, the Soviet Union, or China—wanted to directly face one another in battle over Korea. And yet the Korean conflict presented a situation in which neither rival could clearly see its position or that of its opponent. Such situations may lead to the escalation of limited conflict into total war. Kennan warned in August 1950 that operations north of the 38th parallel risked drawing the Russians and the Chinese into the war to defend North Korea.[48] He criticized American actions that he believed risked bringing about the scenario he most feared. "There was never the slightest doubt in my mind, and I fail to see how anyone could have entertained any, that the demand for permission to bomb beyond the Yalu was equivalent to a demand for expansion of the Korean War into a full-fledged war with both the Soviet Union and China."[49] Despite the course of the war, the armistice that ended the Korean conflict conformed to the limited war model. Kennan commented that the Korean armistice "seems to me to have been, despite all the attendant difficulties, preferable to the alternative with which we were then confronted: to press on with hostilities on the Korean peninsula in the pursuit of military and political objectives which, to the extent their realization was approached, would almost certainly have brought the Russians in against us and would probably have assured the outbreak, then and there, of World War III."[50]

Kennan drew a number of lessons from the war in Korea, as he had done from earlier conflicts. These lessons reinforced his view that war must be subordinate to political objectives. He wrote that Korea illustrated "the terrible danger of letting national policy be determined by military considerations alone. Had the military been given their head (and this goes for the entire combination of MacArthur and the Joint Chiefs of Staff in Washington)—had they not been restrained by the wise discipline exercised, in the face of unprecedentedly savage political opposition, by President Truman, Secretary of State Acheson, and General Marshall—disaster would almost certainly have ensued."[51] These points underscored the imperative to have the military subordinate to political considerations, as discussed earlier. Second, Kennan learned "the great and sometimes crucial value—so seldom heeded, so difficult perhaps to heed, in American statesmanship—of wholly secret, informal and exploratory contacts even between political and military adversaries, as adjuncts to the overt and formal processes of international diplomacy."[52] This observation reflected Kennan's appreciation that war is needed to establish a new psychological relationship, renewed diplomacy, and a negotiated political settlement.

The importance of the balance of power as the American national interest also was reinforced by the Korean War. Kennan faulted U.S. post–World War II neglect of the balance of power in Asia, which, in turn, laid the geopolitical foundation for the Korean War. He observed that

The martial fervor of the war in the Pacific, however—that strange weakness of understanding that causes Americans, once at war, to idealize their associates, to make inhuman demons of their opponents, and to become wholly oblivious to the long-term requirements of any balance of power—impelled us to exploit our victory as a means of removing the Japanese from Korea as well, thus leaving that unfortunate country, insofar as we would not protect it ourselves, at the mercy of the Russians and—within three or four years—of the Russians and Communist Chinese together. Having self-righteously expelled the Japanese from their positions in Korea, we now found ourselves, in the postwar period, faced with the necessity of shouldering the burden they had long borne of containing rival mainland power—once Russian, now Russian and Chinese-Communist combined—on that peninsula.[53]

The Korean War, moreover, is illustrative of Kennan's view that major errors in peacetime statesmanship lay the groundwork for future conflict. As discussed earlier, foreign policy is best conducted when statesmen keep their eyes fixed on long-run objectives, such as nurturing balances of power, as they struggle with short-term problems.

The Korean War had an enormous impact on political relationships well beyond the peninsula, and helped fuel the U.S.-Soviet Cold War. Kennan related in retrospect that the "North Korean attack came soon to appear to a great many people in Washington as merely the first move in some 'grand design,' as the phrase then went, on the part of the Soviet leaders to extend their power to other parts of the world by the use of force. The unexpectedness of this attack—the fact that we had no forewarning of it—only stimulated the already existent preference of the military planners for drawing their conclusions only from the assessed *capabilities* of the adversary, dismissing his *intentions*, which could be safely assumed to be hostile."[54] This perception fueled the militarization of the U.S.-Soviet rivalry. Kennan commented that "All this tended to heighten the militarization of thinking about the cold war generally, and to press us into attitudes where any discriminate estimate of Soviet intentions was unwelcome and unacceptable. In addition, it encouraged the military planners in another tendency against which I had fought long and bitterly but generally in vain: the tendency, namely, to view Soviet intentions as something existing quite independently of our own behavior. It was difficult to persuade these men that what people in Moscow decided to do might be in reaction to things we had done."[55] Korea as a watershed event in the evolution of the Cold War will be explored in greater depth in the next chapter. Suffice it to note here that the Korean War entailed unforeseen consequences for the tension in the bipolar international system of nation-states.

The Vietnam War was a legacy of the Korean conflict, in that the United States again intervened militarily in Asia to stem the expansion of communism. Kennan, however, believed that Vietnam was significantly less important than the Korean peninsula to the balance of power in Asia. Vietnam was not one of the five critical regions of industrial-military power of the world, and South Vietnam's defeat at the hands of the North Vietnamese did not adversely affect the balance of power in Asia. In contrast, Kennan viewed a hostile power in control of the Korean peninsula as a threat to Japan, one of the military-industrial centers of the world.

Although beyond the periphery of U.S. geopolitical interests, the Vietnam War risked drawing the superpowers into direct confrontation. The United States—frustrated in its efforts to suppress an insurgency in South Vietnam backed by North Vietnam—was tempted to press the war on the ground to the north, but the legacy of the drive north of the 38th parallel in the Korean War, in part, counseled against such a move in Vietnam. Kennan argued in the early stages of American involvement in 1966 that

Vietnam is not a region of major industrial-military importance. It is difficult to believe that any decisive development of the world situation is going to be determined by what happens on that territory. Were it not for the considerations of prestige that arise out of our existing involvement, even a situation in which South Vietnam was controlled exclusively by the Vietcong, while regrettable and no doubt morally unwarranted, would not present, in my opinion, dangers great enough to justify our direct military intervention . . . I think it should be our Government's aim to liquidate this involvement just as soon as this can be done without inordinate damage to our own prestige or to the stability of conditions in that area.[56]

These statements reflected Kennan's preference in policy to more heavily weigh the national interest, in large measure defined by geopolitical factors, than moral goals, which overlook the limits of American power and translate to open-ended commitments.

Kennan's assessment of the Vietnam War demonstrated his consistent application of the litmus test of policy—to equate ends and means in strategy. Bernard Brodie detected this strategic calculus in Kennan's testimony to the Senate in 1966. In Brodie's judgment, Kennan expressed "a conception that ought to be utterly commonplace in strategic discourse and in related national policy decisions but that seems on the contrary to be often neglected or omitted. It is the conception simply of reasonable price, and of its being applied to strategy and national policy—the idea that some ends or objectives are worth paying a good deal for and others are not. The latter include ends that are no doubt desirable but which are worth attempting to achieve only if the price can *with confidence* be kept relatively low."[57]

The course of combat in Vietnam again showed the impact of emotionalism in a democratic society. Kennan privately expressed his concern about U.S. policy in Vietnam as early as 1966:

I have a feeling of miserable unhappiness and helplessness about this whole situation. I see a series of catastrophic possibilities, and no favorable ones, at the end of the path on which we are now advancing. And it is particularly shocking to see the President and the Secretary of State doing all in their power to stimulate and to enlist behind this hopeless effort the most violent sort of American patriotic emotionalism—conveying the impression that what we are now involved in is a great national cause, that we have passed the point where any useful purpose could be served by discussion about the desirability of our action, that we must now all stand together behind the boys on the battlefield, that we are full of "determination," etc.[58]

Kennan was pessimistic that military means alone could bring an end to the conflict. "I have, at the same time, great misgivings about any deliberate expansion of hostilities on our part directed to the achievement of something called victory—if, by the use of that term, we envisage the complete disappearance of the recalcitrance with which we are now faced, the formal submission by the adversary to our will, and the complete realization of our present stated political aims. I doubt that these things can be achieved even by the most formidable military successes."[59] His assessment would years later prove to be remarkably accurate.

SPECTER OF ABSOLUTE WAR: THE AMERICAN-SOVIET NUCLEAR STANDOFF

American military intervention in Southeast Asia was in pursuit of peripheral interests in the Cold War competition with the Soviet Union. The primary theater for the Cold War rivalry was Europe, the fulcrum of the world balance of power in Kennan's geopolitical framework. Soviet domination of Europe would have represented the consolidation of a preponderance of power in the Eurasian land mass and would have represented an intolerable threat to the security of the United States in the Western Hemisphere. The specter of absolute war with nuclear weapons hung over the maintenance of the Cold War balance of power in Europe.

Kennan's main Cold War concern was that the Soviet Union would seek to exploit political instabilities and weaknesses in Western Europe to expand its political power on the continent. Kennan assessed that an overt Soviet military threat to Western Europe was secondary to this political threat. As Kennan in 1967 recalled, "I did not believe in the reality of a Soviet military threat to Western Europe. Not believing in it, I was concerned not so much to provide protection against the possibility of such an attack (although I recognized the need for some sort of military facade to quiet the anxieties of the jittery Western Europeans) as to facilitate the retirement of Soviet forces, and with them dominant Soviet political influence, to limits closer to the traditional boundaries of the Russian state."[60]

This sober analysis about the prospects for Soviet military invasion of Western Europe was influenced by Kennan's World War II experiences and his study of history. While assigned as a young diplomat to Prague in 1939, Kennan wrote in a dispatch that "one can predict no successful future for the German attempt to rule the Historic Provinces. Inflation, impoverishment, economic disruption, bitterness, lack of confidence, and the moral disintegration of public administration can reap no good harvest either for victors or vanquished."[61] These eyewitness observations bolstered in Kennan's mind lessons drawn from his study of the Roman Empire. As Kennan viewed German's occupational problems in 1939 to 1941, he "was brought to recognize the continued and undiminished relevance in the modern world of Gibbon's assertion that 'there is nothing more contrary to nature than the attempt to hold in obedience distant provinces.' Out of this grew my feeling that one must not be too frightened of those who aspire to world domination. No one people is great enough to establish a world hegemony. There are built-in impediments to the permanent exertion by any power of dominant influence in areas which it is unable to garrison and police, or at least to overshadow from positions of close proximity, by its own troops."[62] Kennan therefore reasoned that the Soviets would face formidable obstacles to the forcible occupation of Western Europe similar to those experienced by the German military in World War II. Indeed, the collapse of the Soviet Union attested to the validity of Gibbon's insight on the problems inherent in maintaining an empire.

Nevertheless, Kennan acknowledged that Europe needed to maintain a conventional military posture to balance Soviet forces. He believed that Europe had sufficient resources to meet the requirements for sufficiency in conventional weapons without the United States. "If the Western European peoples fail to maintain military forces commensurate with those that confront them to the east, this is because they are *unwilling* to make the attendant sacrifices, not because they *couldn't* make them."[63] The propensity of West European states to resist increases in defense spending for conventional forces, however, compelled NATO to increasingly rely on comparatively cheaper nuclear weapons to balance Soviet power on the continent.

This reliance on nuclear weapons in NATO's defense posture alarmed Kennan, who viewed the use of nuclear weapons against Japan in 1945 "as a regrettable extremism, born of the bad precedent of the conventional strategic bombings of the war just then ended and of the military fixations to which the war had conduced."[64] Nuclear weapons, in his judgment, were unsuitable instruments for waging limited war for political objectives. The only useful role nuclear weapons could fulfill was deterrence. In a Department of State memorandum in 1950, Kennan noted that "barring some system of international control and prohibition of atomic weapons, it is not questioned that some weapons of mass destruction must be retained in the national arsenal for purposes of deterrence and retaliation."[65]

In the event that deterrence failed, intercontinental exchanges of nuclear weapons could not have advanced any American political interests. From Kennan's perspective, "the weapon of mass destruction is a sterile and hopeless weapon which may for a time serve as an answer of sorts to itself and as an uncertain sort of shield against utter cataclysm, but which cannot in any way serve the purposes of a constructive and hopeful foreign policy. The true end of political action is, after all, to affect the deeper convictions of men; this the atomic bomb cannot do."[66]   Kennan elaborated on these thoughts in private correspondence in 1966 to his friend Louis Halle: "The aim of warfare, if it is to be anything more than sheer unreasoning panic or madness, must be to affect in some way the political realities in a given part of the world: the behavior of another political regime, the political domination of territory, the reactions and policies of governing elites. This is not done just by acts of blind destruction."[67] Kennan's bottom-line assessment was essentially that nuclear weapons in the Cold War rivalry could not have been used to fulfill Clausewitz's dictum that war is an extension of politics by other means.

Adherents to the realist school share a skeptical view of the utility of nuclear weapons in foreign policy. There is a strong consensus on this point among traditional realists. Bernard Brodie, in his groundbreaking study on nuclear weapons, outlined the position of many realists, including Kennan, on the use of the weapon in modern statecraft. Brodie argued in 1946 that "Thus far the chief purpose of our military establishment has been to win wars. From now on its chief purpose must be to avert them. It can have almost no other useful purpose."[68] Hans Morgenthau assessed that "The atomic revolution has made an end to this rational relationship between violence and foreign policy; for under the conditions of all-out atomic war the use of all-out violence is a contradiction in terms, making war a perfectly irrational, senseless, self-defeating, and self-destructive act."[69] Henry Kissinger argued that the doctrine of massive retaliation deprived the United States of flexibility because it posed risks out of proportion to the objectives to be achieved.[70] Kissinger concluded that "The destructiveness of modern weapons deprives victory in an all-out war of its historical meaning. Even the side which inflicts a greater devastation than its opponent may not retain sufficient resources to impose its will."[71]

The challenge faced by statesmen in the Cold War was to prevent conventional conflict from escalating to nuclear war. Kennan was emphatic that a "firebreak" between conventional and nuclear weapons had to be preserved in Europe. He worried that the use of nuclear weapons in Europe could not be limited and would quickly escalate into general nuclear war between the superpowers. Kennan argued, along with other influential figures, that "any use of nuclear weapons in Europe, by the Alliance or against it, carries with it a high and inescapable risk of escalation into the general nuclear war which would bring ruin to all and victory to none. The one clearly definable firebreak against the worldwide disaster of general nuclear war is the one that stands between all other kinds of conflict and any use whatsoever of nuclear weapons."[72]

A NATO pledge of no-first-use of nuclear weapons was viewed by Kennan as a means to strengthen the firebreak between conventional and nuclear warfare as well to increase West European emphasis on conventional forces. Kennan and his colleagues in 1982 maintained, "An Allied posture of no-first-use would have one special effect that can be set forth in advance: it would draw new attention to the importance of maintaining and improving the specifically American conventional forces in Europe."[73] They and others reasoned in 1986 that "NATO's strategy of relying on the first use of nuclear weapons has, in our view, not only diminished its ability to respond with conventional forces but also increased the likelihood that at the height of a crisis NATO would resort to nuclear weapons."[74] This view was consistent with the one that Kennan espoused in 1959 when he called for a rejection of the principle of first use to set the stage for strengthening conventional forces and the eventual abolition of nuclear weapons.[75]

Kennan's advocacy of no-first-use is plagued with problems. The ambiguity over NATO's use of nuclear weapons increased the level of uncertainty in Soviet calculations and arguably increased the deterrent value of these weapons. Moreover, a decreased emphasis on nuclear weapons in NATO planning would not necessarily have been matched with an increased emphasis on conventional forces. Instead, West European states might have coupled decreased American reliance on nuclear weapons with decreased European conventional force expenditures, to reduce NATO's overall military preparedness level and to perhaps embolden Soviet political behavior.

Above and beyond the nuts-and-bolts discussions of defense strategy in Europe, Kennan believed that war between the superpowers—even if it were limited in its conduct to conventional weapons—could serve no political purpose. A war between the superpowers would have damaged rather than advanced the national interests of each state. Kennan speculated that in such a war there could never be a military victory for either combatant, as "Neither country was occupiable by the forces of the other. Both were simply too large, too different—linguistically, culturally, and in every other way."[76] He reasoned, moreover, that since there was no "tradition or psychology of the Soviet leaders to surrender to an adversary who had occupied any sizable portion of their territory," the United States eventually "would have to come to some sort of terms with them, if the war was to end; and these terms would have to be based on a compromise of conflicting interests. But for this, one would have to formulate at some point limited objectives--objectives short, that is, of unconditional surrender."[77] This being the case, it would have been nonsensical to allow a war to start between the superpowers that would have run exceedingly high risks of escalating to nuclear weapons and crossing the threshold from total to absolute war, completely beyond the control of political purpose.

MODERN WAR AND MAJOR POWERS

Kennan extrapolated from his analysis of the Cold War potential for war between the superpowers and his work as a diplomatic historian on World War I some generalizations about modern war between major powers in the international system of nation-states. His generalizations reflected a realist tension between an appreciation for the ubiquity of force and war in politics and a disgust at the destructiveness of modern weapons. Kennan hoped against the odds that war between major powers could be ruled out in modern international politics because he doubted that such conflict could conform to his model of limited war.

The use of the means and ends litmus test led Kennan to question the overall utility of total war between major powers. Kennan in 1964 judged that "World War I still looms on the historical horizon as *the* great determining tragedy of our century. There are many lessons to be gained from it for our own generation. But one stands out in importance. It is the lesson of the unsuitability of major war as an instrument of policy in the modern age. In that period of 1914 to 1918, thirty years before the development of the nuclear weapon, it was demonstrated that war, conducted in the grand manner and as a means of achieving major political objectives, was no longer a rational means of procedure."[78] He argued that "all-out war, involving the total commitment of a nation's manpower and resources and aimed at the total destruction of an enemy's will to resist and the complete power to order his life and to shape his behavior, had already, in 1914, lost its rationale. It had lost its rationale because of the terrible destructiveness of modern weapons, because of the enormous cost of cultivating and employing such weapons, because of the great complexity of modern society, because of the impossibility, the sheer technical impossibility, of one great country holding another great country in subjection for any long period of time and shaping its life in ways contrary to the will of the people."[79]

Kennan was emotionally and intellectually torn between the recognition of the ubiquity of war in international relations and the realization that modern conventional war between major powers was so destructive that it could serve no rational political end.

The best that humanity can hope for, it seems to me, is an even and undramatic muddling along on its mysterious and unknowable paths, avoiding all that is abrupt, avoiding the great orgies of violence that acquire their own momentum and get out of hand—continuing, to be sure, to live by competition between political entities, but being sophisticated and wise about the relationships of power: recognizing and discounting superiority of strength, in the good old Christian manner, rather than putting it suicidally to the test of the sword—imagining the great battles rather than fighting them; seeing to it that armies, if they must be employed at all, are exercised, as Gibbon put it, "by temperate and indecisive contests"; remembering at all times that civilization has become a fragile thing that must be kept right-side up and will not stand too much jolting and abuse.[80]

The challenge for statesmen is to harness political wisdom to maintain precarious balances of power and thus avoid the outbreak of war between major powers. Kennan placed the priority on major power relations and even hoped that war between major powers could be banned. "War itself, as a means of settling differences at least between the great industrial powers, will have to be in some way ruled out; and with it there will have to be dismantled (for without this the whole outlawing of war would be futile) the greater part of the vast military establishments now maintained with a view to the possibility that war might take place." He hastened to add that "No one could be more aware than I am of the difficulty of ruling out war among great powers. It is not possible to write any sure prescription as to how this might be achieved, particularly because the course of international life is not, and cannot be determined over the long term by specific treaties or charters agreed upon at a single moment in history and reflecting only the outlooks and circumstance of that particular moment. It is the ingrained habits and assumptions of men, and above all men in government, which alone can guarantee any enduring state of peaceful relations among nations."[81] Kennan in this passage suggested that international institutions and law were insufficient to preclude major war, but stressed the importance of making peace a habit among the leaders of major powers. In so doing, Kennan showed his affinity for Edmund Burke's emphasis on traditions, customs, and history as the foundation for moderation and prudence in international relations and his rejection of a Kantian or institutional approach to world politics.

A RETURN TO LIMITED WAR AFTER THE COLD WAR?

Today there is an absence of rivalries between major powers that threaten to soon erupt into armed conflict. Nevertheless, in the aftermath of the Cold War the United States has turned to military force as an instrument of policy against lesser powers in the Persian Gulf, the Horn of Africa, the Caribbean, and, most recently, the Balkans. The American rationale for employing force in each of these interventions has varied. Kennan has not treated each of these American interventions in depth, but some cursory thoughts suggest potential pitfalls in the American use of force in the post–Cold War period.

The use of American force in the post–Cold War period in some instances—although limited—has not conformed with Kennan's principle of war and foreign policy. The national interests at stake have been ambiguous, and it has been unclear that military means could be used to achieve the poorly defined political objectives in many of these cases. American military force in the case of Somalia, for example, could not have been used to fulfill the loosely defined political objective of imposing a democratic form of government there. Kennan commented in his diary that U.S. intervention in Somalia in 1992 was flawed: "The situation we are trying to correct has its roots in the fact that the people of Somalia are wholly unable to govern themselves and that the entire territory is simply without a government. The starvation that we are seeing on television is partly the result of drought (or so we are told), partly of overpopulation, and partly of the chaotic conditions flowing from the absence of any government authority. What we are doing holds out no hope of coming to terms with any of those situations."[82] Kennan's thoughts on Somalia probably are applicable to some extent to the use of American military force in Haiti. In that situation, foreign policy failed to contain a clearly articulated national interest, assess that limited force could achieve any such interest, and anticipate that the costs of the military intervention would be commensurate with political objectives.

The United States preponderance of power enables it in the post–Cold War period to intervene militarily in or against weaker nation-states without the threat of entanglement in a conflict with a major power. Nevertheless, Kennan cautioned in general against the use of American military power in small states. The United States should remember that "the great country has a vulnerability to dreams of power and glory to which the smaller state is less easily inclined. Such dreams can be, and usually are, benevolent in intent, at least in the minds of their authors. But since the belief that one country can do much good for another country by intervening forcefully in the latter's internal affairs is almost invariably an illusion in the first place, the entertainment of such dreams is usually no more than another example of the proverbial road to hell, paved with good intentions."[83] The incremental American military intervention in the Balkans, for example, although undertaken with humanitarian concern for innocent civilians caught in the crossfire, may yet evolve into a major military undertaking with costs not commensurate with the American national interest there.

Although Kennan supported limited U.S. involvement in the Balkans, he was concerned about the potential for an overcommitment of American power there. He wrote that "while this Balkan situation is one to which the United States cannot be indifferent, it is primarily a problem for the Europeans. It is their continent, not ours, that is affected."[84] Kennan further elaborated that "it is clear that no one—no particular country and no group of countries—wants, or should be expected, to occupy the entire distracted Balkan region, to subdue its excited peoples, and to hold them in order until they can calm down and begin to look at their problems in a more orderly way. Conceivably, such an occupation might be momentarily helpful but even that is not certain; and in any case any effort along that line could be only the most tenuous and temporary of improvisations. In the long run, no region can solve any other region's problems. The best the outsider can do is to give occasional supplementary help in the pinches."[85] These views reflect Kennan's skepticism about the ability of great powers to occupy other lands, born in his study of Gibbon and in his experience in World War II. Nevertheless, Kennan concluded that the crisis in the Balkans would require "outside mediation, and in all probability outside force, to devise a reasonable settlement and to bring the various parties to accept and observe it."[86] Kennan probably had in mind limited airstrikes, but ground occupation probably was beyond the scope of operations that he envisioned to promote a negotiated settlement to mitigate the devastation.

Beyond the regional balance of power in Europe and Asia upon which the equilibrium of the global balance rested, Kennan saw little vital American interest at stake that justified intervention in small nation-states. Relations among major powers, for Kennan, was the key to the maintenance of the global equilibrium of power, and he worried that commitments to small nation-states would divert attention from major power relationships. Relations with major powers place "more important demands on our attention, policies, and resources. The present moment is marked, most happily, by the fact that there are no great conflicts among the great powers."[87] In congressional testimony, Kennan remarked that "we have worried about a great many more things than we needed seriously to worry about in recent years or at least . . . we have felt it necessary to take action in more situations than we needed to take action in. I think that we must realize that this world is not going to be without violence—not in our time, not in any time that we can conceive of."[88] These comments were made in connection with his concern over American policy in Vietnam in the 1960s, but they remain pertinent, as the United States today appears increasingly eager to contemplate military action in small nation-states.

CONCLUSION

The preceding discussion reveals that Kennan had a coherent principle for governing the use of force and war in American foreign policy. Kennan clearly shared Clausewitz's view that war is a continuation of policy by other means. The ultimate end of war is to change an adversary's psychology to create the conditions suitable for a negotiated settlement that restores a balance of power.

Drawing from Kennan's analysis, if compelled to resort to force, American statesmen need to equate ends and means to conform to the limited war model in advancing the national interest. The United States went beyond the bounds of the limited war model in the world wars with demands for unconditional surrender, which may have prolonged the conflicts and increased the costs. The military means used, particularly in the Second World War, targeted civilian populations, which escalated the conflict to total war. Although the Korean War ended in an armistice consistent with the limited war model, the American military in the course of the conflict threatened to usurp political leaders and to escalate the conflict into total war between major powers. The United States became embroiled in a limited but costly conflict in Vietnam, the outcome of which had little impact on the balance of power in Asia. The use of nuclear weapons in a conflict between the Cold War superpowers would have resulted in absolute war, which would have defeated the national interests of both belligerents. Kennan hoped that an appreciation of limited war would ameliorate the prospects for total war between major powers. The use of American military force against weaker powers in the post–Cold War period will be insufficient to obtain moral objectives such as the promotion of democracy.

Kennan's thoughts on war and foreign policy contain signposts to help guide American policy makers in the post–Cold War period. The challenge for American statesmen is to manipulate power relationships to forestall the imbalances of power that are susceptible to outbreaks of violence. Policy makers need to stand ready to work diplomatically to limit the sweep and destructiveness of periodic outbreaks of hostilities. Kennan called for an

American foreign policy approach "not predicated on any hope for the early total abolition of violence from the affairs of nations, but concerned primarily to reduce the scope and dangerousness of such violence where it cannot be avoided."[89] Kennan's principle of war and foreign policy does not prescribe ready-made answers for American statesmen grappling with the dilemmas of war and peace. What Kennan's thought does represent, however, is a body of questions to be posed in the policy deliberation process. American statesmen, in contemplating intervention, should articulate the national interest, assess whether the national interest could be achieved through the use of force, and weigh the costs anticipated against the national interest at stake. The use of such a framework might help to bring Kennan's realist hope for prudence and a steady course in American foreign policy to fruition.

NOTES

1. George F. Kennan, *Russia, the Atom and the West* (New York, NY: Harper & Brothers Publishers, 1958), 56.

2. George F. Kennan, *Realities of American Foreign Policy* (Princeton, NJ: Princeton University Press, 1954), 37.

3. George F. Kennan, *The Nuclear Delusion: Soviet-American Relations in the Atomic Age* (New York, NY: Pantheon Books, 1982), xxvi.

4. George F. Kennan, "Is War with Russia Inevitable?" in Hans J. Morgenthau and Kenneth W. Thompson (eds.), *Principles and Problems of International Politics* (Washington, DC: University Press of America, 1950), 375.

5. George F. Kennan, "The Price We Paid for War," *Atlantic* 214, no. 4 (October 1964): 52.

6. Kennan, "The Price We Paid for War," 53.

7. "Correspondence to Professor Norman A. Graebner," 26 February 1960, George F. Kennan Papers, Box 31, Seeley G. Mudd Manuscript Library, Department of Rare Books and Special Collections, Princeton University Library.

8. Kennan, *Realities of American Foreign Policy*, 36.

9. Carl von Clausewitz, *On War*, Edited and Translated by Michael Howard and Peter Paret (Princeton, NJ: Princeton University Press, 1989), 87.

10. John Lewis Gaddis, "Introduction: The Evolution of Containment," in Terry L. Deibel and John Lewis Gaddis, *Containing the Soviet Union: A Critique of U.S. Policy* (Elmsford, NY: Pergamon-Brassey's International Defense Publishers, 1987), 10.

11. George F. Kennan, *Around the Cragged Hill: A Personal and Political Philosophy* (New York, NY: W.W. Norton & Company, 1993), 221. Kennan later in this passage partly acknowledged his debt to Clausewitz for this thought: "It was Clausewitz, after all, who maintained that the amount of the military effort put forward should be determined by the political, not the purely military, goals to be achieved."

12. Hans J. Morgenthau and Kenneth W. Thompson, *Politics among Nations: The Struggle for Power and Peace*, Sixth Edition (New York, NY: McGraw-Hill Publishing Company, 1985), 33.

13. Kenneth W. Thompson, "Power, Force and Diplomacy," *Review of Politics* 43, no. 3 (July 1981): 412.

14. George F. Kennan, *The Fateful Alliance: France, Russia, and the Coming of the First World War* (New York, NY: Pantheon Books, 1984), 235.

15. Kennan, *The Fateful Alliance*, 235.

16. Kennan, *The Fateful Alliance*, 248.

17. Edmund Burke, *Reflections on the Revolution in France*, Edited by J. G. A. Pocock (Indianapolis, IN: Hackett Publishing Company, 1987), 186.

18. George F. Kennan, *Memoirs, 1925–1950* (New York, NY: Pantheon Books, 1967), 310.

19. Kennan, *The Fateful Alliance*, 254.

20. Kennan, *The Fateful Alliance*, 255–256.

21. Kennan, *The Fateful Alliance*, 256.

22. George F. Kennan, *American Diplomacy*, Expanded Edition (Chicago, IL: University of Chicago Press, 1984), 89.

23. Kennan, *Realities of American Foreign Policy*, 81.

24. Kennan, "The Price We Paid for War," 54.

25. Henry A. Kissinger, *Nuclear Weapons and Foreign Policy* (New York, NY: Harper & Brothers, 1957), 140.

26. Bernard Brodie, *Strategy in the Missile Age* (Princeton, NJ: Princeton University Press, 1965), 309.

27. Kennan, *Around the Cragged Hill*, 212.

28. Clausewitz discussed his conceptualizations of limited, total, and absolute war in Book I, Chapter 1, in *On War*. In pure theory, absolute "war is an act of force, and there is no logical limit to the application of that force. Each side, therefore, compels its opponent to follow suit; a reciprocal action is started which must lead, in theory, to extremes." See page 77. Clausewitz eventually dismissed absolute war and concluded that in practice political objectives set for military operations result in wars that "can have all degrees of importance and intensity, ranging from a war of extermination down to simple armed observation." See page 81. He might have revisited the concept, however, had he lived to see the advent of nuclear weapons.

29. Kennan, *Realities of American Foreign Policy*, 23.

30. George F. Kennan, *Memoirs, 1950–1963* (New York, NY: Pantheon Books, 1972), 95.

31. Kennan, *Memoirs, 1950–1963*, 95.

32. Kennan, *American Diplomacy*, 175.

33. Kennan, *American Diplomacy*, 102.

34. Kennan, *American Diplomacy*, 175.

35. George F. Kennan, *Sketches from a Life* (New York, NY: Pantheon Books, 1989), 121.

36. David Mayers, *George Kennan and the Dilemmas of U.S. Foreign Policy* (New York, NY: Oxford University Press, 1988), 283.

37. Kennan, *Memoirs, 1925–1950*, 437.

38. "Correspondence to Dr. R. Paul Ramsey," 11 November 1959, George F. Kennan Papers, Box 31, Seeley G. Mudd Manuscript Library, Department of Rare Books and Special Collections, Princeton University Library.

39. Just war theory encompasses two sets of tests: *jus ad bellum*, or the justice of war, and *jus in bello*, or justice in war. "*Jus ad bellum* requires us to make judgments about aggression and self-defense; *jus in bello* about the observance or violation of the customary and positive rules of engagement. The two sorts of judgment are logically

independent. It is perfectly possible for a just war to be fought unjustly and for an unjust war to be fought in strict accordance with the rules." See Michael Waltzer's *Just and Unjust Wars: A Moral Argument with Historical Illustrations*, Second Edition (USA: BasicBooks, 1992), 21.

40. Kennan, *American Diplomacy*, 61.

41. Kennan, *American Diplomacy*, 62–63.

42. Kennan, *American Diplomacy*, 65–66.

43. Reinhold Niebuhr, *The Structure of Nations and Empires* (New York, NY: Charles Scribner's Sons, 1959), 197.

44. Herbert Butterfield, *International Conflict in the Twentieth Century: A Christian View* (Westport, CT: Greenwood Press, 1960), 114.

45. Kennan, *Memoirs, 1925–1950*, 437.

46. Kennan, *Memoirs, 1950–1963*, 23.

47. Kennan, *Memoirs, 1950–1963*, 23.

48. Kennan, *Memoirs, 1950–1963*, 24.

49. Kennan, *Memoirs, 1950–1963*, 93.

50. Kennan, *Memoirs, 1950–1963*, 38.

51. Kennan, *Memoirs, 1950–1963*, 38.

52. Kennan, *Memoirs, 1950–1963*, 38.

53. Kennan, *Memoirs, 1950–1963*, 48.

54. Kennan, *Memoirs, 1925–1950*, 497.

55. Kennan, *Memoirs, 1925–1950*, 497.

56. "Testimony of George Kennan on American Foreign Policy," Hearing before the Committee on Foreign Relations, United States Senate, Eighty-ninth Congress, Second Session, 10 February 1966, *Congressional Record*, Volume 112, Part 3, 2984.

57. Bernard Brodie, *War and Politics* (New York, NY: Macmillan Publishing Company, 1973), 159.

58. "Correspondence to Emmet John Hughes," 31 May 1966, George F. Kennan Papers, Box 31, Seeley G. Mudd Manuscript Library, Department of Rare Books and Special Collections, Princeton University Library.

59. "Testimony of George Kennan on American Foreign Policy," 2984.

60. Kennan, *Memoirs, 1925–1950*, 464–465.

61. George F. Kennan, *From Prague after Munich: Diplomatic Papers, 1938–1940* (Princeton, NJ: Princeton University Press, 1968), 170–171. Kennan's primary reason for publishing these diplomatic papers was to help "illustrate for a modern public both the hideousness and the futility of the effort by one people to dominate another one, and to ride roughshod over its national feelings, in the circumstances of the modern age." See page viii.

62. Kennan, *Memoirs, 1925–1950*, 129–130.

63. George F. Kennan, "Europe's Problems, Europe's Choices," *Foreign Policy* 14 (Spring 1974): 13.

64. Kennan, *The Nuclear Delusion*, xiv.

65. George F. Kennan, "International Control of Atomic Energy," in *Foreign Relations of the United States 1950*, Volume I (Washington, DC: U.S. Government Printing Office, 1977), 29. Kennan wrote this policy paper in January 1950 for Secretary of State Dean Acheson and later characterized it as "the most important paper, in its implications, that I ever wrote; and the thoughts it set forth have been basic to my attitude towards the nuclear weapons problem ever since." See Kennan's *The Nuclear*

Delusion, xvi.

66. Kennan, *Russia, the Atom and the West*, 54.

67. "Correspondence to Louis J. Halle," 20 April 1966, George F. Kennan Papers, Box 31, Seeley G. Mudd Manuscript Library, Department of Rare Books and Special Collections, Princeton University Library.

68. Bernard Brodie, "Implications for Military Policy," in Bernard Brodie (ed.), *The Absolute Weapon: Atomic Power and World Order* (New York, NY: Harcourt, Brace and Company, 1946), 76.

69. Hans J. Morgenthau, *Politics in the Twentieth Century*, Abridged Edition (Chicago, IL: University of Chicago Press, 1971), 100.

70. Henry A. Kissinger, "Force and Diplomacy in the Nuclear Age," *Foreign Affairs* 34, no. 3 (April 1956): 350. Interestingly, Kennan privately wrote to Kissinger, "In general, I can only say 'three cheers' to your article." "Correspondence to Kissinger," 10 April 1956, George F. Kennan Papers, Seeley G. Mudd Manuscript Library, Department of Rare Books and Special Collections, Princeton University Library. Although Kennan's correspondence with Kissinger indicates that he considered the latter's intellectual endeavor laudable, Kennan was not sanguine about the prospects for the limitation of war after the nuclear threshold had been crossed in combat.

71. Kissinger, *Nuclear Weapons and Foreign Policy*, 90.

72. McGeorge Bundy, George F. Kennan, Robert S. McNamara, and Gerard Smith, "Nuclear Weapons and the Atlantic Alliance," *Foreign Affairs* 60, no. 4 (Spring 1982): 757.

73. Bundy et al., "Nuclear Weapons and the Atlantic Alliance," 760–761.

74. McGeorge Bundy, Morton H. Haperin, William W. Kaufmann, George F. Kennan, Robert S. McNamara, Madalene O'Donnell, Leon V. Sigal, Gerard C. Smith, Richard H. Ullman, and Paul C. Warnke, "Back from the Brink," *Atlantic* 258, no. 2 (August 1986): 37.

75. George F. Kennan, "A Proposal for Western Survival," *The New Leader*, 16 November 1959, 14.

76. Kennan, *Memoirs, 1950–1963*, 95.

77. Kennan, *Memoirs, 1950–1963*, 95–96.

78. Kennan, "The Price We Paid for War," 53–54.

79. Kennan, "The Price We Paid for War," 54.

80. "Correspondence to Arnold Toynbee," 7 April 1952, George F. Kennan Papers, Box 29, Seeley G. Mudd Manuscript Library, Department of Rare Books and Special Collections, Princeton University Library.

81. Kennan, *The Nuclear Delusion*, xxix.

82. George F. Kennan, "Somalia, Through a Glass Darkly," *New York Times*, 30 September 1993, A25.

83. Kennan, *Around the Cragged Hill*, 146.

84. George F. Kennan, "The Balkan Crisis: 1913 and 1993," *New York Review of Books*, 15 July 1993, 6.

85. Kennan, "The Balkan Crisis," 6–7.

86. Kennan, "The Balkan Crisis," 7.

87. George F. Kennan, "On American Principles," *Foreign Affairs* 74, no. 2 (March/April 1995): 125–126.

88. George F. Kennan, "The Communist World in 1967," *Hearing before the Committee on Foreign Relations*, United States Senate, Ninetieth Congress, First Session, 30 January 1967 (Washington, DC: U.S. Government Printing Office, 1967), 56.

89. Kennan, *Realities of American Foreign Policy*, 60.

7

MAJOR POWER RIVALRY: THE AMERICAN-SOVIET SECURITY DILEMMA

The relationships between major powers have enormous impact on the stability of the international system. The importance that Kennan attached to the relationships between major powers has been alluded to in the discussions of the balance of power, diplomacy—particularly in regard to international law and institutions—and war. A closer look at the dynamics at play in relations between major powers competing for power in the international arena is in order. Most of Kennan's career—both as a diplomat and as a scholar—was devoted to the study of the American-Soviet relationship in the Cold War. It is in the American-Soviet context that many of the principles in Kennan's thought were used to inform his policy recommendations. As we will see, Kennan's political theory, geopolitical thought, and principles of diplomacy and war were all brought to bear in his analysis of the American-Soviet relationship.

A review of Kennan's writings on the Cold War reveals a pronounced concern over heightened tensions, or the "security dilemma," in the American-Soviet relationship. The pursuit of power by rival nation-states causes a spiral of insecurity referred to in international relations theory literature as the security dilemma. Statesmen are aware of the high costs of miscalculation and try to hedge their bets and overcompensate for potential shortcomings in their power, according to Hans Morgenthau and Kenneth Thompson. A nation will "try to have at least a margin of safety which will allow it to make erroneous calculations and still maintain the balance of power."[1] That margin of power, in turn, causes a rival nation-state to be insecure and leads it to seek its own margin of power, thereby creating a spiral of escalating tension in the relationship. Although Kennan never explicitly articulated and treated the security dilemma concept to the extent that Morgenthau and Thompson had, a concern for the dynamics of the security dilemma is a thread that implicitly runs through Kennan's analysis of American-Soviet relations. Kennan was acutely concerned that the security dilemma would propel the Cold War rivals down the path toward war. As Robert Jervis remarked, "the security dilemma can not only create conflicts and tensions but also provide the dynamics triggering war."[2]

Although there is no escape from the dynamics of the security dilemma, wise statesmanship can ease its effects and keep international rivalries within bounds short of war. In Morgenthau's view, what a statesman needs is the ability to see clearly "himself, the enemy, and then himself again as the enemy sees him. To see clearly means to see without passions, without the passion of pride, of hatred, and of contempt. The statesman must master the paradox of wanting passionately to win over the enemy to whom he feels passionately superior, and of having to view his relations with the enemy with the detachment and objectivity of the scholar."[3] To a remarkable degree, Kennan's analysis of the Soviet-American relationship achieved these qualities.

This chapter explores the security dilemma in the American-Soviet relationship during the Cold War as viewed through Kennan's eyes. It initially discusses the factors that Kennan believed were the most significant in the formulation of Soviet foreign policy and his understanding of the role of Soviet ideology and Russian national interest in foreign policy decision making as well as strengths and weaknesses of the Soviet state. An appreciation of Soviet power and its limits allowed Kennan initially to take a confident view of the West's ability to meet the Soviet challenge—a view that eventually led, in part, to his departure from government service. This chapter then looks at Kennan's recommendations for American foreign policy, from the Truman to the Reagan administrations, which flowed from his view of the Soviet Union and his desire to ameliorate the security dilemma between the superpowers. It concludes with an assessment—with the advantage of twenty-twenty hindsight—of Kennan's analysis of the Cold War Soviet-American relationship.

SOVIET IDEOLOGY AND RUSSIAN NATIONAL INTEREST

The sophisticated understanding of the Soviet Union that enabled Kennan to view the American-Soviet relationship from a detached perspective was developed and nurtured over a period of years. As Martin Wight related, "Kennan stands out in the public life of the West as a foreign policy publicist who was most scrupulous and respectful in considering the interests of Russia. He tried to see each situation through Soviet eyes, condemning and discarding elements of doctrinal imperialism, and isolating and emphasizing a core of

Soviet national interest which he urged the United States to respect."[4] Kennan wrote preliminary papers to sort out his own thinking on Soviet foreign policy long before he drafted the Long Telegram cable from his Moscow post, the message that propelled him to stature within government.[5] These studies, in turn, were the basis for his *Foreign Affairs* X article, which elevated him to public fame. Henry Kissinger opined that "Of the thousands of articles written since the end of the Second World War, Kennan's 'The Sources of Soviet Conduct' stands in a class by itself. In this lucidly written, passionately argued literary adaptation of his 'Long Telegram,' Kennan raised the Soviet challenge to the level of philosophy of history."[6] These works collectively were the foundation for Kennan's subsequent analysis of Soviet foreign policy.

Soviet foreign policy was derived from a mix of Marxist-Leninist ideology and Russian national interests. Kennan argued that Soviet policy "is the product of ideology and circumstances: ideology inherited by the present Soviet leaders from the movement in which they had their political origin, and circumstances of the power which they now have exercised for nearly three decades in Russia."[7] The task for American statesmen was to "try to trace the interaction of these two forces and the relative role of each in the determination of official Soviet conduct" in order to effectively counter Soviet moves.[8]

Marxism significantly colored the worldview of leaders in the Kremlin. Kennan warned that the view that dismissed Soviet ideology as "mere window dressing" and ignored its "political content and implications" was dangerously inaccurate.[9] He believed, however, that "the role of ideology in Soviet political psychology, while of tremendous importance, is not primarily that of a basic determinant of political action. It is rather a prism through which Soviet eyes must view the world, and an indispensable vehicle for the translation into words and actions of impulses and aspirations which have their origin deeper still. It colors what the Russians see and what they do."[10] Kennan judged that this ideological prism led Soviet leaders to think that "the capitalist powers, and above all the United States, will eventually be inclined to seek a war with the Soviet Union as a way out of the political frustrations and difficulties to which capitalism is supposed to be subjected in ever-increasing degree."[11]

Soviet leaders exaggerated the threat posed by Western powers as a political expedient to aid in their internal struggle for power. From Kennan's perspective, "circumstances of the immediate post-revolution period—the existence in Russia of civil war and foreign intervention, together with the obvious fact that the Communists represented only a tiny minority of the Russian people—made the establishment of dictatorial power a necessity."[12] To consolidate control internally, the Soviet regime used the fear of external threats to justify dictatorship. Kennan wrote that "since capitalism no longer existed in Russia and since it could not be admitted that there could be serious or widespread opposition to the Kremlin springing spontaneously from the liberated masses under its authority, it became necessary to justify the retention of the dictatorship by stressing the menace of capitalism abroad."[13]

Ideology coupled with the internal power struggle caused Soviet leaders to have a distorted view of the world. "The Soviet concept of power, which permits no focal points of organization outside the Party itself, requires that the Party leadership remain in theory the sole repository of truth. For if truth were to be found elsewhere, there would be justification for its expression in organized activity. But it is precisely that which the Kremlin cannot and will not permit."[14] Consequently, the "Soviet diplomatic representative or journalist abroad has no choice but to cast his analytical report in the terms of Marxist-Leninist ideology whether this is applicable or not in the given instance. In this way the Soviet leaders find themselves committed to a badly distorted image of the outside world."[15] Kennan maintained in 1967 that it would be long before "the image of the Western world that projects itself onto the Russian-Communist vision will be devoid of some measure of distortion through the prism of Marxist assumptions."[16]

Marxism was grafted onto Russia's political, historical, and cultural heritage. Indeed, the advent of Marxism was fueled by Russian history: "It was no coincidence that Marxism, which had smoldered ineffectively for half a century in Western Europe, caught hold and blazed for the first time in Russia. Only in this land which had never known a friendly neighbor or indeed any tolerant equilibrium of separate powers, either internal or international, could a doctrine thrive which viewed economic conflicts of society as insoluble by peaceful means."[17] Kennan observed that "Many of the characteristic features of Soviet attitudes (the strong instinct for orthodoxy, the claim to political infallibility and to a monopoly of ideological or religious truth, messianic dreams of world ascendancy, an exaggerated sense of prestige, a morbid suspiciousness toward outside powers, a determination to isolate the Russian people from contacts with the West, etc.) were characteristic features of pre-Petrine Russia."[18] He noted that in 1839, the Marquis de Custine had observed these same Russian tendencies of "the disrespect for the truth, the deliberate mystification, the studied silence," which reflected "awareness of backwardness, a distrust of one's own people, a shame for the tyranny one dared not live without—qualities that made Russians quail at the thought of any free and true comparison with Western conditions."[19]

Traditional national interests—which are primarily derived from a nation-state's geopolitical circumstances and remain constant regardless of the nature of the regime in power—and Marxism blended to form the signposts for Soviet foreign policy.

At bottom of [the] Kremlin's neurotic view of world affairs is [the] traditional and instinctive Russian sense of insecurity. Originally, this was insecurity of a peaceful agricultural people trying to live on vast exposed plain in a neighborhood of fierce nomadic peoples. To this was added, as Russia came into contact with economically advanced West, fear of more competent, more powerful, more highly organized societies in that area. But this latter type of insecurity was one which afflicted rather Russian rulers than Russian people; for Russian rulers have invariably sensed that their rule was relatively archaic in form, fragile and artificial in its psychological foundation, unable to stand comparison or contact with political systems of Western countries.[20]

Soviet policy in many respects paralleled that which Russia pursued under the tsars. Kennan consciously drew historical parallels between communist and aristocratic Russia: "The Soviet state has now repeated in the brief space of two decades much of the history of Tsardom in its last two centuries. Stalin in the first ten years of his rule relived the era of Peter the Great. The outbreak of the war in Europe found him already enjoying Russian power in the grand manner of Catherine II. The end of the war finds him in a position strikingly similar to that of Alexander I at the close of the Napoleonic era. And the shades of Nicholas I are already present in the growing ponderousness and inelasticity of Russian police power, in many of the aims and methods of Russian policy."[21] The Soviet regime represented a "police regime par excellence, reared in the dim half world of Tsarist police intrigue, accustomed to think primarily in terms of police power."[22]

THE LIMITS OF SOVIET POWER

Kennan combined his assessment of the interplay between ideology and national interest in Soviet foreign policy with a keen appreciation of both the strengths and weaknesses of the Soviet state. Kennan's assessment of Soviet power was more tempered than that held by many of his contemporaries. The assessment was the baseline from which Kennan made his recommendations for prudent American foreign policies to meet the Soviet challenge and to dampen the destabilizing effects of the security dilemma in the American-Soviet relationship.

The Soviet Union of course was a major world power. Kennan wrote in admiration that the Soviet regime possessed the "energies of one of world's greatest peoples and resources of world's richest national territory, and is borne along by deep and powerful currents of Russian nationalism."[23] These qualities had been strengthened in the aftermath of World War II. "Prior to 1939 the military strength of Russia, while formidable in certain areas and for certain purposes, was not of such a nature that it appeared as any great immediate threat to the security of central and western Europe."[24] Its growth in power was due to Soviet "control of the physical and technical and manpower resources of the Baltic states, of eastern Germany, and of the satellite countries of eastern Europe."[25] The strength of the Soviet Union in the world balance of power also was a function of the prostration of Germany and Japan after World War II.[26]

Despite these strengths, Kennan identified economic, political, societal, and military shortcomings that limited the power of the Soviet Union in international politics and called into question its long-term viability. Kennan prophetically hypothesized in 1947 that "the possibility remains (and in the opinion of this writer it is a strong one) that Soviet power, like the capitalist world of its conception, bears within it the seeds of its own decay, and that the sprouting of these seeds is well advanced."[27]   Kennan's speculation was not to come to fruition until some forty years later, with the dissolution of the Soviet Union.

The Soviet Union was economically backward. In the wake of the Second World War, the country had a primitive road and rail infrastructure, and its labor force had nothing like the "general culture of production and technical self-respect which characterizes the skilled worker of the west."[28]   Kennan predicted in 1947 that "Russia will remain economically a vulnerable, and in a certain sense an impotent, nation, capable of exporting its enthusiasms and of radiating the strange charm of its primitive political vitality but unable to back up those articles of export by the real evidences of material power and prosperity."[29]

The Communist Party, the center for foreign policy deliberations, contained potential fissures. Kennan speculated that "if disunity were ever to seize and paralyze the Party, the chaos and weakness of Russian society would be revealed in forms beyond description. For we have seen that Soviet power is only a crust concealing an amorphous mass of human beings among whom no independent organizational structure is tolerated," and if "anything were ever to occur to disrupt the unity and efficacy of the Party as a political instrument, Soviet Russia might be changed overnight from one of the strongest to one of the weakest and most pitiable of national societies."[30]   Events in Chechnya in the 1990s were dramatic evidence of the deterioration of the Russian state after the collapse of the Communist Party.

Many in the West were alarmed at the size of the Soviet military in the aftermath of World War II, but Kennan saw historical reasons for the Soviet retention of a large force structure. He observed that "Soviet naval and air forces were regarded at the end of the war as so inferior to the comparable Western contingents that no policy was conceivable in Moscow except one of the most vigorous continued expansion of these arms. As for the rest—the maintenance in peacetime of ground forces of forbidding and, to all outward appearances, quite excessive strength was traditional not only to the Soviet government but to the Russian governments generally."[31]   The Soviets sought to use numerical advantages to compensate for technological inferiorities, while traditional Russian concern over internal security also contributed to the Soviet need for large ground forces. "Russian political leaders have usually operated against a background of uncertainty and anxiety with respect to domestic political and economic conditions which heightened their congenital sense of insecurity and caused them to wish for a larger margin of numerical safety in armed strength than would be thought necessary elsewhere. The maintenance of land armies in Russia has generally been cheap financially, and has had certain domestic political advantages insofar as it kept a good portion of the young male population in a regimented and controlled status."[32]

The principal foreign policy role for the large Soviet military was political intimidation. The Soviets, in other words, appeared to have a firmer grasp of

Clausewitz's wisdom of using military means to achieve political objectives than the West. Kennan judged that "Soviet leaders, interested in extending their real power by measures short of general war, have not been oblivious to the possibilities of such things as threats and intimidation—the possibilities of the use of the shadow of armed strength rather than its substance—as a means of influencing the political behavior of peoples elsewhere."[33] Kennan stressed that Soviet leaders wanted to avoid general war with the West and "to conduct the attack on the capitalist world in a much more cautious manner, representing what Lenin termed a 'state of partial war,' and involving the elastic and opportunistic use of a wide variety of tactics including outstandingly such things as deception, concealed penetration and subversion, psychological warfare, and above all the adroit exploitation of every conceivable form of division in capitalist society, whether on the international scale or within the domestic framework of capitalist states."[34]

Most observers in the West during the Cold War did not share Kennan's subtle analysis of the origins of the Soviet military. Consequently, the massive Soviet army was a major source of insecurity that compelled Western states to devote substantial resources to military defenses to counter the perceived threat. These factors set the security dilemma in motion in the American-Soviet relationship.

THE CHALLENGE FOR AMERICAN STATESMEN

Setting aside for the moment the reasons behind the massive Soviet military, there was no denying that the Soviet Union posed a formidable challenge to the West. Kennan viewed this challenge primarily as political and placed secondary emphasis on the military threat. In his words, the United States and its allies faced "a political force committed fanatically to the belief that with us there can be no permanent *modus vivendi,* that it is desirable and necessary that the internal harmony of our society be disrupted, our traditional way of life be destroyed, the international authority of our state be broken, if Soviet power is to be secure."[35] Soviet policy consisted "primarily of a determination to exploit every element of disunity, of confusion, of short-sightedness in our society, with a view to causing us to eliminate ourselves as rivals to Soviet power and influence everywhere."[36]

The primary thrust of Soviet foreign policy was in Europe. Kennan argued that Soviet expansionist efforts after World War II concentrated on Europe, where there "was a greater economic and military potential" than in Asia "and greater danger of the resurgence of forces capable of reacting against Soviet pressure if they were not immediately crushed. Europe was the greater prize if won, and the more serious loss if not."[37] He told a National War College audience in 1947 that the aim of Soviet leaders was "to reduce rival power everywhere and to make the Kremlin the most powerful force militarily and politically in the world. Being landpower-minded, the men in the Kremlin are most immediately concerned with breaking up all other serious concentrations of power on the Eurasian land mass and gaining dominant influence over the governments of that territory. Their policies in other continents outside of Eurasia are basically subordinate to that aim at this time."[38]

What were the implications of Kennan's assessment of Soviet power and interests for American foreign policy? Above all, Kennan viewed the Soviet-American rivalry as a test of the latter's strength. He wrote that "Much depends on the health and vigor of our own society. World communism is like a malignant parasite which feeds only on diseased tissue. This is the point at which domestic and foreign policies meet. Every courageous and incisive measure to solve internal problems of our own society, to improve self-confidence, discipline, morale and community spirit of our own people, is a diplomatic victory over Moscow worth a thousand diplomatic notes and joint communiques."[39] Kennan cautioned that "the greatest danger that can befall us in coping with this problem of Soviet communism, is that we shall allow ourselves to become like those with whom we are coping."[40] He confidently assessed that "To avoid destruction the United States need only measure up to its own best traditions and prove itself worthy of preservation as a great nation."[41] Kennan, therefore, viewed United State domestic prosperity as the key to the international struggle for power with the Soviet Union. The deterioration of our own society would cause a loss of American power relative to that of the Soviet Union. Conversely, the nurturing of American society would increase our power and ability to withstand Soviet political pressure while systemic Soviet internal deficiencies eroded Moscow's power and ability to project influence abroad, particularly in Europe.

The West needed to marshal sufficient military strength and patient political will to mount a long-term effort to contain the political expansion of Soviet power. Kennan argued that the "main element of any United States policy toward the Soviet Union must be that of a long-term, patient but firm and vigilant containment of Russian expansive tendencies."[42] Kennan—in probably the most controversial sentence he ever wrote—stated that "Soviet pressure against the free institutions of the western world is something that can be contained by the adroit and vigilant application of counter-force at a series of constantly shifting geographical and political points, corresponding to the shifts and maneuvers of Soviet policy, but which cannot be charmed or talked out of existence."[43] He was confident of the West's ability to meet this challenge because the Soviet Union was "by far the weaker party," which should have given the United States "reasonable confidence" that a "policy of firm containment, designed to confront the Russians with unalterable counter-force at every point where they show signs of encroaching upon the interests of a peaceful and stable world" would be successful.[44] A long-term Western strategy of containment, in Kennan's view, would either moderate Soviet policy or contribute to the demise of the Soviet Union. Kennan suggested that "the United States has it in its power to increase enormously the strains under which Soviet policy must operate, to force upon the Kremlin a far greater degree of moderation and circumspection than it has had to observe in recent years, and in this way to promote tendencies which must eventually find their outlet in either the break-up or the gradual mellowing of Soviet power."[45] Few observers were willing at the birth of the Cold War to share Kennan's bold hypothesis.

Kennan's use of the term "counter-force" and his reference to "constantly shifting geographical and political points" evoked strong criticism. Kennan's most vocal critic, columnist Walter Lippmann, argued that Kennan advocated the use of force to stop the expansion of Soviet power even in areas of the world of no strategic consequence to the United States, a position that would have failed to recognize the limits of American power. Kennan wrote in a letter to Lippmann to refute the latter's criticisms that "I am a little nonplussed to find myself sternly rebuked as the author of the 'Truman doctrine' and confronted with the Marshall Plan as an example of constructive statesmanship from which I might derive a useful lesson and improve my ways."[46]

The wording of the X article was ambiguous and subject to misinterpretation, but Kennan's remarks at the National War College at roughly the same time indicate that he opposed the indiscriminate and global commitments of American resources implied in the Truman Doctrine. Before that forum, Kennan commented that there was "a great difference in the danger of communism in areas which are contiguous to Soviet military power and the danger of communism in areas remote from it, as for example, in South America. There is a difference in the danger of communism in highly strategic areas such as Greece or Austria or Germany—where a communist victory might have very, very serious results for us and for our allies—and a communist victory in other places where it is not apt to have those results."[47] Kennan's remarks here clearly show that what he had in mind was a policy of challenging Soviet power in those areas that he believed were strategically important to the United States, not a global containment strategy that would have committed the United States to intervene anywhere the Soviets were poised to gain a foothold—whether political, military, or economic—regardless of a country's geopolitical significance to the United States.

Kennan was critical of the Truman Doctrine because of its failure to equate means and ends in foreign policy. He implicitly criticized the doctrine at one of his National War College lectures when he suggested that "we may have undertaken too much; there may be a serious gap in peacetime policy between the things we have set out to do and our capabilities for doing them."[48] Kennan wrote years later that he objected to the Truman Doctrine because it "placed our aid to Greece in the framework of a universal policy rather than in that of a specific decision addressed to a specific set of circumstances. It implied that what we had decided to do in the case of Greece was something we would be prepared to do in the case of any other country, provided only that it was faced with the threat of 'subjugation by armed minorities or by outside pressure.'"[49] In contrast, the Marshall Plan was consistent with Kennan's recognition of the need to equate ends and means in foreign policy to protect Western Europe from Soviet domination. He believed, moreover, that the Marshall Plan in 1947 frustrated any Soviet ambitions for the political takeover of Western Europe.[50]

MILITARIZATION OF AMERICAN-SOVIET RELATIONS

Kennan's confidence in the West's ability to manage the Cold War superpower rivalry waned from the 1950s through the 1980s. He increasingly believed during the course of this period that the American-Soviet rivalry had been transformed from a political into a military contest that ran a high risk of leading to armed conflict. Kennan wanted American foreign policy crafted in such a way as to avoid exaggeration that could unnecessarily contribute to the spiral of tension in the relationship. Such a nuanced foreign policy was a tightrope for policy makers to walk, as many American domestic voices preferred to cast the American-Soviet relationship in stark terms.

Kennan implicitly traced the security dilemma at play in the policies that littered the Cold War landscape. He wrote from a vantage point in 1976 that the course of Soviet-American relations "was determined by a series of spontaneous misinterpretations and misread signals which would have been comical had it not been so dangerous. The Marshall Plan, the preparations for the setting up of a West German government, and the first moves toward the establishment of NATO, were taken in Moscow as the beginnings of a campaign to deprive the Soviet Union of the fruits of its victory over Germany."[51] On the other hand,

The Soviet crackdown on Czechoslovakia and the mounting of the Berlin blockade, both essentially defensive (and partially predictable) reactions to these Western moves, were then similarly misread on the Western side. Shortly thereafter there came the crisis of the Korean War, where the Soviet attempt to employ a satellite military force in civil combat to its own advantage, by way of reaction to the American decision to establish a permanent military presence in Japan, was read in Washington as the beginning of the final Soviet push for world conquest; whereas the active American military response, provoked by this Soviet move, appeared in Moscow (and not entirely without reason) as a threat to the Soviet position in both Manchuria and in eastern Siberia."[52]

As Kennan saw the relationship, it moved "tragically and unnecessarily, into the respective misinterpretations of such later events as the bringing of the Germans into NATO, the launching of the first Sputnik, the decision to introduce nuclear weapons into the continental components of NATO, the second and prolonged Berlin crisis provoked by Khrushchev in the late fifties and early sixties, and finally the Cuban missile crisis. Each misreading set the stage for the next one. And with each of them, the grip of military rivalry on the minds of policy makers on both sides was tightened and made more formal."[53] These quotes capture the remarkable ability Kennan possessed to see the dynamics at work in the American-Soviet competition from the perspectives of statesmen both in Washington and in Moscow.

The Korean War was a watershed event in the Cold War, and it shifted the focus in Washington from political and economic measures to military means as the primarily policy tools of the containment strategy. The United States misread North Korea's invasion of the South Korea as an opening Soviet-sponsored military bid against the West. "The attack in Korea, even though Soviet troops were not involved, was viewed as another 'Austria'—as the first move in a supposed 'grand design' of world conquest."[54] Kennan complained that American policy makers "could not free themselves from the image of Hitler and his timetables. They viewed Soviet leaders as absorbed with the pursuit of something called a 'grand design'—a design for the early destruction of American power and for world conquest."[55] The Korean conflict spurred the United States to adopt a policy document entitled "United States Objectives and Programs for National Security" (NSC 68) to guide the policy of containment. NSC 68 defined the American-Soviet competition primarily in military rather than political terms. As Wilson Miscamble observed, the "adoption of the more militarily oriented approach of NSC 68 marked a firm rejection of the geopolitical views" of Kennan.[56] The Korean conflict raised the specter of miscalculation, which could have brought the superpowers into direct conflict.

Worst-case analysis for military contingencies contributed to the deterioration of American-Soviet political relations and risked becoming a self-fulfilling prophecy. Kennan warned that "History shows that belief in the inevitability of war with a given power affects behavior in such a way as to cripple all constructive policy approaches towards that power, leaves the field open for military compulsions, and thus easily takes on the character of a self-fulfilling prophecy."[57] Kennan's historical research reinforced his view that worst-case scenarios could contribute to conflict. Bismarck late in his career had to fight "the tendency of the German military leaders, and many senior political officials in his country, to regard a German-Russian war as inevitable just because the elaborate preparations of the military establishments on both sides of the line made it appear so. In vain, he pleaded with people to understand that Germany had no objectives with regard to Russia that were worth the sacrifices of a war—that war would bring disaster to both parties—such disaster that at the end of it people would no longer even remember the relatively trivial bones of contention out of which it had arisen."[58]

On the other side of the coin, Kennan also faulted the Soviets for their imprudent behavior—particularly in the Korean War—which heightened Western insecurity and fueled the Soviet-American security dilemma. "Soviet leaders seem either unwilling or unable to take any proper account of the true measure of the shock wrought to the Western pubic by their exploitation, for purposes of political aggrandizement, of their military position in Eastern and Central Europe in the period 1945-1948; by their failure to match the demobilization of the Western armies; by the political attack launched by the Communists in

Western Europe in the years 1947 and 1948; by the imposition of the Berlin blockade, and above all by the launching of the Korean War."[59]

The Korean conflict increased fears of Soviet military ambitions in Europe, the main theater of Cold War competition. NATO, the birth of which in part reflected the alarm caused by the Korean conflict, was riddled with shortcomings from Kennan's point of view. Although he accepted the need for a robust conventional defense capability of Western Europe to redress European insecurities due to the Soviet military posture, he wanted the alliance cast in a different light. Kennan argued that "we should try to portray our military preparations as prudent minimal responses to the *political* threat posed by the power and attitudes of the Soviet leaders—not as responses to an alleged or implied Soviet intention to attack the West, and not as reflections of a conclusion on our part that the only possible outcome of our political differences with the Russians was a major war."[60] Second, he argued that "we should attempt to establish a proper balance in our policy between political and military considerations and should not let the prospects for the preservation of peace be diminished by pursuit of the ideal military posture in an imaginary and not inevitable war."[61] He was aware "that many of the military measures on our part that disturbed me were viewed by their authors as defensive in inspiration. But any given pattern of military preparations was always bound, I pointed out, to appear to others as the reflection of a given pattern of calculations and intentions."[62] Kennan clearly worried that the formation of NATO constituted a step up on the security dilemma ladder.

The establishment of NATO and the subsequent formation of the Warsaw Pact polarized Europe into two competing power blocs. Kennan feared that the standoff between opposing military forces standing "eyeball to eyeball" at the heart of Europe was a quick fuse that could ignite a major armed conflict. He wanted both alliances to withdraw forces from Europe to ease tension in the superpower military rivalry as well as to allow the states of Europe more autonomy from the great powers. In the late 1950s, Kennan proposed the "disengagement" of American and Soviet forces from the heart of Europe to defuse the military standoff created by the opposing alliances. He argued that it was "far more desirable in principle to get the Soviet forces out of Central and Eastern Europe than to cultivate a new German army for the purpose of opposing them while they remain there."[63] In Kennan's view, a more stable European future rested in the "possibility of separating geographically the forces of the great nuclear powers, of excluding them as direct factors in the future development of political relationships on the Continent, and of inducing the continental peoples, by the same token, to accept a higher level of responsibility for the defense of the Continent than they have recently borne."[64]

Kennan's proposals were too late to be practical. Soviet forces had already created "facts on the ground" in Central and Eastern Europe, and Stalin probably would have been unwilling to relinquish direct control there with a negotiated withdrawal. Secretary of State Dean Acheson sharply rebuked

Kennan's plan and argued that "there is no precedent in history for, or does there seem to me to be any possibility of, the successful insulation of a large and vital country situated, as Germany is, between two power systems and with ambitions and purposes of its own."[65] Moreover, Acheson argued that "there would be no Power in Europe capable of opposing Russian will after the departure of the United States from the Continent and the acceptance of a broad missile-free area. Then, it would not be long, I fear, before there would be an accommodation of some sort or another between an abandoned Germany and the great Power to the East."[66] Kennan's proposed disengagement also favored the Soviets in that they could more readily redeploy forces into Eastern and Central Europe after a withdrawal than the United States could across the Atlantic.

Kennan eventually came to denounce the policy of containment that he is credited to have fathered. The policy had by the late 1970s outlived its usefulness, in his view. "The world communist movement, once a monolithically controlled instrument of Stalinist power, is now widely fragmented; only a portion of it retains a relationship to Moscow which could cause it to serve as a vehicle for Russian policies . . . the highest priority in Soviet policy appears to be given today to the effort to resist encroachments by the Chinese on Soviet influence among radical-socialist and 'anti-imperialist' movements across the world--an undertaking which does not greatly concern the United States and does not represent a field of conflict in Soviet-American relations."[67] To Kennan's dismay, however, Washington and the American public had accepted the policy of containment as the guiding foreign policy framework beyond the circumstances of its origin. Louis Halle noted the irony of this turn of events: "His vision had, inevitably, to be reduced to the level of the common mind in the great bureaucracy and, beyond it, in the nation at large."[68]

In the absence of major political disputes between the United States and the Soviet Union, the continuation of the Cold War was largely a manifestation of inertia. Kennan in 1972 remarked that "today the military rivalry, in naval power as in nuclear weaponry, is simply riding along on its own momentum, like an object in space. It has no foundation in real interests—no foundation, in fact, but in fear, and in an essentially irrational fear at that. It is carried not by any reason to believe that the other side *would*, but only by an hypnotic fascination with the fact that it *could*. It is simply an institutionalized force of habit."[69] Kennan saw no major conflict of real interests between the Cold War powers that could justify war. He judged that there were "no political issues between the Soviet Union and the United States which could conceivably be susceptible of solution by war, even if the state of weaponry had not made any major military conflict between the two powers unthinkable. And this being the case, the weapons race—a race which, admittedly, is not confined just to nuclear weapons alone—has to be regarded as essentially devoid of political justification."[70]

Although Kennan favored an easing of tensions in the American-Soviet relationship, he had reservations about the policy of detente initiated in the

Nixon administration. "The idea that there was some sort of sharp change in policy and in the relationship between the U.S. and the Soviet Union in the early 1970's was a myth propagated by the Nixon administration for its own internal-political purposes, eagerly supported and inflated by the Western press—or large parts of it, and happily sustained by the Soviet government—once again, for purposes of its own."[71] Kennan observed that "there was never any general agreement envisaging a basic change in relations" and that the Soviets never encouraged "us to believe that 'detente' would mean the end of their efforts to promote the success of left-wing forces in the Third World; on the contrary, they reminded us a hundred times, if they did so once, that 'detente' did not apply in the ideological field."[72] Moscow wanted good relations with the West but was afraid to lose its ideological credentials in its rivalry with China. Consequently, what the Soviets understood by the concept of detente was a "relaxation of tensions and greater collaboration on the *bilateral* plane, while insisting on the right to behave like a traditional communist power in their relations with third countries and areas."[73]

Soviet meddling in the Third World, for the most part, was peripheral to core American national interests. Kennan viewed Soviet policy in the Third World, such as in Angola and Ethiopia, more as an irritant than a threat to the United States: "these places are mostly remote from our own defensive interests," and they "will do lip service to a political affinity with Moscow precisely as long as it suits their interest to do it and not a moment longer. Where the Russians acquire bases or other substantial military facilities, this has, of course, greater military significance."[74] Kennan consistently maintained throughout the Cold War that the primary interest of the United States was to ensure that none of the world's major industrial-military centers fell under Soviet domination. Countries such as Vietnam, Angola, and Ethiopia were located outside these vital regions and consequently should not have required significant commitments of American assistance to fight internal wars against Soviet-backed forces. American-Soviet relations took a downturn late in the Nixon administration. The Nixon administration, having oversold its ability to influence Soviet foreign policy and being plagued by Soviet activity in the Third World, could not maintain domestic support for the policy of detente.

The Carter administration's policy of normalized relations with the Soviet Union was shattered by the Soviet invasion of Afghanistan. Kennan, for his part, viewed Afghanistan as part of the Soviet's sphere of influence and the military action as consistent with the Soviet Union's need to maintain security along its borders. He did not view the Soviet action as an opening military bid for access to the warm-water ports of the Persian Gulf. Kennan actually saw the Soviet military move as evidence that a younger, more aggressive Soviet leadership was assuming the reins of power in Moscow, because it was not consistent with the conservative behavior of older Soviet statesmen such as Brezhnev and Gromyko.[75] The old Soviet guard, however, had indeed orchestrated the invasion. Kennan's flawed analysis showed a weak spot in his ability to gauge Soviet intentions and gave weight to his critics, who argued that the United States—without a means to confidently divine Soviet intentions—needed to closely watch Soviet military capabilities. The American public's alarm over the Soviet invasion, coupled with the perceived incompetent handling of the American hostage situation in Iran at the same time, led to the downfall of Carter's presidency. These circumstances created a domestic political environment in the United States ripe for a confrontational American foreign policy toward the Soviet Union.

The Reagan administration's commitment to the development of strategic defenses against intercontinental ballistic missiles threatened to bring the security dilemma to a higher plane of competition and insecurity. Kennan and other distinguished figures with whom he associated his position—McGeorge Bundy, Robert McNamara, and Gerard Smith—objected to the Reagan administration's vigorous pursuit of the Strategic Defense Initiative (SDI) on the grounds that it was technically impossible and prohibitively costly. The program, "openly aimed at making Soviet missiles 'impotent,' while at the same time our own hard-target killers multiply" was bound to alarm the Soviet Union and lead to "an intensification of both its offensive and defensive strategic efforts."[76] Kennan and his colleagues concluded that "There is simply no escape from the reality that Star Wars offers not the promise of greater safety, but the certainty of a large-scale expansion of both offensive and defensive systems on both sides."[77]

Arms control was a means to defuse the American-Soviet security dilemma. Kennan pleaded for both superpowers to reassess their threat perceptions to make them more realistic and to settle for reasonable security rather than to drive for absolute security, which could never be achieved. In 1980 he argued that statesmen needed to muster greater courage and "take their military establishments in hand and insist that these should become the servants, not the masters and determinants, of political action. On both sides, one must learn to accept the fact that there is no security to be found in the quest for military superiority; that only in the reduction, not the multiplication, of the existing monstrous arsenals can the true security of any nation be found."[78]

Kennan called for a bold, unilateral American initiative in nuclear arms reduction to cut through the Gordian knot in arms control negotiations. In 1981 he argued for the American president to "propose to the Soviet government an immediate across-the-boards reduction by 50 percent of the nuclear arsenals now being maintained by the two superpowers," to be followed by a second reduction of at least two-thirds of what would be left.[79] Kennan judged that the risks of such a bold, unilateral move were outweighed by the chance that the Soviet Union would reciprocate the initiative. These moves, in turn, could then be legitimized in arms control treaties. Kennan assessed on this score that the United States "*can* conclude useful agreements with the Soviet side, and they *will* respect them—on condition, however, that the terms be clear and specific, not general; that as little as possible be left to interpretation; that questions of motivation, and particularly professions of noble principle, be left aside; and that the other contracting party show a serious and continued interest in their observance."[80]   Although the Reagan administration did not act on Kennan's proposal directly, President Reagan eventually made an even more ambitious proposal for the elimination of nuclear weapons, although the Soviets refused to accept it because Reagan would not sacrifice SDI as Gorbachev demanded.

The Cold War in fact came to a peaceful close on Reagan's watch. As Professor Gaddis has observed, "it fell to Ronald Reagan to preside over the belated but decisive success of the strategy of containment George F. Kennan had first proposed more than four decades earlier."[81]   Even Kennan, who at the time had been terribly alarmed by what he believed were reckless policies of the Reagan administration, in retrospect could faintly praise Reagan for his role in ending the Cold War.[82]   The praise probably is due to several factors. First, Kennan underestimated the value to the U.S. arms control negotiating position of Reagan's strategic forces buildup and commitment to SDI. These programs enabled the American side to negotiate with an upper hand; the Soviets knew that they lacked the industrial, economic, and technological wherewithal to compete on an equal footing with the United States arms buildup and were eager to negotiate a deal before the Soviet Union's rough military parity with the United States was eclipsed by Reagan's programs. Second, Kennan at the time simply underestimated Reagan's personal and emotional desire to get rid of nuclear weapons as well as his willingness to make a bold gesture in that direction. Third, Kennan apparently came to a belated intellectual appreciation of the Cold War role nuclear weapons played in inducing superpower caution and inhibiting them from taking risks that could have brought them to the brink of war.[83]   Despite this reconsideration, one suspects that Kennan continued to see nuclear weapons as a threat to humanity, given his worry that, if they were ever used—for whatever irrational purposes—their destructiveness would make what he witnessed firsthand in Germany's post–World War II ruins pale by comparison.   Given his personal revulsion to the thought of mass civilian casualties in combat, Kennan in the end probably rejected the reliance on nuclear weapons as a sound basis for national security.

CONCLUSION

Kennan's insight into American-Soviet relations was due, in part, to his ability to view objectively the national interests and power of each rival. His analysis of the origins of Soviet behavior and the strengths and weaknesses of the Soviet state enabled him to recognize both American and Soviet policies that were based on exaggerated perceptions of the other, policies that in turn fueled insecurity and the security dilemma. The superpower relationship was plagued with ambiguity, which created insecurity and drove both states to seek surpluses of power to hedge their bets in their competition. The drive for absolute security manifested itself in Cold War competition in Europe, Asia, the Third

World, and the nuclear arms race. Kennan feared that the security dilemma increased the risk that missteps would draw the superpowers into direct conflict. His paramount concern from 1946 to the mid-1980s was the need to prevent the security dilemma from escalating into general war. Kennan advocated American policies such as disengagement in Europe and drastic reduction in nuclear arsenals as diplomatic measures to dampen the spiraling security dilemma and reduce tension in the Soviet-American relationship.

The amelioration of the security dilemma in American-Soviet relations ultimately had to await the arrival of prudent statesmanship in Moscow. American policy makers may have been without an enlightened Soviet counterpart who was capable of reciprocating moderate gestures until the rise of Gorbachev. Gorbachev's leadership enabled the security dilemma in American-Soviet relations to be defused and substantially reduced the risk of inadvertent armed conflict between the superpowers. As Gorbachev emerged in the mid-1980s to leadership in Moscow, it became clear that he was the leader for whom Kennan had hoped. Gorbachev broke with the Soviet worldview of a hostile West and redefined the security requirements of the Soviet state to "sufficiency" instead of absolute security, paving the way for the amelioration of political tension and substantial progress in arms control measures.[84]

The international system of nation-states after the Cold War has evolved in a direction that Kennan had hoped would be more conducive to peace between major powers. The Soviet Union both mellowed and collapsed, as Kennan had speculated in his 1947 X article. Russia has embarked on a moderate foreign policy course, primarily due to its preoccupation with internal troubles, much as Kennan had envisioned in 1951 as a possible scenario for Russia.[85] Germany is unified and moving toward integration in a European framework, as Kennan had hoped in 1957, although Germany remains firmly entrenched in NATO. Finally, the United States and the Soviet Union have negotiated major across-the-board reductions in strategic and tactical nuclear weapons as well as in conventional weapons, well beyond the scope of Kennan's hopes.

NOTES

1. Hans J. Morgenthau and Kenneth W. Thompson, *Politics among Nations: The Struggle for Power and Peace*, Sixth Edition (New York, NY: McGraw-Hill Publishing Company, 1985), 227.

2. Robert Jervis, *Perception and Misperception in International Politics* (Princeton, NJ: Princeton University Press, 1976), 67.

3. Hans J. Morgenthau, *Politics in the Twentieth Century*, Abridged Edition (Chicago, IL: University of Chicago Press, 1971), 30.

4. Martin Wight, *International Theory: The Three Traditions*, Edited by Gabriele Wight and Brian Porter (Leicester, UK: Leicester University Press, 1991), 120.

5. Kennan in September 1944 wrote an essay, "Russia—Seven Years Later," in which "I poured forth, as in nothing else I ever wrote, the essence of what I knew about Russia generally, and Stalin's Russia in particular, as a phenomenon on the horizon of

American foreign policy makers. It was a broader, more balanced, and more specific than the so-called X-Article, written two and a half years later, which went in part over the same ground and in fact drew heavily on the earlier statement." George F. Kennan, *Memoirs, 1925–1950* (New York, NY: Pantheon Books, 1967), 225. He wrote in May 1945 another essay entitled "Russia's International Position at the Close of the War with Germany," which contained "the basic elements of the containment doctrine, as it was to be enunciated two years later in the X-Article." Kennan noted that his "views about the problem faced by the West as it confronted Soviet power in the postwar years were ones arrived at not in the anxieties and disillusionments of 1947, when they first became publicly known, but rather in the impressions of wartime service in Moscow itself, and in the effort to look ahead from that vantage point, on the heels of the Allied victory, into the uncertain future of Russia's relationship to the West." See his *Memoirs, 1925–1950*, 251.

6. Henry Kissinger, "Reflections on Containment," *Foreign Affairs* 73, no. 3 (May/June 1994): 120.

7. X [George F. Kennan], "The Sources of Soviet Conduct," *Foreign Affairs* 25, no. 4 (July 1947): 566.

8. Kennan, "The Sources of Soviet Conduct," 566.

9. George F. Kennan, *Russia, the Atom and the West* (New York, NY: Harper & Brothers Publishers, 1958), 17.

10. George F. Kennan, "The Soviet Way of Thought and Its Effect on Foreign Policy," 24 January 1947, in Giles D. Harlow and George C. Maerz (eds.), *Measures Short of War: The George F. Kennan Lectures at the National War College, 1946–47* (Washington, DC: National Defense University Press, 1991), 114. This paper, unpublished at the time it was written, probably was another analytic foundation for the X article published in *Foreign Affairs*.

11. George F. Kennan, *Realities of American Foreign Policy* (Princeton, NJ: Princeton University Press, 1954): 70.

12. Kennan, "The Sources of Soviet Conduct," 568.

13. Kennan, "The Sources of Soviet Conduct," 570.

14. Kennan, "The Sources of Soviet Conduct," 573.

15. Kennan, *Russia, the Atom and the West*, 22.

16. George F. Kennan, "The Russian Revolution—Fifty Years After: Its Nature and Consequences," *Foreign Affairs* 46, no. 1 (October 1967): 17.

17. The Chargé in the Soviet Union [George F. Kennan] to the Secretary of State, Moscow Cable # 511, 22 February 1946, in *Foreign Relations of the United States, 1946*, Volume VI (Washington, DC: U.S. Government Printing Office, 1969), 700. Hereafter referred to as The Long Telegram.

18. Kennan, "The Russian Revolution—Fifty Years After," 15.

19. George F. Kennan, *The Marquis de Custine and His Russia in 1839* (Princeton, NJ: Princeton University Press, 1971), 83.

20. Kennan, The Long Telegram, 699.

21. George F. Kennan, "Russia's International Position at the Close of the War with Germany," May 1945, published in his *Memoirs, 1925–1950*, 535.

22. Kennan, The Long Telegram, 706.

23. Kennan, The Long Telegram, 706.

24. Kennan, *Realities of American Foreign Policy*, 66.

25. Kennan, *Realities of American Foreign Policy*, 66.

26. Kennan, *Realities of American Foreign Policy*, 67.

27. Kennan, "The Sources of Soviet Conduct," 580.

28. Kennan, "The Sources of Soviet Conduct," 578.

29. Kennan, "The Sources of Soviet Conduct," 578. Kennan was later to acknowledge that "Soviet economic progress in these intervening years, in the face of all these handicaps has surpassed anything I then thought possible." See his *Russia, the Atom and the West*, 2.

30. Kennan, "The Sources of Soviet Conduct," 579–580.

31. George F. Kennan, "The Soviet Union and the Atlantic Pact," Moscow Telegram #116, 8 September 1952, published in his *Memoirs, 1950–1963* (New York, NY: Pantheon Books, 1972), 334.

32. Kennan, "The Soviet Union and the Atlantic Pact," 335.

33. Kennan, "The Soviet Union and the Atlantic Pact," 335.

34. Kennan, "The Soviet Union and the Atlantic Pact," 333.

35. Kennan, The Long Telegram, 706.

36. Kennan, *Russia, the Atom and the West*, 18.

37. George F. Kennan, "What Is Policy?" 18 December 1947, in Harlow and Maerz (eds.), *Measures Short of War*, 299.

38. Kennan, "What Is Policy?" 299.

39. Kennan, The Long Telegram, 708.

40. Kennan, The Long Telegram, 709.

41. Kennan, "The Sources of Soviet Conduct," 582.

42. Kennan, "The Sources of Soviet Conduct," 575.

43. Kennan, "The Sources of Soviet Conduct," 576.

44. Kennan, "The Sources of Soviet Conduct," 581.

45. Kennan, "The Sources of Soviet Conduct," 582.

46. "Draft Correspondence to Walter Lippmann," 6 April 1948, George F. Kennan Papers, Box 17, Seeley G. Mudd Manuscript Library, Department of Rare Books and Special Collections, Princeton University Library. Kennan never sent this letter to Lippmann. The State Department—where Kennan was then employed—was reluctant to have one of its own engaged in an open policy debate with a columnist and would not authorize Kennan to send it.

47. George F. Kennan, "Problems of US Foreign Policy after Moscow," 6 May 1947, in Harlow and Maerz (eds.), *Measures Short of War*, 198–199. The lecture was delivered at the National War College only one week after General Marshall had ordered Kennan to set up the Policy Planning Staff at the Department of State.

48. George F. Kennan, "Planning of Foreign Policy," 18 June 1947, in Harlow and Maerz (eds.), *Measures Short of War*, 213.

49. Kennan, *Memoirs, 1925–1950*, 319–320.

50. George F. Kennan, "America's Unstable Soviet Policy," *Atlantic* 250, no. 5 (November 1982): 72.

51. George F. Kennan, "The United States and the Soviet Union, 1917–1976," *Foreign Affairs* 54, no. 4 (July 1976): 683.

52. Kennan, "The United States and the Soviet Union, 1917–1976," 683–684.

53. Kennan, "The United States and the Soviet Union, 1917–1976," 684.

54. Kennan, *Memoirs, 1950–1963*, 91.

55. Kennan, *Memoirs, 1950–1963*, 92.

56. Wilson D. Miscamble, "Rejected Architect and Master Builder: George Kennan, Dean Acheson and Postwar Europe," *Review of Politics* 58, no. 3 (Summer 1996): 453. For an insightful treatment of Kennan's interpretation of the policy of containment versus those who espoused NSC 68, see John Lewis Gaddis, *Strategies of Containment: A Critical Appraisal of Postwar American National Security Policy* (New York, NY: Oxford University Press, 1982).

57. George F. Kennan, *The Cloud of Danger: Current Realities of American Foreign Policy* (Boston, MA: Little, Brown and Company, 1977), 201–202.

58. Kennan, *The Cloud of Danger*, 169.

59. George F. Kennan, "Peaceful Coexistence: A Western View," *Foreign Affairs* 38, no. 2 (January 1960): 183.

60. Kennan, *Memoirs, 1950–1963*, 139–140.

61. Kennan, *Memoirs, 1950–1963*, 140.

62. Kennan, *Memoirs, 1950–1963*, 140.

63. Kennan, *Russia, the Atom and the West*, 45.

64. Kennan, *Russia, the Atom and the West*, 61.

65. Dean Acheson, "The Illusion of Disengagement," *Foreign Affairs* 36, no. 3 (April 1958): 377. For an excellent analysis of the personal and professional relationship between Kennan and Acheson, as well as their policy disagreements related to postwar Europe, see Miscamble's "Rejected Architect and Master Builder."

66. Acheson, "The Illusion of Disengagement," 377.

67. George F. Kennan, "After the Cold War: American Foreign Policy in the 1970s," *Foreign Affairs* 51, no. 1 (October 1972): 219–220.

68. Louis J. Halle, "George Kennan and the Common Mind," *Virginia Quarterly* 45, no. 1 (Winter 1969): 55.

69. George F. Kennan, "Interview with George F. Kennan," *Foreign Policy* 7 (Summer 1972): 11.

70. Kennan, "After the Cold War," 220.

71. George F. Kennan, "Western Decadence and Soviet Moderation," in Martin F. Herz (ed.), *Decline of the West? George Kennan and His Critics* (Washington, DC: Ethics and Public Policy Center of Georgetown University, 1978), 4.

72. Kennan, "Western Decadence and Soviet Moderation," 4–5.

73. Kennan, "Western Decadence and Soviet Moderation," 6.

74. George F. Kennan, "Containment Then and Now," *Foreign Affairs* 65, no. 4 (Spring 1987): 888.

75. George F. Kennan, *The Nuclear Delusion: Soviet-American Relations in the Atomic Age* (New York, NY: Pantheon Books, 1982), 161–165.

76. McGeorge Bundy, George F. Kennan, Robert S. McNamara, and Gerard Smith, "The President's Choice: Star Wars or Arms Control," *Foreign Affairs* 63, no. 2 (Winter 1984/85): 271.

77. Bundy et al., "The President's Choice," 273.

78. Kennan, *The Nuclear Delusion*, 146.

79. Kennan, *The Nuclear Delusion*, 180.

80. George F. Kennan, "Breaking the Spell," *The New Yorker*, 3 October 1983, 53.

81. John Lewis Gaddis, *The United States and the End of the Cold War: Implications, Reconsiderations, Provocations* (New York, NY: Oxford University Press, 1992), 131.

82. Kennan revealed this sentiment to John Lewis Gaddis during a June 1995 interview. Gaddis Correspondence to the Author, 24 October 1996.

83. The author is indebted to Professor Gaddis for this point.

84. For a treatment of Gorbachev's redefinition of Soviet security policy, see Coit D. Blacker, *Hostage to Revolution: Gorbachev and Soviet Security Policy, 1985–1991* (New York, NY: Council on Foreign Relations, 1993). Also see Allen Lynch's *Gorbachev's International Outlook: Intellectual Origins and Political Consequences* (New York, NY: Institute for East-West Security Studies, 1989).

85. See George F. Kennan, "America and the Russian Future," *Foreign Affairs* 29, no. 3 (April 1951).

8

KENNAN'S REALISM
AS A THEORY OF
AMERICAN FOREIGN POLICY

When Peace returns after the present war, and a wave of well-earned Idealism sweeps through our English-speaking Nations, an appeal for a counter-balancing Realism will be the more willingly listened to, if it retains the form which has been exposed to the criticism of subsequent events.

—Sir Halford J. MacKinder, 1942

This chapter brings together the elements in Kennan's thought that were discussed in discrete parts in the preceding chapters, to examine the entire corpus. It initially places Kennan's worldview in context with the realist tradition of international politics as delineated by Hans Morgenthau, illuminates the principles embedded in Kennan's worldview, and evaluates the collective set of principles against the requirements for a classical theory. Finally, this chapter turns to the question posed at the onset of this study: What relevance does Kennan's theory have for American foreign policy beyond the Cold War? The study concludes that Kennan's classical realist theory and principles nurtured during the Cold War continue to have relevance as a guide to contemporary American foreign policy.

A REALIST'S WORLDVIEW

Kennan's realist appreciation of the dynamics of international politics is the foundation for his principles of American foreign policy. This underlying conception of international relations nurtured his pursuit of guiding principles for

American foreign policy. One must look at Kennan's conceptualization of international relations in general before coming to a full appreciation of the body of principles for American foreign policy in particular that are implicit in his diplomatic and scholarly work.

Throughout the discussions in preceding chapters, references were cited to similarities of thought between Kennan and other thinkers in the American realist tradition. As is fitting for a concluding chapter of a study on Kennan's strategic thought, it is useful to step back from the details examined in the preceding chapters and juxtapose Kennan's views with those key principles of realist thought delineated by the godfather of the American realist school, Hans Morgenthau. Although other thinkers have helped develop the American school of political realism, no one articulated the school's underlying principles as clearly and explicitly as Morgenthau. Consequently, Morgenthau's work is the benchmark for measuring other realists. Such an effort moves beyond the mere assertion that Kennan was a realist thinker to explicitly lay out the grand principles that he shared with Morgenthau's model of political realism.

It will be recalled from chapter 1 that a theory or philosophy is comprised of a set of interrelated principles. Such principles are the fabric of classical conservative thought. In the classical tradition of theory—as understood by traditional conservatives—an appreciation of the importance of principle was exemplified in the works of Carl von Clausewitz and Edmund Burke. It was with this understanding of the importance of principles as guides to political action that Morgenthau labored over his formulation of a theory of international politics and his six principles of political realism.

Kennan, like Morgenthau, took the nature of man as the starting point for the study of politics and stressed the critical importance of human nature for understanding the dynamics of politics in the international arena. For Morgenthau, "Political realism believes that politics, like society in general, is governed by objective laws that have their roots in human nature."[1] Realism holds that human nature has remained constant since antiquity and has not progressed as technology has advanced, contrary to the assertions of the Enlightenment philosophers. As discussed in chapter 2, Kennan saw little evidence that man has progressively improved his condition. To the contrary, modern man is riddled with the same imperfections that plagued ancient man. Despite the rapid pace of technological advances, human nature—with its potential for good and as well as for evil—has remained constant. Kennan observed the bitter irony that modern technology has enabled man to inflict evil on an unprecedented scale, as witnessed in two world wars in this century. This strongly conservative philosophy rejects the Enlightenment philosophy which held out the prospect of the progressive development of human nature and the elimination of evil.

The concepts of interest and power for Kennan and Morgenthau were the bedrock of both domestic and international politics. Morgenthau's second principle of realism held that "The concept of interest defined as power imposes intellectual discipline upon the observer, infuses rational order into the subject of politics, and thus makes the theoretical understanding of politics possible."[2] Morgenthau acknowledged that contingent elements of personality and emotions prevent foreign policies from always following a purely rational course. Nevertheless, he stressed "the rational elements of political reality; for it is these rational elements that make reality intelligible for theory. Political realism presents the theoretical construct of a rational foreign policy which experience can never completely achieve."[3] Kennan recognized the difficulty in defining the national interest of nation-states but argued forcefully that it existed. His analysis of American and Soviet foreign policies was predicated on assumptions of national interest. Kennan recognized along with Morgenthau that nation-state behavior deviated from rational behavior due, in part, to powerful emotions, as evident in modern nationalism—a manifestation of the individual's will to experience power vicariously through the nation-state, as discussed in chapter 2. Emotionalism led to extreme policies that neglected the tools of diplomacy and compromise to advance the national interest without resort to force and war, the costs of which in many cases outweighed the potential benefits to the national interest.

Rationality was the normative goal for Morgenthau in international politics and for Kennan in American foreign policy. From Morgenthau's normative stance, if more nation-states were to accept rational policy goals and appreciate limits of power and interest, greater moderation in foreign policy and order in the international system of nation-states would result. For Kennan, the normative aim was to impose rationality on American foreign policy with an appreciation of power and interest to reduce the American zeal for moralism and crusades, which resulted from an idealistic philosophy that divorced the calculation of interest and power from foreign policy. Kennan was frustrated that the domestic contest for power in the United States influenced the formulation and implementation of foreign policy and in many cases forced the policy to deviate from a rational course on the world scene, as discussed in chapter 4. Through this prism, Kennan criticized American policy for excesses in the world wars, the Korean War, the Vietnam War, and several post–Cold War interventions. Kennan's general policy advocacy, although criticized by many for being one of isolationism, was more accurately depicted as a call to make American power and interest move in lockstep.

Interest and power were universal concepts in the study of politics for both Kennan and Morgenthau. Power is both a means and an end in politics. In other words, nation-states seek power in and of itself as well as for use in achieving the national interest. According to Morgenthau's third principle, "Realism assumes that its key concept of interest defined as power is an objective category which is universally valid, but it does not endow that concept with a meaning that is fixed once and for all. The idea of interest is indeed of the essence of politics and is unaffected by the circumstances of time and place."[4] For Kennan, Morgenthau, and Reinhold Niebuhr, power was the currency of politics—domestic and international—as discussed in chapter 2. Man's individual drive for power, which is magnified in the competition between nation-states, is the broad generalization that characterized Kennan's understanding of politics. Power is a necessity of civilization, in Kennan's view, "flowing from certain facts about human nature—certain imperfections if you will—that are basic and that are not going to be corrected by any man-made device, whether institutional or educational. These basic facts provide one of the main keys to understanding history."[5] Power and interest, for Kennan, were the core subjects of politics, and they remained valid beyond circumstances of time and place, as Morgenthau had argued.

Kennan shared with Morgenthau the appreciation that political prudence is necessary to weigh the demands of power and interest against those of morality. In his fourth principle, Morgenthau argued that "Realism maintains that universal moral principles cannot be applied to the actions of states in their abstract universal formulation, but that they must be filtered through the concrete circumstances of time and place . . . There can be no political morality without prudence; that is, without consideration of the political consequences of seemingly moral action. Realism, then, considers prudence—the weighing of the consequences of alternative political actions—to be the supreme virtue in politics."[6] Kennan's thought sidestepped the deep philosophic grappling with the tension between power, interest, and morality in foreign policy evident in the work of realists such as Morgenthau, Niebuhr, and Kenneth Thompson. Instead, Kennan dealt with the more concrete, and he criticized Wilsonianism's placement of morality as the central goal for foreign policy with indifference to power, interest, and prudence. Kennan argued that a framework that ignored these features was bound to fail at potentially high costs.

Kennan's thoughts on morality might best be viewed as a call for an American principle of Christian humility in foreign policy. It is a call, in other words, for Americans to candidly recognize that we do not have all of the answers to the political and moral dilemmas in the world. Kennan counseled the United States to strengthen its own society and polity to improve the condition of American citizens so that the United States might serve as an example to other nation-states to try to emulate in the context of their own political communities if they so desired. These thoughts mirrored those of Morgenthau, who in a fifth principle asserted that "Political realism refuses to identify the moral aspirations of a particular nation with the moral laws that govern the universe."[7]

Political realism's principles form a lens through which scholars and practitioners can more readily see the world and understand its fundamental elements at work. The realist school strenuously argues that statesmen must recognize the ubiquity of the struggle for power to fashion policies that balance competing drives for power to promote international order. Kenneth Thompson captured the essence of realist thought when he wrote that "On the international scene, rivalries among states remain largely uncontrolled by effective law or government.   The business of statesmanship and diplomacy under these conditions is to limit the struggles and restrict their scope. The means available are a mixture of military power and diplomacy employed in the unceasing pursuit of new balances of power and rough equilibriums among contending parties."[8] Thompson concluded that realism "accepts for the guide and premise of its thought the permanence and ubiquity of the struggle for power. But it strives unceasingly through every means at its disposal to contain and limit concentrations of power and to compose and relieve tensions that could lead to a situation of war."[9]

Kennan's lifetime commitment was to the prudent exercise of American power in pursuit of the national interest to strengthen the American polity at home and foster political order abroad. Kennan, in an echo of Morgenthau and Thompson, called for "a careful examination of our national interest, devoid of all utopian and universalistic pretensions; and . . . a sober, discriminating view of the world beyond our borders—a view that takes account of the element of relativity in all antagonisms and friendships, that sees in others neither angels nor devils, neither heroes nor blackguards; a concept, finally, which accepts it as our purpose not to abolish all violence and injustice from the workings of international society but to confine those inevitable concomitants of the human predicament to levels of intensity that do not threaten the very existence of civilization."[10] Kennan sought to use diplomacy with the backing of modest military means, where appropriate, to shape and channel—albeit only at the margins in many cases—the forces of nature rather than to radically alter them. He pleaded that "we must be gardeners and not mechanics in our approach to world affairs. We must come to think of the development of international life as an organic and not a mechanical process. We must realize that we did not create the forces by which this process operates. We must learn to take these forces for what they are and to induce them to work with us and for us by influencing the environmental stimuli to which they are subjected, but to do this gently and patiently, with understanding and sympathy, not trying to force growth by mechanical means, not tearing the plants up by the roots when they fail to behave as we wish them to."[11] This passage captures the essence of Kennan's realist approach to foreign policy and the hope for a more orderly international system of nation-states.

By juxtaposing Morgenthau's theory of international relations with Kennan's thought, one comes to a fuller appreciation of political realism. This appreciation, in turn, underscores Morgenthau's sixth and final principle, that the difference "However much of the theory of political realism may have been misunderstood and misinterpreted, there is no gainsaying its distinctive intellectual and moral attitude to matters political."[12] The similarities in the political thought of Morgenthau, Kennan, and other realist thinkers are extensive and indicate a consistent theory common to their worldviews. It is possible in some instances to trace the roots of Kennan's realist philosophy, particularly to Niebuhr, but in most cases the trail is faint. The task of determining where one realist thinker's thought ends and another's begins is difficult. The school resembles an interlocking web of thought rather than an easily compartmented discipline. Kennan shared many of the views held by Morgenthau, Niebuhr, Thompson, Nicholas Spykman, and Henry Kissinger. John Lewis Gaddis, for example, concluded in assessing the similarities in thought between Kennan and Kissinger that "their congruent approaches seem to have grown out of a shared commitment to the 'realist' tradition in American foreign policy, and intellectual orientations solidly grounded in the study of European diplomatic history, a degree of detachment from the academic and policy-making elites of the 1950's and 1960's, and, above all, a sense of strategy—an insistence on the importance of establishing coherent relationships between ends and means."[13] Nevertheless, perhaps Kenneth Thompson put his finger on why the trail of the origins of Kennan's thoughts is faint when he judged that Kennan was "too self-conscious of the need to distinguish his own mode of thinking to share in any depth ideas he has drawn from historians and philosophers."[14]

REALIST PRINCIPLES OF AMERICAN FOREIGN POLICY

In light of the preceding discussion, Kennan's worldview falls squarely in the realist tradition of international politics. His thoughts are consistent with the six principles of political realism established by Morgenthau. Morgenthau devoted his energy to the illumination of a theory of international politics, but Kennan confined his search to a narrower subfield in international relations and sought to discover the underlying principles of a theory for American foreign policy. Morgenthau constructed the overarching theoretical principles of international relations, and Kennan implicitly related these principles to the conduct of American foreign policy. Morgenthau laid the broad tenets of the theory or philosophy of political realism, while Kennan's principles were more closely tied to the practice of American foreign policy. On a spectrum where theory lies at the left end and practice lies on the right end, Morgenthau's thought lies closer to the left and Kennan's lies closer to the right. Although Kennan's thought bore the markings of Morgenthau's six principles of political realism, he failed to articulate it as a theory with the comprehensiveness and clarity that Morgenthau provided.

Beyond the consistency of Kennan's realist thought with that of Morgenthau on the nature of politics in general, embedded within Kennan's worldview are realist principles to govern the conduct of American foreign policy. Kennan was a vocal advocate of principles to govern the conduct of American foreign policy. The search for principles was at the heart of Kennan's quest for a classical theory to underpin American foreign policy. Principles are closer to the demands of practice than universal abstractions. Kennan confessed that "I am afraid that when I think about foreign policy, I do not think in terms of doctrines. I think in terms of principles."[15] He defined a principle as "a general rule of conduct by which a given country chooses to abide in the conduct of its relations with other countries. "[16] In the conservative tradition, Kennan explained his conceptualization of principle as a general rule of conduct, not as an absolute one. Instead, established principle, he believed, should have the first and most authoritative claim on the attention and respect of the policy maker.[17] Kennan—like Burke, Clausewitz, and Morgenthau—was too aware of the forces of circumstance and the contingent to look to universal laws or absolutes to govern the course of policy.

On the basis of the discussions in the preceding chapters, we must try to synthesize and make explicit the principles that composed Kennan's worldview. These principles fall into four broad categories. First, Kennan's worldview contains principles for understanding the basis for the political behavior of man and nation-states. These principles were discussed in the preceding section in conjunction with Morgenthau's principles. These primary or fundamental principles illuminate the driving factors behind the behavior of nation-states, including the United States, to help scholars and practitioners see the most salient features of international politics. Second, Kennan's principles encompass a hierarchy of American interests that govern foreign policy and also take into account the impact of domestic politics. Third, Kennan's principles address the policy instruments available to the United States—primarily diplomacy and force—for maneuvering in international politics to realize the national interest. Fourth, Kennan's principles warn of the pitfalls in the dynamics of relations between major powers in international politics.

The United States must strive to evaluate ever-changing international power relationships and to manage the global balance of power. This is the central principle of Kennan's thought—the appreciation of power and the articulation of the national interest in American foreign policy. For Kennan, foreign policy was a function of domestic needs. Foreign policy is not an end in of itself, but rather a means to strengthen American society. Domestic vitality is the source of power on the international stage, and a rational, prudent foreign policy, in turn, strengthens American power abroad and supports the nurturing of the domestic polity.

Kennan's thought embodies a geostrategic framework for the American national interest. It is a hierarchy of interests that focuses on the relations between major nation-states in the international system. Kennan viewed the maintenance of balances of power between the five core areas of industrial-military significance—North America, Japan, Russia, Germany, and the United Kingdom—as the key to international order. Imbalances among the five core areas would destabilize the international system and pose a threat to American sovereignty, our core national interest. Kennan's emphasis was more on the international behavior of major powers and less on the internal composition of their polities. Less powerful nation-states—unless they have an impact on the five core areas—play insignificant roles in the global balance of power and were not treated by Kennan as central to the American national interest.

Kennan, much like his realist contemporaries, tended to view economics as a critical component of power, but he did not delve deeply into the realm of political economy to the extent that many contemporary scholars do.[18] Despite the increasingly interconnected global economy, politics reign supreme, and political calculations dictate the behavior of nation-states more heavily than purely economic considerations. Critics might assert that Kennan's geopolitical framework does not accurately take into account today's movement from the industrial to the technological revolution. Such criticism, however, would overlook the fact that most of the five political-military-industrial centers that Kennan identified early in the Cold War are the powerhouses in the technological revolution.

China's contemporary position seriously calls into question the secondary importance that Kennan attributed to it in the global balance of power. China—with its natural resources, military power, experimentation with economic liberalization, and geopolitical position—is poised to become a major regional, if not world, power. In light of these circumstances, one might update Kennan's geopolitical worldview to conclude that Japan will play an increasingly important role for U.S. interests by acting as a balancing power against potential Chinese expansion in Asia.

Kennan's attention to power and national interest concentrated his thought on means and ends in foreign policy. A central strand that runs through the web of his thought is a realist appreciation of the critical importance of relating ends and means in foreign policy. Kennan wrote, for example, that "the value of any policy purporting to reflect the national interests of the United States cannot be greater than the ability of the U.S. government to carry it out."[19] Kennan's thought was in the tradition of Clausewitz, who identified this relationship as critical to grand strategy when he wrote that "It is the task of theory, then, to study the nature of ends and means."[20] Kennan's appreciation of strategy has not escaped astute observers. Professor Gaddis, for example, pointed out that "Kennan is not often regarded as a strategist, but if 'strategy' is thought of as the rational relationship of national objectives to national capabilities, then he has as good a claim as anyone to having devised a coherent American strategy for dealing with the postwar world."[21] David Mayers also argued that "What was truly impressive about Kennan during the period of early Cold War, and set him apart from most ranking members of the Truman administration, was his sense—in the best conservative tradition of proportionality—of the limits of American power."[22]

Prudent statesmanship is needed to articulate the national interest to Americans and to override the domestic struggle for power that causes a drift from a rational course in foreign policy. For Kennan, the struggles for power within the United States—or within any nation-state, for that matter—could not be divorced from the international struggle for power between nation-states. In the American context, Kennan looked for gifted statesmen to rise above the fray of the domestic struggle for power to see and articulate the national interest and governing principles of foreign policy. Statesmanship was required to overrule domestic parochial political interests to guide the United States toward the national interest. For Kennan, the national interest, beyond the maintenance of the world balance of power, was a method of conducting foreign policy. He believed that the style and conduct of American foreign policy abroad needed to be consistent with our own moral standards, but that those moral standards were not to be imposed on other nation-states. Kennan firmly believed that the president was best positioned institutionally to give context to the governing principles to advance the national interest.

Diplomacy is a tool for advancing the American national interest through bargaining and compromise in a world of conflicting power and interest, not for converting other nation-states to democracy. Kennan warned of the dangers posed to American foreign policy in the glorification of democracy as a universal cure-all for the shortcomings of political societies. He emphasized the unique cultural and historical basis of American democracy, which reduces its universal applicability, as well as the unsuitability of military force for imposing democracy on other societies. "Democracy is a matter of tradition, of custom, of what people are used to and expect. It is something that cannot be suddenly grafted onto an unprepared people—particularly not from outside, and not by precept and preaching and pressure rather than example."[23] Above all, Kennan prudently warned against looking abroad to promote democracy while neglecting its nurture at home. Such neglect could lead to the failure of our own democratic experiment and with it our power to influence world affairs. Traditional diplomatists such as Kennan and the Founding Fathers viewed the international behavior of nation-states rather than their internal form of government as the focus for diplomacy.

Diplomacy must be backed up by the ability to use force and wage war to achieve political objectives and to reestablish severed political relationships of power. The challenge for statesmen is to use limited force to achieve the national interest when psychological power to influence events has stalled. In these circumstances, force should complement diplomatic efforts to arrive at a negotiated settlement to conflict commensurate with the national interest. Kennan was a student of Clausewitz in that he viewed war as a continuation of politics by other means. The United States needs to refrain from the use of force in circumstances in which no national interest is at stake. The limited use of force in some situations, however, may be essential to ensure a diplomatic resolution that protects the American national interest.

American statesmen must weigh American power and interest against that of other major powers, ever mindful of the destabilizing effects of the security dilemma, which could propel major powers into armed conflict. Kennan implicitly argued that wise statecraft was needed to ease the security dilemma that heightened the insecurity and fueled the superpower arms race between the United States and the Soviet Union. Expanding nuclear and conventional arsenals increased tension in the relationship, and Kennan worried that a spiraling series of miscalculations would move the superpowers along the path to nuclear war. Kennan looked to skilled statecraft informed by a prudent conception of American national interest and power and a levelheaded assessment of Soviet interest and power to dampen the spiral in tensions, stabilize the U.S.-Soviet political relationship, and lessen the prospects for an inadvertent war.

Kennan's analysis was devoted to the American-Soviet relationship, but power relationships between major powers have not ceased with the end of the Cold War. Kennan's concern about a post–Cold War security dilemma led him to oppose in 1997 the enlargement of NATO membership as "the most fateful error of American policy in the entire post–cold war era" on the grounds that it was likely to "inflame the nationalistic, anti-Western and militaristic tendencies in Russian opinion; to have an adverse effect on the development of Russian democracy; to restore the atmosphere of the cold war to East-West relations, and to impel Russian foreign policy in directions decidedly not to our liking."[24] Although observers might reasonably take issue with the consequences of NATO enlargement that Kennan anticipated, statesmen would be well advised to be alert to the dynamics of the security dilemma in the post–Cold War period. The management of major power relationships in the future will require that statesmen seek to dampen the effects at work in the balance of power. Major power relations will need to be maintained on an even keel via diplomacy to prevent them from deteriorating into more dangerous zones of the security dilemma, which could propel major nation-states to armed conflict.

KENNAN'S REALIST PRINCIPLES AS A THEORY

The preceding realist principles constitute the essence of Kennan's worldview. We now must ask whether these principles taken collectively constitute a coherent, consistent theoretical framework for American foreign policy. Do Kennan's realist principles measure up to the demands of a theory able to inform the conduct of American foreign policy?

Kennan's thoughts are best viewed from the perspective of the classical approach to international politics, which draws on history, philosophy, and value judgments. Kennan in particular unceasingly sought to draw analogies, parallels, and lessons from history to guide the conduct of contemporary foreign policy. His lectures delivered at the University of Chicago in 1950, for example, were, in his words, "an attempt to look back from a present full of uncertainty and controversy and unhappiness, to see whether a study of the past will not help us to understand some of our present predicaments."[25] More recently, he wrote that "I fancy myself to perceive, in these records of the past, lessons that, if they were closely looked at, could help us all to identify the hopeful roads into the future and to refrain from entering, and from pulling others along with us, on those paths at the end of which there is no hope, and from which no one ever returns."[26] Kennan's study of history probed for the recurrent as well as for the unique in human affairs and international politics.

Although Kennan relied heavily on his study of history to help him interpret international politics, he was aware of the technique's limitations. His scholarship underscored the complexity of human affairs, which severely limits the prospects for using history to predict the future. In his detailed accounts of diplomatic history, Kennan observed that statecraft has been riddled by factors such as "personality, coincidence, communication and the endless complexity" which "all combine to form a process beyond the full vision or comprehension of any single contemporary."[27] Given the complexity of the contingent, "it is useful to be reminded that there is none who understands fully the stuff of which international affairs are made, none who is not being constantly surprised by the turns it actually takes."[28] Kennan concluded that "in the field of international affairs one should never be so sure of his analysis of the future as to permit it to become a source of complete despair. The greatest law of human history is its unpredictability."[29]

Statesmen, therefore, are rarely, if ever, able to fully anticipate the consequences of their actions. Kennan drew a lesson that "Nothing is written more clearly into the record of history than the inability of men to take the full measure of their situation either as members of a society or as individuals, to see that situation in all its aspects, to comprehend its dynamics, to forecast its future. The great English historian, Herbert Butterfield, has pointed out the irony that invariably marks the relationship between what statesmen—even the best of them—mean to achieve, when they take their various actions, and the actual consequences those actions ultimately have."[30] Kennan's personal experiences as a diplomat and policy maker reinforced his awareness of the unintended consequences of policy: "I can testify from personal experience that not only can one never know, when one takes a far-reaching decision in foreign policy, precisely what the consequences are going to be, but almost never do these consequences fully coincide with what one intended or expected."[31] Consequently, Kennan rejected the proposition, advanced by proponents of the contending scientific approach to politics, that a successful theory of international politics should have strong predictive capabilities for the behavior of nation-states. From Kennan's perspective, the complexities of reality and the intricacies of the contingent in human affairs are beyond mathematic quantification and preclude a high confidence in the prediction of the future.

Although Kennan had no confidence in any scientific theory's capability to predict the course of social behavior, his own worldview enabled him to anticipate the broad course of events in international politics. That worldview—informed by the study of Gibbon—projected as early as 1947 that the Soviet Union would eventually collapse, given its internal structural weaknesses.[32] Kennan's projection was a substantial departure from those of his contemporaries and the "common mind" that prevailed in 1947. Kennan's worldview also enabled him to envision as early as the 1950s the Cold War's end, a scenario that was unthinkable by conventional wisdom. Such a profound restructuring of international politics was not envisioned by neorealism—the scientific version of realism—which assumed the perpetual continuation of the bipolar world and dismissed the internal politics of nation-states as inconsequential to international relations theory.

Kennan's principles of American foreign policy, derived from his worldview, meet the criteria for a classical theory. First, they constitute a general framework that illuminates the essential features of the struggle for power in the international system of nation-states. Second, Kennan's principles provide explicit criteria for the selection of problems for intensive analysis. He explicitly and implicitly formed a hierarchy of American national interests and recognized the opportunities as well as the limits of American power to achieve these interests via diplomacy and force. Third, Kennan recognized that the dual nature of man and nationalism cause statesmen to deviate from rational moderation in foreign policy. Kennan's general principles help statesmen and policy makers reduce the complexity of international politics to more manageable proportions. Taken collectively, they constitute a sophisticated prism or theory through which scholars and policy makers can view the world and America's place and role in it.

Most important, Kennan's realist theory of foreign policy meets the practicality test for American statesmen. A theory or philosophy consisting of a general body of principles that simplify reality may lack the specificity demanded by many scholars, but this shortcoming is overshadowed by its potential practicality for policy makers. Kennan's theory, grounded in history and philosophy, is composed of a body of principles that could be readily grasped by hurried policy makers who are not experts in all the problems they are forced to face. It is a way of thinking about problems, not a formula in a scientific sense. Scientific approaches are either too narrow or too technical for policy makers to use to help make strategic decisions in the rush of tactical day-to-day events. Kennan's principles help narrow the gap between theory and practice to improve the quality of American foreign policy and reduce the chances for policy debacles.

KENNAN'S THEORETICAL RELEVANCE BEYOND THE COLD WAR

The explication of Kennan's work reveals a model of a realist approach to American foreign policy. Much of the previous scholarship on Kennan has either examined a limited portion of his life's work or has not related it to the realist theory literature as an overarching guide to American foreign policy. The present study has taken a fresh look at Kennan as a realist thinker to clear the misconceptions and misrepresentations of a foreign policy based on realist principles that have accumulated during the Cold War and its aftermath. In other words, this study has sought to clear the underbrush of this literature to begin a reexamination of political realism and American foreign policy from a solid footing.

Kennan's theory and principles can inform the contemporary debate in international relations theory in general and American foreign policy in particular. The struggle between the contending classical approaches of liberalism and conservatism or realism is alive and active today in the aftermath of the Cold War. President Clinton's former national security adviser, Anthony Lake, for example, characterized the liberalism of Woodrow Wilson as the guiding philosophy for the administration's foreign policy.[33] On the other hand, administration observers and scholars have criticized President Clinton's foreign policy from a realist framework, although they may not have explicitly referred to their views as such. Professor Michael Mandelbaum has likened the Clinton administration's approach to foreign policy to "social work." He has been critical of the administration's intervention in "peripheral areas" such as Bosnia, Somalia, and Haiti and its preoccupation "not with the relations with neighboring countries, the usual subject of foreign policy, but rather with the social, political, and economic conditions within borders."[34] Former Bush administration official Richard Haass has called for a modified realist approach to foreign policy to fill the void left after the loss of the policy of containment as an overarching philosophic guide for American foreign policy.[35]

Kennan's principles are not concrete rules of action. They are guidelines to help policy makers through the inevitable maze of policy dilemmas. Political realists such as Kennan do not claim to have ready-made answers for the unceasing dilemmas posed by foreign policy. They have too great an appreciation for the role of the contingent in human affairs to aspire to a scientific theory to dictate policy. Instead, they look for the recurrent amongst the mass of unique events in the course of human affairs for the substance of their theory. As Professor Gaddis concluded, both Kennan and Kissinger "understood the existence of a strategic 'logic' transcending time and circumstance; a way of thinking that can make ideas formulated in one context relevant to very different ones; that can make it possible for thoughtful men, separated in their periods of public responsibility by a quarter of a century, to apply with some success similar strategies to vastly dissimilar situations."[36] The realist tradition offers a broad framework for interpreting international politics coupled with a sense of the tools needed for practitioners to grapple with foreign policy challenges. Kennan's theory is a set of principles that can be used to critically examine the assumptions and premises on which the Wilsonian approach to foreign policy is based or can act as a standard of measurement for assessing the merits and liabilities of alternative foreign policy courses.

An American foreign policy based on realist principles such as Kennan's would lend a consistency and steadiness to American foreign policy, which is frequently characterized by broad changes in direction. American foreign policy this century has been influenced by a crusade for exporting democracy and pursuing objectives that lie beyond our interest and power to achieve at reasonable costs. Such was the case in World War I, when the United States sought to remodel the world in its own self-image. Kennan pointed to the Treaty of Versailles—which planted the seeds for World War II—as evidence of the dangers posed by attempts to break with the forces of history in crafting foreign policy. He referred to the interwar period as "the sort of peace you got when you allowed war hysteria and impractical idealism to lie down together in your mind, like the lion and the lamb; when you indulged yourself in the colossal conceit of thinking that you could suddenly make international life over into what you believed to be your own image; when you dismissed the past with contempt, rejected the relevance of the past to the future, and refused to occupy yourself with the real problems that a study of the past would suggest."[37] The temporary realization that we could not remold the rest of the world in our own image led to a period of American isolationism after World War I. The withdrawal of the United States from world politics, in part, fostered an imbalance of power in Europe, which contributed to the rise of Nazi Germany and consequent threat to the American national interest.

An American foreign policy based on Kennan's principles would plot a course between the extremes of crusade and isolationism to more ably serve our interests at home, which, in Kennan's view, was the ultimate purpose of foreign policy. Realist principles place a theoretical foundation under American foreign policy and give it a stability and consistency conducive to the promotion of the American national interest and international order. They collectively are a framework that can be overlaid on the rush of day-to-day events to separate the significant from the insignificant and to focus policy attention on those concerns that pose the greatest danger to American interests. Conversely, use of Kennan's theory would reduce the diversion of policy attention and American power to intractable problems that lie beyond our means ever to fully correct and do not merit the costs in power in attempting to do so. A realistic foreign policy, moreover, would be within the limits of American power to achieve and would not overburden our resources to the detriment of our society. A commonality in the theoretical conceptualizations of international politics and recommendations for American foreign policy among realist thinkers attests to a link between theory and practice. As Thompson has pointed out, for instance, it could be no accident that realist thinkers such as Morgenthau, Kennan, and Niebuhr rejected American participation in the Vietnam War.[38] For the realists, Vietnam was not a geopolitical threat to the United States and, therefore, did not warrant a significant commitment of American military power and the loss of tens of thousands of American lives.

Although Kennan is most studied in connection with the Cold War policy of containment, this book has sought to reveal a more general theory, which may be his most enduring legacy. Kennan was disheartened by the commonly held interpretations of the policy of containment, which, in his view, lacked the diplomatic and political subtleties that he had envisioned for the policy. He grew to see the misinterpretation of the policy—with an overly heavy emphasis on the military dimension of the rivalry—as an engine that propelled the superpowers toward confrontation rather than as a set of governing principles to manage the American-Soviet competition and thus enhance international order. Although Kennan concluded that the policy of containment as he envisioned it had become obsolete by the 1970s, it was some twenty years later, in 1989, when events made that conclusion self-evident to all observers. It would be a further tragic twist of fate if the full body of Kennan's work were neglected. This study reveals that Kennan's corpus was underpinned by a body of principles that, taken collectively, constitute a theory of foreign policy that remains valid today as the United States continues to compete in the international struggle for power.

NOTES

1. Hans J. Morgenthau and Kenneth W. Thompson, *Politics among Nations: The Struggle for Power and Peace*, Sixth Edition (New York, NY: McGraw-Hill Publishing Company, 1985), 4.

2. Morgenthau and Thompson, *Politics among Nations*, 5.

3. Morgenthau and Thompson, *Politics among Nations*, 10.

4. Morgenthau and Thompson, *Politics among Nations*, 10.

5. George F. Kennan, "Training for Statesmanship," *Atlantic* 191, no. 5 (May 1953): 41.

6. Morgenthau and Thompson, *Politics among Nations*, 12.

7. Morgenthau and Thompson, *Politics among Nations*, 13.

8. Kenneth W. Thompson, *Political Realism and the Crisis of World Politics: An American Approach to Foreign Policy* (Lanham, MD: University Press of America, 1982), 69.

9. Thompson, *Political Realism*, 69–70.

10. George F. Kennan, "The Quest for Concept," *Harvard Today*, Autumn 1967, 17.

11. George F. Kennan, *Realities of American Foreign Policy* (Princeton, NJ: Princeton University Press, 1954), 93.

12. Morgenthau and Thompson, *Politics among Nations*, 13.

13. John Lewis Gaddis, *Strategies of Containment: A Critical Appraisal of Postwar American National Security Policy* (New York, NY: Oxford University Press, 1982), 308.

14. Kenneth W. Thompson, *Schools of Thought in International Relations: Interpreters, Issues, and Morality* (Baton Rouge, LA: Louisiana State University Press, 1996), 70.

15. George F. Kennan, *Memoirs, 1925–1950* (New York, NY: Pantheon Books, 1967), 364.

16. George F. Kennan, "On American Principles," *Foreign Affairs* 74, no. 2 (March/April 1995): 118.

17. Kennan, "On American Principles," 119.

18. I am indebted to Professor Gaddis for underscoring this point to me. Interview with the Author, 26 October 1995, Woodrow Wilson International Center for Scholars, Washington, DC.

19. George F. Kennan, *Around the Cragged Hill: A Personal and Political Philosophy* (New York, NY: W.W. Norton & Company, 1993), 186.

20. Carl von Clausewitz, *On War*, Edited and Translated by Michael Howard and Peter Paret (Princeton, NJ: Princeton University Press, 1989), 142.

21. John Lewis Gaddis, "Containment: A Reassessment," *Foreign Affairs* 55, no. 4 (July 1977): 886–887.

22. David Mayers, *George Kennan and the Dilemmas of U.S. Foreign Policy* (New York, NY: Oxford University Press, 1988), 10.

23. George F. Kennan, *At a Century's Ending: Reflections, 1982–1995* (New York, NY: W.W. Norton & Company, 1996), 91.

24. George F. Kennan, "A Fateful Error," *New York Times*, 5 February 1997, A23.

25. George F. Kennan, *American Diplomacy*, Expanded Edition (Chicago, IL: University of Chicago Press, 1984), 55.

26. Kennan, *At a Century's Ending*, 42.

27. George F. Kennan, *Soviet-American Relations, 1917–1920: Volume I: Russia Leaves the War* (Princeton, NJ: Princeton University Press, 1956), viii.

28. Kennan, *Soviet-American Relations, 1917–1920*, viii.

29. Kennan, *Realities of American Foreign Policy*, 92.

30. George F. Kennan, "Why Do I Hope?" *University: A Princeton Quarterly* 29 (Summer 1966): 4.

31. George F. Kennan, "Foreign Policy and Christian Conscience," *Atlantic* 203, no. 5 (May 1959): 44.

32. See X [George F. Kennan], "The Sources of Soviet Conduct," *Foreign Affairs* 25, no. 4 (July 1947): 580.

33. Cited from John J. Mearsheimer, "The False Promise of International Institutions," *International Security* 19, no. 3 (Winter 1994/95): 5.

34. Michael Mandelbaum, "Foreign Policy as Social Work," *Foreign Affairs* 75, no. 1 (January/February 1996): 17.

35. See Richard N. Haass, "Paradigm Lost," *Foreign Affairs* 74, no. 1 (January/February 1995).

36. Gaddis, *Strategies of Containment*, 308.

37. Kennan, *American Diplomacy*, 69.

38. Kenneth W. Thompson, Conversation with the Author, 24 April 1996, Miller Center of Public Affairs, University of Virginia, Charlottesville, Virginia.

SELECTED BIBLIOGRAPHY

BOOKS BY GEORGE F. KENNAN

Realities of American Foreign Policy. Princeton: Princeton University Press, 1954.

Soviet-American Relations, 1917–1920: Volume I: Russia Leaves the War. Princeton: Princeton University Press, 1956.

Russia, the Atom and the West. New York: Harper & Brothers Publishers, 1958.

Soviet-American Relations, 1917–1920: Volume II: The Decision to Intervene. Princeton: Princeton University Press, 1958.

Soviet Foreign Policy, 1917–1941. Princeton: D. Van Nostrand Company, Inc., 1960.

Russia and the West under Lenin and Stalin. New York: Mentor, 1961.

On Dealing with the Communist World. New York: Harper & Row Publishers, 1964.

Memoirs, 1925–1950. New York: Pantheon Books, 1967.

From Prague after Munich: Diplomatic Papers, 1938–1940. Princeton: Princeton University Press, 1968.

Democracy and the Student Left. Boston: Little, Brown and Company, 1968.

The Marquis de Custine and His Russia in 1839. Princeton: Princeton University Press, 1971.

Memoirs, 1950–1963. New York: Pantheon Books, 1972.

The Cloud of Danger: Current Realities of American Foreign Policy. Boston: Little, Brown and Company, 1977.

The Decline of Bismarck's European Order: Franco-Russian Relations, 1875–1890. Princeton: Princeton University Press, 1979.

The Nuclear Delusion: Soviet-American Relations in the Atomic Age. New York: Pantheon Books, 1982.

American Diplomacy. Expanded Edition. Chicago: University of Chicago Press, 1984.

The Fateful Alliance: France, Russia, and the Coming of the First World War. New York: Pantheon Books, 1984.

Sketches from a Life. New York: Pantheon Books, 1989.

Around the Cragged Hill: A Personal and Political Philosophy. New York: W.W. Norton & Company, 1993.

At a Century's Ending: Reflections, 1982–1995. New York: W.W. Norton & Company, 1996.

ARTICLES, INTERVIEWS, PAPERS, AND TESTIMONIES BY GEORGE F. KENNAN

Papers. Seeley G. Mudd Manuscript Library, Department of Rare Books and Special Collections, Princeton University Library.

Chargé in the Soviet Union [George F. Kennan] to the Secretary of State, Moscow Cable # 511 [The Long Telegram], 22 February 1946. In *Foreign Relations of the United States, 1946*, Volume VI. Washington: U.S. Government Printing Office, 1969.

X [George F. Kennan], "The Sources of Soviet Conduct." *Foreign Affairs* 25, no. 4 (July 1947).

"Current Problems in the Conduct of Foreign Policy." *Department of State Bulletin*, 15 May 1950.

"How New Are Our Problems?" *Illinois Law Review* 45, no. 6 (January–February 1951).

"The National Interest of the United States." *Illinois Law Review* 45, no. 6 (January–February 1951).

"Let Peace Not Die of Neglect." *New York Times Magazine*, 25 February 1951.

"America and the Russian Future." *Foreign Affairs* 29, no. 3 (April 1951).

"Training for Statesmanship." *Atlantic* 191, no. 5 (May 1953).

"The Future of Our Professional Diplomacy." *Foreign Affairs* 33, no. 4 (July 1955).

"The Challenge of Freedom." *The New Leader*, 26 December 1955.

"History and Diplomacy as Viewed by a Diplomatist." *Review of Politics* 18, no. 2 (April 1956).

"America's Administrative Response to Its World Problems." *Daedalus* 87, no. 2 (Spring 1958).

"Disengagement Revisited." *Foreign Affairs* 37, no. 2 (January 1959).

"Foreign Policy and Christian Conscience." *Atlantic* 203, no. 5 (May 1959).

"A Proposal for Western Survival." *The New Leader*, 16 November 1959.

"Peaceful Coexistence: A Western View." *Foreign Affairs* 38, no. 2 (January 1960).

"Diplomacy as a Profession." *Foreign Service Journal* 38, no. 5 (May 1961).

"Polycentrism and Western Policy." *Foreign Affairs* 42, no. 2 (January 1964).

"The Price We Paid for War." *Atlantic* 214, no. 4 (October 1964).

"Testimony of George Kennan on American Foreign Policy." Hearing before the Committee on Foreign Relations, United States Senate, Eighty-ninth Congress, Second Session, 10 February 1966. *Congressional Record*, Volume 112, Part 3.

"Why Do I Hope?" *University: A Princeton Quarterly* 29 (Summer 1966).

"The Communist World in 1967." *Hearing before the Committee on Foreign Relations*, United States Senate, Ninetieth Congress, First Session, 30 January 1967. Washington: U.S. Government Printing Office, 1967.

"The Quest for Concept." *Harvard Today*, Autumn 1967.

"The Russian Revolution--Fifty Years After: Its Nature and Consequences." *Foreign Affairs* 46, no. 1 (October 1967).

"The Relation of Religion to Government." *Princeton Seminary Bulletin* 62, no. 1 (Winter 1969).

"To Prevent a World Wasteland: A Proposal." *Foreign Affairs* 48, no. 3 (April 1970).

"Interview." *Foreign Service Journal* 47, no. 8 (August 1970).

"Interview with George F. Kennan." *Foreign Policy* 7 (Summer 1972).

"After the Cold War: American Foreign Policy in the 1970s." *Foreign Affairs* 51, no. 1 (October 1972).

"Europe's Problems, Europe's Choices." *Foreign Policy* 14 (Spring 1974).

"George F. Kennan Replies." *Slavic Review* 35, no. 1 (March 1976).

"The United States and the Soviet Union, 1917–1976." *Foreign Affairs* 54, no. 4 (July 1976).

"International Control of Atomic Energy" [written in 1950]. In *Foreign Relations of the United States, 1950*, Volume I. Washington: U.S. Government Printing Office, 1977.

"A Last Warning." *Encounter* 51, no. 1 (July 1978).

"Foreign Policy and the Professional Diplomat." In Louis J. Halle and Kenneth W. Thompson (eds.), the Geneva Papers, *Foreign Policy and the Democratic Process*. Washington: University Press of America, 1978.

Kennan, George F., McGeorge Bundy, Robert S. McNamara, and Gerard Smith. "Nuclear Weapons and the Atlantic Alliance." *Foreign Affairs* 60, no. 4 (Spring 1982).

"America's Unstable Soviet Policy." *Atlantic* 250, no. 5 (November 1982).

"Breaking the Spell." *The New Yorker*, 3 October 1983.

Kennan, George F., McGeorge Bundy, Robert S. McNamara, and Gerard Smith. "The President's Choice: Star Wars or Arms Control." *Foreign Affairs* 63, no. 2 (Winter 1984/85).

"Morality and Foreign Policy." *Foreign Affairs* 64, no. 2 (Winter 1985/86).

Kennan, George F., McGeorge Bundy, Morton H. Halperin, William W. Kaufmann, Robert S. McNamara, Madalene O'Donnell, Leon V. Sigal, Gerard C. Smith, Richard H. Ullman, and Paul C. Warnke. "Back from the Brink." *Atlantic* 258, no. 2 (August 1986).

"Containment Then and Now." *Foreign Affairs* 65, no. 4 (Spring 1987).

"The Balkan Crisis: 1913 and 1993." *New York Review of Books*, 15 July 1993.

"Somalia, Through a Glass Darkly." *New York Times*, 30 September 1993, A25.

"The Failure in Our Success." *New York Times*, 14 March 1994, A17.

"On American Principles." *Foreign Affairs* 74, no. 2 (March/April 1995).

"A Fateful Error." *New York Times*, 5 February 1997, A23.

RELATED BOOKS

Bailyn, Bernard (ed.). *The Debate on the Constitution: Federalist and Antifederalist Speeches, Articles, and Letters during the Struggle over Ratification*. Parts One and Two. New York: Literary Classics of the United States, 1993.

Blainey, Geoffrey. *The Causes of War*. Third Edition. New York: The Free Press, 1988.

Bredvold, Louis I., and Ralph G. Ross (eds.). *The Philosophy of Edmund Burke: A Selection from His Speeches and Writings*. Ann Arbor: University of Michigan Press, 1967.

Brodie, Bernard (ed.). *The Absolute Weapon: Atomic Power and World Order*. New York: Harcourt, Brace and Company, 1946.

———. *Strategy in the Missile Age*. Princeton: Princeton University Press, 1965.

———. *War and Politics*. New York: Macmillan Publishing Company, 1973.

Burke, Edmund. *Reflections on the Revolution in France*. Edited by J. G. A. Pocock. Indianapolis: Hackett Publishing Company, 1987.

————. *Pre-Revolutionary Writings*. Edited by Ian Harris. New York: Cambridge University Press, 1993.

Butterfield, Herbert. *International Conflict in the Twentieth Century: A Christian View*. Westport, CT: Greenwood Press, 1960.

————. *The Whig Interpretation of History*. New York: AMS Press, 1978.

Butterfield, Herbert, and Martin Wight (eds.). *Diplomatic Investigations: Essays in the Theory of International Politics*. Cambridge: Harvard University Press, 1966.

Carr, Edward Hallett. *The Twenty Years' Crisis, 1919–1939: An Introduction to the Study of International Relations*. Second Edition. New York: St. Martin's Press, 1966.

Clausewitz, Carl von. *On War*. Edited and Translated by Michael Howard and Peter Paret. Princeton: Princeton University Press, 1989.

Claude, Inis L., Jr. *Power and International Relations*. New York: Random House, 1962.

Deibel, Terry L., and John Lewis Gaddis. *Containing the Soviet Union: A Critique of U.S. Policy*. Elmsford, NY: Pergamon-Brassey's International Defense Publishers, 1987.

Fox, William T. R. (ed.). *Theoretical Aspects of International Relations*. Notre Dame: University of Notre Dame Press, 1959.

Gaddis, John Lewis. *Strategies of Containment: A Critical Appraisal of Postwar American National Security Policy*. New York: Oxford University Press, 1982.

————. *The United States and the End of the Cold War: Implications, Reconsiderations, Provocations*. New York: Oxford University Press, 1992.

Gellman, Barton. *Contending with Kennan: Toward a Philosophy of American Power*. New York: Praeger Publishers, 1984.

George, Alexander L. *Bridging the Gap: Theory and Practice in Foreign Policy*. Washington: United States Institute of Peace Press, 1993.

Gibbon, Edward. *The History of the Decline and Fall of the Roman Empire*. Volumes I and II. Edited by David Womerly. New York: Penguin Books, 1994.

Graebner, Norman A. (ed.). *Ideas and Diplomacy: Readings in the Intellectual Tradition of American Foreign Policy*. New York: Oxford University Press, 1964.

Halle, Louis J. *Civilization and Foreign Policy: An Inquiry for Americans*. New York: Harper & Brothers Publishers, 1955.

————. *American Foreign Policy: Theory and Reality*. London: Bradford & Dickens, 1960.

————. *Men and Nations*. Princeton: Princeton University Press, 1962.

————. *The Cold War as History*. New York: HarperPerennial, 1991.

Harlow, Giles D., and George C. Maerz (eds.). *Measures Short of War: The George F. Kennan Lectures at the National War College, 1946–47*. Washington: National Defense University Press, 1991.

Herz, John H. *Political Realism and Political Idealism: A Study in Theories and Realities*. Chicago: University of Chicago Press, 1951.

Herz, Martin F. (ed.). *Decline of the West?: George Kennan and His Critics*. Washington: Ethics and Public Policy Center of Georgetown University, 1978.

Hixson, Walter L. *George F. Kennan: Cold War Iconoclast*. New York: Columbia University Press, 1989.

Hobbes, Thomas. *Leviathan*. Edited by C. B. MacPherson. New York: Penguin Books, 1985.

Howard, Michael. *The Causes of Wars.* Second Edition. Cambridge: Harvard University Press, 1983.

Jervis, Robert. *Perception and Misperception in International Politics.* Princeton: Princeton University Press, 1976.

Keohane, Robert O. (ed.). *Neorealism and Its Critics.* New York: Columbia University Press, 1986.

Kissinger, Henry A. *Nuclear Weapons and Foreign Policy.* New York: Harper & Brothers, 1957.

———. *American Foreign Policy.* New York: W.W. Norton & Company, 1969.

———. *Diplomacy.* New York: Simon & Schuster, 1994.

Lassman, Peter, and Ronald Speirs (eds.). *Weber: Political Writings.* New York: Cambridge University Press, 1994.

Lippmann, Walter. *Essays in the Public Philosophy.* Boston: Little, Brown and Company, 1955.

MacKinder, Halford J. *Democratic Ideals and Reality.* New York: Henry Holt and Company, 1942.

Mayers, David. *George Kennan and the Dilemmas of U.S. Foreign Policy.* New York: Oxford University Press, 1988.

Miscamble, Wilson D. *George F. Kennan and the Making of American Foreign Policy, 1947–1950.* Princeton: Princeton University Press, 1992.

Morgenthau, Hans J. *Scientific Man vs. Power Politics.* Chicago: University of Chicago Press, 1946.

———. *Politics in the Twentieth Century.* Abridged Edition. Chicago: University of Chicago Press, 1971.

———. *In Defense of the National Interest: A Critical Examination of American Foreign Policy.* Lanham, MD: University Press of America, 1982.

———. *The Purpose of American Politics.* Lanham, MD: University Press of America, 1982.

Morgenthau, Hans J., and Kenneth W. Thompson (eds.). *Principles and Problems of International Politics.* Washington: University Press of America, 1950.

Morgenthau, Hans J., and Kenneth W. Thompson. *Politics among Nations: The Struggle for Power and Peace.* Sixth Edition. New York: McGraw-Hill Publishing Company, 1985.

Niebuhr, Reinhold. *Christianity and Power Politics.* New York: Charles Scribner's Sons, 1940.

———. *The Children of Light and the Children of Darkness: A Vindication of Democracy and a Critique of its Traditional Defense.* New York: Charles Scribner's Sons, 1944.

———. *The Structure of Nations and Empires.* New York: Charles Scribner's Sons, 1959.

———. *Moral Man and Immoral Society: A Study in Ethics and Politics.* New York: Charles Scribner's Sons, 1960.

———. *The Irony of American History.* New York: Charles Scribner's Sons, 1962.

———. *Christian Realism and Political Problems.* Fairfield, NJ: Augustus M. Kelley Publishers, 1977.

Polley, Michael. *A Biography of George F. Kennan: The Education of a Realist.* Lewiston, NY: Edwin Mellon Press, 1990.

Rosenthal, Joel H. *Righteous Realists: Political Realism, Responsible Power, and American Culture in the Nuclear Age*. Baton Rouge: Louisiana State University Press, 1991.

Rossiter, Clinton. *Conservatism in American*. Second Edition. Cambridge: Harvard University Press, 1982.

Russell, Greg. *John Quincy Adams and the Public Virtues of Diplomacy*. Columbia: University of Missouri Press, 1995.

Smith, Michael Joseph. *Realist Thought from Weber to Kissinger*. Baton Rouge: Louisiana State University Press, 1986.

Spykman, Nicholas John. *America's Strategy in World Politics: The United States and the Balance of Power*. New York: Harcourt, Brace and Company, 1942.

Stephanson, Anders. *Kennan and the Art of Foreign Policy*. Cambridge: Harvard University Press, 1989.

Thompson, Kenneth W. *American Diplomacy and Emergent Patterns*. New York: New York University Press, 1962.

———. *Masters of International Thought*. Baton Rouge: Louisiana State University Press, 1980.

———. *Morality and Foreign Policy*. Baton Rouge: Louisiana State University Press, 1980.

———. *Political Realism and the Crisis of World Politics: An American Approach to Foreign Policy*. Lanham, MD: University Press of America, 1982.

———. *Traditions and Values in Politics and Diplomacy*. Baton Rouge: Louisiana State University Press, 1992.

———. *Schools of Thought in International Relations: Interpreters, Issues, and Morality*. Baton Rouge: Louisiana State University Press, 1996.

Tocqueville, Alexis de. *Democracy in America*. Volumes I and II. Henry Reeve Text as Revised by Francis Bowen, Further Corrected and Edited by Phillips Bradley. New York: Vintage Books, 1990.

Walt, Stephen M. *The Origins of Alliances*. Ithaca, NY: Cornell University Press, 1987.

Waltz, Kenneth N. *Man, the State and War*. New York: Columbia University Press, 1959.

———. *Theory of International Politics*. Reading, MA: Addison-Wesley Publishing Company, 1979.

Watson, Adam. *Diplomacy: The Dialogue between States*. New York: Routledge, 1991.

Wight, Martin. *International Theory: The Three Traditions*. Edited by Gabriele Wight and Brian Porter. Leicester, UK: Leicester University Press, 1991.

Wolfers, Arnold, and Laurence W. Martin. *The Anglo-American Tradition in Foreign Affairs*. New Haven, CT: Yale University Press, 1956.

RELATED ARTICLES AND PAPERS

Acheson, Dean. "The Illusion of Disengagement." *Foreign Affairs* 36, no. 3 (April 1958).

Armstrong, Hamilton Fish. Papers. Seeley G. Mudd Manuscript Library, Department of Rare Books and Special Collections, Princeton University Library.

Aron, Raymond. "What Is a Theory of International Relations?" *Journal of International Affairs* 21, no. 2 (1967).

Bull, Hedley. "International Theory: The Case for a Classical Approach." *World Politics* 18, no. 3 (April 1966).

Ferguson, Yale H., and Richard W. Mansbach. "Between Celebration and Despair: Constructive Suggestions for Future International Theory." *International Studies Quarterly* 35, no. 4 (December 1991).

Gaddis, John Lewis. "Containment: A Reassessment." *Foreign Affairs* 55, no. 4 (July 1977).

———. "International Relations Theory and the End of the Cold War." *International Security* 17, no. 3 (Winter 1992/93).

George, Alexander. "The 'Operational Code': A Neglected Approach to the Study of Political Leaders and Decision-Making." *International Studies Quarterly* 13, no. 2 (June 1969).

Graebner, Norman A. "The President as Commander in Chief: A Study in Power." *Journal of Military History* 57, no. 1 (January 1993).

Haass, Richard N. "Paradigm Lost." *Foreign Affairs* 74, no. 1 (January/February 1995).

Halle, Louis J. "George Kennan and the Common Mind." *Virginia Quarterly* 45, no. 1 (Winter 1969).

Jervis, Robert. "Cooperation under the Security Dilemma." *World Politics* 30, no. 2 (January 1978).

Joffe, Josef. "Europe's American Pacifier." *Foreign Policy* 54 (Spring 1984).

Kissinger, Henry A. "Force and Diplomacy in the Nuclear Age." *Foreign Affairs* 34, no. 3 (April 1956).

———. "Reflections on Containment." *Foreign Affairs* 73, no. 3 (May/June 1994).

Mandelbaum, Michael. "Foreign Policy as Social Work." *Foreign Affairs* 75, no. 1 (January/February 1996).

Mearsheimer, John J. "The False Promise of International Institutions." *International Security* 19, no. 3 (Winter 1994/95).

Miscamble, Wilson D. "Rejected Architect and Master Builder: George Kennan, Dean Acheson and Postwar Europe." *Review of Politics* 58, no. 3 (Summer 1996).

Morgenthau, Hans J. "Another 'Great Debate': The National Interest of the United States." *American Political Science Review* 66, no. 4 (December 1952).

———. "Common Sense and Theories of International Relations." *Journal of International Affairs* 21, no. 2 (1967).

Newsom, David D. "Foreign Policy and Academia." *Foreign Policy* 101 (Winter 1995–96).

Thompson, Kenneth W. "Toward a Theory of International Politics." *American Political Science Review* 49, no. 3 (September 1955).

———. "Liberalism and Conservatism in American Statecraft." *Orbis* 2, no. 4 (Winter 1959).

———. "Normative Theory in International Relations." *Journal of International Affairs* 21, no. 2 (1967).

———. "Power, Force and Diplomacy." *Review of Politics* 43, no. 3 (July 1981).

———. "Unity and Contradiction in the Theory and Practice of International Relations." *Review of Politics* 44, no. 3 (July 1982).

INDEX

About the Author

RICHARD L. RUSSELL is a lecturer on American national security policy at the Washington Center of the University of California, Berkeley. He is a member of the International Institute for Strategic Studies.

ISBN 0-275-96402-7

90000>

EAN

9 780275 964023

HARDCOVER BAR CODE